Leaders of Their Race

Leaders of Their Race

Educating Black and White Women in the New South

SARAH H. CASE

UNIVERSITY OF
ILLINOIS PRESS
Urbana, Chicago, and Springfield

Library of Congress Cataloging-in-Publication Data
Names: Case, Sarah H.
Title: Leaders of their race : educating black and white women in the
    new South / Sarah H. Case.
Description: Urbana : University of Illinois Press, 2017. | Series:
    Women in American history | Includes bibliographical references
    and index. |
Identifiers: LCCN 2017011655 (print) | LCCN 2017033662 (ebook) | ISBN
    9780252099847 (ebook) | ISBN 9780252041235 (hardback) | ISBN
    9780252082795 (paper)
Subjects: LCSH: Women—Education—Southern States—History. |
    Women—Education—United States—History. | African American
    women—Education—Southern States—History. | Women,
    White—Education—Southern States—History. | Women—
    Southern States—Social conditions. | Lucy Cobb Institute (Athens,
    Ga.)—History. | Spelman Seminary (Atlanta, Ga.)—History. |
    BISAC: SOCIAL SCIENCE / Women's Studies. | EDUCATION /
    History. | HISTORY / United States / 20th Century.
Classification: LCC LA230.5.S6 (ebook) | LCC LA230.5.S6 C37 2017
    (print) | DDC 370.820975—dc23
LC record available at https://lccn.loc.gov/2017011655

For Julia and Katharine

Contents

Acknowledgments

I am indebted to many who have assisted me in the project. Special thanks go to Jane Sherron De Hart, for her insightful comments and critiques of the manuscript, and to Carl Harris, for his inspiring commitment to the study of southern history. John Majewski had clear and helpful advice, and Erika Rappaport made many suggestions that sharpened my thinking. Thanks also to Ann Plane, Mary Furner, Patricia Cline Cohen, Alice O'Connor, Otis L. Graham Jr., and Lisa Jacobson, and to Beverly Schwartzberg, Jay Carlander, Anne Rapp, and Anne Petersen. Thanks also to Dean Maarten Pereboom of Salisbury University, for granting a Dean's research award and a semester sabbatical that assisted my work on this project.

Deep appreciation goes to the anonymous readers for the University of Illinois Press, who offered critiques and advice that improved the project tremendously. Thanks also to those who have read or commented on conference papers or other work related to this manuscript, including Ann Short Chirhart, John Inscoe, and Jacqueline Jones. I am very appreciative of the patience, support, and clear advice of my editors at University of Illinois Press, Dawn Durante and Laurie Matheson.

I especially want to thank the archivists and librarians who assisted my research. The late Taronda Spencer at Spelman had an encyclopedic knowledge of the college, equaled only by her kindness and generosity with her time. Holly Smith and Kassandra Ware have been equally helpful, professional, and expert in their assistance with the finishing stages of the project. I'd like to also thank the archivists of the Hargrett Library at the University of Georgia who helped me navigate the university's extensive collections during several visits, especially Chuck Barber; special thanks also to Mary

Linneman for helping with reproductions and images. Thanks also to the staff of the Athens-Clarke County Heritage Foundation, the Agnes Scott College Library, the Auburn Avenue Research Library on African American Culture and History, the Robert W. Woodruff Library at Emory University, and the Robert W. Woodruff Library at the Atlanta University Center. My appreciation also goes to the late Phyllis Jenkins Barrow for sharing her memories of Lucy Cobb with me at her home in Athens.

Many thanks to the editors of *The Public Historian*, Randy Bergstrom and James F. Brooks, who have been extraordinarily supportive of my work on this book. Thanks also to my family for their love and support.

Leaders of Their Race

Introduction

Women, Education, and the New South

The June 1896 edition of the *Spelman Messenger*, the school's monthly newsletter, was almost entirely devoted to an essay by Henry Morehouse, president of Spelman's board and the executive secretary of the American Baptist Education Society, titled "The Worth of Spelman Seminary to the World." In this essay marking the fifteenth anniversary of the Atlanta school, Morehouse celebrated the seminary's accomplishments and "character," stating that it had contributed to southern, African American, and national progress. Most notably, he asserted, Spelman had created women who would become "leaders of their own race"—the female half of the "talented tenth" that would aid in both "the civilization of the southern Negro" and "the establishment of right relations between the two races."[1] The mix of condescension and support for African American women apparent in Morehouse's essay was typical of white supporters of the seminary, but it also points to an assumption shared by Spelman students and alumnae themselves—the central purpose of their education was to create women who would take a leading role in contributing to racial advancement in the post-Civil War, or "New" South.

The following year, in December of 1897, a newspaper described the Lucy Cobb Institute of Athens, Georgia, as the best college for women south of Baltimore, noting both the rigorous academic program and the "atmosphere of refinement and good breeding that bespeaks the nature of the patronage of the school."[2] The unidentified observer here neatly summed up the uncertainty of the purpose of advanced education for elite southern white women—was it to teach manners and etiquette in the "finishing school" tradition, or provide them with serious academic study? Lucy Cobb tried to do both, and in fact viewed them as mutually compatible and reinforcing.

"Lucies," as they were known, would be well educated but also unquestionably feminine and modest in manner and appearance, which would protect them from criticism as they stepped into public life. As a 1903 catalogue boasted, the school was "proud to claim among her alumnae many of the leading and most influential Christian women in the South."[3] Like Spelman, Lucy Cobb alumnae would be "leaders of their race"—but for the Athens school, "race leadership" meant maintaining white supremacy, not breaking it down. Both Spelman and Lucy Cobb viewed women's education as crucial to racial, regional, and national progress, but their vision of progress diverged sharply by race.

Leaders of Their Race: Educating Black and White Women in the New South analyzes the educational objectives of the founders, faculty, students, and alumnae of two schools that sought to prepare young women for the new circumstances of the postwar South. Founded in 1881 in a church basement by two white northern women, Sophia Packard and Harriet Giles, representatives of the Woman's American Baptist Home Missionary Society, Spelman Seminary viewed its mission as Christian education for black women in a cloistered, single-sex environment. Chartered in 1859 by politician, lawyer, and pro-slavery theorist T.R.R. Cobb as a place to educate the young white ladies of Athens, Lucy Cobb Institute evolved significantly after 1880, when his nieces Mildred Rutherford and Mary Ann Lipscomb took on the administration of the school. A close examination of these two private secondary schools for young women, one for African Americans, one for whites, provides a way to explore beliefs about women's roles and duties, racial and class divisions between women, and changes in expectations of women's citizenship rights and duties. Giving particular attention to the years between 1880 and 1925, and focusing on two Georgia schools—the Lucy Cobb Institute of Athens, and Spelman Seminary (now College) of Atlanta—this book demonstrates the importance of secondary-level female education in refashioning women's identity, and analyzes the significance of race, gender, sexuality, and region in shaping that education. It identifies the social and ideological backgrounds of founders and influential faculty members of each school, and their goals in teaching young women. Additionally, it examines who attended both schools, the motivations and agenda of students, and how alumnae used their education after leaving school. Using a comparative approach, it explores what female education indicates about the multiple and complex ways that racial and gender ideology functioned in the New South. It especially analyzes the attention given to cultivating modesty and sexual restraint in both schools, and argues that concerns about female sexuality and respectability united the two schools, despite their very different student populations. Further, by highlighting the actions of women as teachers, students, and alumnae, it analyzes how southern women used their education to negotiate the political, economic, and social upheavals of the New South. Both black and white women had new responsibilities as "leaders of their race"—and both viewed these new expectations in specifically race-conscious ways.

Scholars have long recognized the historical significance of education and have shown that educational goals can reveal significant insights about social ideologies and aspirations. The expansion of urban public primary school systems in the late nineteenth and early twentieth century has long been a focus of scholars, many of them critical of the "one best system" model of standardized elementary instruction.[4] Whereas northeastern school systems standardized and expanded in the Progressive Era, in many areas of the South, public school systems were in their infancy. Former slaves, viewing education as the key to empowerment, opened their own schools in churches or homes just after emancipation. James Anderson and others have emphasized the role of African Americans in creating educational opportunity for themselves in the Reconstruction era, and the lasting legacy of schools founded in the immediate postwar era. As Anderson argued, freedmen and women were the first southerners to attempt to create a public school system in the South.[5] New South promoters also understood the value of education in their program to modernize the South economically and socially. Educational reformers worked to replace one-room schoolhouses with graded institutions taught by well-trained, if poorly paid, female teachers. By stressing understanding over rote memorization, and a sense of duty over fear of authority, these modern schools sought to educate an intelligent, efficient, self-disciplined populace able to compete in a new, nationally integrated economy. Communities often resisted these changes, preferring local to state control, and even the best-planned and funded systems developed unevenly, especially in rural areas. Scholars have analyzed the complexity of attempting to modernize the South through compulsory public education.[6] Studies specifically on southern education have frequently focused on inequalities in the development of a postwar public education system, especially the founding of a segregated system that was anything but equal.[7]

Historians of women, too, have given attention to education, and have identified the expansion of literacy and access to print culture across the nineteenth century as a major transformation in women's lives. Yet women's experiences with education varied widely across the nineteenth century, by region, race, and class, and over time. Whereas as early as the end of the eighteenth century, New England women had near universal basic literacy, the rate in 1850 for southern white women was under 80 percent, and as low as 64 percent in some states.[8] The number of women who attended school in the antebellum South remained quite small. Planter women often received their education at home, with tutors. Yeomen women, for the most part, did not attend school, and slave women were prohibited by custom and often by law from acquiring even basic literacy.[9] Yet some elite southern women received educations superior to that of northern women. Historian Christie Anne Farnham found that before the Civil War, the South actually led the nation in the number of female "colleges" and schools. Northern women sought education to gain employment, usually as teachers. But southern schools for elite girls did not prepare them for professional work, and therefore did not threaten gender hierarchy. Southern education for women, especially knowledge of French, music, and art, served as a marker of class status rather than as preparation for paid labor.[10]

Women's increasing access to true college-level education in the late nineteenth century has been of particular interest to women's historians. After the founding of Vassar College in Poughkeepsie, New York, credited as the first true college for women, in 1867, several other schools for women revamped their curriculum to model themselves on Vassar. Others opened their doors for the first time. In addition, several large public universities, especially those founded after the passage in 1862 of the Morrill Act, admitted women. Higher education laid the groundwork for the creation of a class of professional women, the settlement house residents, social workers, educators, medical professionals and others active in the Progressive Era. Many of the best known and most influential women of the early twentieth century, such as Florence Kelley, Alice Paul, Carrie Chapman Catt, and Frances Perkins had college (and often, graduate) degrees. Although many large southern universities refused to admit women until required to by the 1972 Higher Education Act, southern women who did not wish to leave their region could attend private women's colleges such as Agnes Scott and Sophie Newcomb or public universities specifically designed to educate teachers, such as the North Carolina State Normal and Industrial School in Greensboro.[11]

Despite scholarly interest in both public primary school systems and college-level education for women at the turn of the twentieth century, much less attention has been paid to private secondary schools in this period. Analyzing two such schools for women in the New South period, this book begins to fill that gap. Although access to college for women expanded significantly over the course of the nineteenth century, and although many of the most prominent female leaders of the time had college degrees, college-level education remained out of the grasp of most women, particularly southern women. Much larger numbers of women could have access to secondary-level education, and the content and meaning of this education deserves attention.

Secondary education for young women witnessed a sharp increase in the years following the Revolutionary War. Whereas the stereotype of an educated woman earlier in the eighteenth century was an unattractive, obnoxious, and unfeminine shrew, attitudes about the appropriateness of education for women began to change around the time of the Revolution. The altered political climate required a rethinking of the role of citizens in a republic; no longer subjects to the crown, Americans began to re-imagine their relationship to the state. Because they viewed republican government as fragile and potentially unstable, political elites viewed civic virtue—putting the good of the republic ahead of private, selfish interest—as essential to its continuation. Historians have termed this idea as "republicanism," and have shown its link with independence and masculinity (they note the linguistic link of "virtue" and "virile"). Yet women too had a role in preserving the republic. Although women continued to be restricted by the law of coverture, which mandated that married women lose their civil and legal identity upon marriage, white women clearly were citizens and part of the body politic. Late eighteenth-century supporters of expanded rights for women, most notabily Judith Sargent Murray, sought new definitions of femininity in the new nation. Key to their re-imagining of women's role was their insistence on the importance of education for women. Only with education, Murray and others insisted, could women raise children suffused with the sort of civic virtue necessary for the continuation of the republic. That is, the health of the nation depended on the ability of the republic's women to mother correctly, and proper education would prepare women for their private civic roles. Support for the idea of "republican motherhood" inspired the expansion of private secondary schools for women in the years following the Revolution.[12]

Secondary-level education also allowed women to become teachers themselves, a female occupation that seemed to not overtly challenge gendered expectations of women's association with the caregiving of children. Beginning in the early nineteenth century, promoters of both "separate spheres" ideology and of female education such as Catherine Beecher and Sarah Josepha Hale viewed teaching as a particularly appropriate occupation for women. For them, secondary education could train unmarried female teachers to be "republican mothers" for many more children than those they might later have themselves.[13] By the late nineteenth century, teaching represented the primary respectable female profession for both white and black women.

Educators also responded to what they viewed as a sexual crisis in the late eighteenth century. In the mid-eighteenth century, it was not at all unusual for young women to marry after becoming pregnant; one study found that nearly one-third of brides in the second half of the 1700s were pregnant on their wedding day. This statistic suggests that not only were couples engaging in premarital intercourse, but that they, willingly or unwillingly, responded to community pressure to marry. Premarital pregnancy, scholars have found, was generally accepted, as long as the couple married. Yet with the increasing opportunity for mobility by the end of the eighteenth century, young men increasingly chose not to marry their sexual partner. In this climate, young women seemed especially vulnerable—burdens to their families and outcasts in their communities.[14]

One of the goals of secondary education for young women was to teach them a new morality of sexual chastity. Founders of female academies, such as Susanna Rowson, best known for her seduction novel *Charlotte Temple*, believed that education for adolescent girls should emphasize the danger of sex. This is the major theme of her novels as well—fifteen-year-old Charlotte, after being seduced by a soldier, suffers from abandonment, ostracism, unwanted pregnancy, mental illness, and eventually death. Simply removing young women to the cloistered protection of the seminary would help preserve their chastity; additionally, in Rowson's schools, and in the textbooks she wrote for other similar schools, young women received clear messages about the dangers of premarital sexual relations to their futures. By the 1830s, this new message had been received; premarital pregnancy rates fell dramatically, and young women understood their sexual reputation to be central to their personal identity.[15]

Views about even marital sexuality and pregnancy began to change in the late eighteenth century. As Susan Klepp found, fertility rates took a sharp decline around the time of the Revolution, and attitudes about pregnancy and childbearing changed dramatically too. Women no longer viewed pregnancy as healthy, natural, and enjoyable, but as physically draining, uncomfortable, and even somewhat embarrassing. No longer did multiple children deserve admiration or even jealously; instead it indicated lack of restraint, the body trumping the mind. Klepp links this shift not to industrialization, but to the rhetoric and ideology of the Revolution, the new emphasis on individualism, freedom, rational thought, and self-determination. Women, despite their secondary status, were to exemplify the new ideology, and the physical body of the pregnant woman belied women's attempt to prove their rationality, their ability to separate body from mind.[16]

In a sense, champions of Revolution-era education for women viewed the female body and the rational mind as fundamentally incompatible; in order to define themselves as sensible republican women, they must control, or even negate, their sexuality. The ideological tension between the bodily and the intellectual continued to shape education for young women across the nineteenth century and made advanced female education itself controversial. Some late-nineteenth-century medical experts, most prominently Dr. Edward Clarke of Harvard, insisted that higher education, particularly college-level study, wrecked women's physical health and took away their ability to reproduce. Clarke believed that as women studied, blood would flow to their brain away from other organs and because of this blood "loss," educated women would cease to menstruate. For Clarke and others, advanced education for women was not only inadvisable, but also destructive.[17] Not all medical experts agreed with Clarke, and advocates for female secondary education viewed their work as preserving female sexual innocence and teaching good moral habits. Promotional material for seminaries and other secondary schools consistently emphasized that they protected their students from sexual temptation; many of them were architecturally designed specifically to enhance the control over the young women in their care.[18]

Concerns about female sexual purity were heightened in the southern states. In the antebellum era, obsession with racial purity and bloodlines meant that white women's sexual reputation could define a family's status. Sexual purity became a defining feature of southern "true womanhood." At the same time, older folk beliefs about the sexual lasciviousness of women were projected onto black women, viewed as "jezebels," lacking in sexual restraint.[19] Most white northern women, even those sympathetic to the antislavery cause, accepted this idea, as it allowed for an ideological bifurcation between their own purity and black women's lewdness.[20] The cultural identification of black women with aggressive sexuality was even more pronounced in the South, where it served as a justification for white male sexual coercion of female slaves. As a result of this historical sexual exploitation and vilification, black women felt a powerful need to prove their own sexual purity.[21] Anxiety about women's sexuality did not end with abolition. Both white and black women continued to feel pressure to prove their sexual respectability in the changed landscape of the postwar era.[22] In some ways these concerns increased as southern women, black and white, sought out new public roles in the rapidly changing New South. The careful attention schools such as Lucy Cobb and Spelman gave to protecting their students from sexual temptation, and trying to get students to internalize chaste and modest behavior, reflect the continuing importance of sexual purity as a marker of female respectability and even racial progress.

In the aftermath of the Civil War and Reconstruction, southern women began renegotiating their place within a rapidly changing society. The end of slavery revolutionized the economy and society of the South. Across the region, the development of cotton mills and other industries threatened to challenge planters' hegemony. Railroads connected once-isolated areas to a national community, and terminals became new urban centers. Urbanization encouraged the growth of a business- and industry-oriented middle class, albeit one that shared familial ties and political interests with the older planter elite.[23] In Georgia, cotton agriculture remained the basis of the economy, and within a few years, production surpassed antebellum levels. This high production represented a problem as low prices, worn-out soil, and overconcentration in one area slowed economic growth. Some "New South boosters," such as the best known, Henry Grady of *The Atlanta Constitution*, promoted industrial development and scientific farming as an antidote. Although railroads, cotton mills, and extractive industries, such as timber production and mining, did make gains in the state in the 1870s and '80s, cotton remained the basis of the economy.[24]

All southerners experienced these changes, yet the lives of African Americans were most dramatically altered in the postwar years. Former slaves sought to reunite families separated by war or sale, and to create institutions—churches, schools, mutual aid societies—that would improve and give meaning to their new status as freedmen and women. Emancipation allowed African Americans more personal freedom and opportunity, but as blacks made economic and political gains, white supremacists responded with violence and legalized disenfranchisement and segregation.[25] Although most former slaves hoped to become landowners, the vast majority became sharecroppers, and by the end of the century, many were locked into a cycle of poverty and debt that made their condition appear materially little better than slavery. Many rural people, especially women, white and black, migrated to cities, swelling the population of Atlanta, the archetypical New South city, from 9554 in 1860 to over 65,000 in 1890. Although segregation laws did not appear until the 1890s, these newly urbanizing areas were, in effect, segregated, and many blacks lived in squalid, overcrowded, and disease-ridden conditions.[26] At the same time, cities provided chances for individual autonomy and organized resistance by African Americans. They also offered educated women new forms of employment. Families of the emerging black bourgeoisie often relied on the contributions of women's income, and professional black women's paid work, especially as teachers and health workers, contributed to the well being of the community.[27]

White women, too, faced new challenges and gained more access to power in the late nineteenth century South. During the war, plantation and yeomen women alike took on more responsibilities as their husbands and fathers left their homes to serve in the Confederate military. Many, left widowed, continued to provide for themselves and their families after the war's end, and to become more involved in political and social reform, particularly on behalf of Confederate veterans and the promotion of the Lost Cause.[28] Just as women took on newly political roles in the aftermath of the Revolution, after the Civil War, many white southerners began to see women's paid work and social activism as essential to sectional growth and improvement.[29] Private secondary schools for girls, still focused on training virtuous mothers, also became more explicit in promoting women as wage earners, especially teachers, and community activists. Across the South women increasingly became involved in politics and reform, and in Georgia, urban areas such as Atlanta and Athens in particular provided both white and black women new opportunities for employment as well as public activism in women's clubs and religious organizations.[30]

Still, politics in Georgia through the end of the nineteenth century largely remained dominated by a small, powerful elite that made reform slow and difficult. In the immediate postwar period, conservative white Democrats took advantage of the lenient terms of presidential Reconstruction, even electing former Confederate Vice President Alexander Stephens as senator, but by 1869, Radical Republicans in Congress put Georgia under military control. Nonetheless, within months, conservative Democrats began to dominate state government, and set about destroying the very limited progress (even in comparison to other former Confederate states) African Americans had made in gaining political influence. By 1877, a convention lacking any black representation adopted a state constitution that limited state power and gave rural areas disproportional representation. Further, by stipulating that only citizens who had paid all of their past and present taxes could vote, the constitution effectively disenfranchised not only the majority of potential black voters, but also many whites as well. This allowed conservative Democrats (known as Bourbons) to effectively create a one-party political system controlled by a small elite of "New South" developers who dominated the state's political system until the 1890s, leaving a legacy of white supremacy, limited government oversight of business, and lack of funding for public services. Notably, the 1877 constitution established a segregated public school system, but also severely limited the amount of money the state could pay for education, restricting state funding to the 1st through 8th grades. In the late decades of the nineteenth century, many areas, especially rural regions, offered no education at all after 6th grade.[31] This fact made private schools essential to the growth of education in postwar Georgia.

Both the poverty of the former Confederate states and specific state policies such as Georgia's that restricted funding help explain southerners' continuing reliance on nonpublic institutions. In isolated rural areas, private schools filled gaps in the still developing southern public system. Another factor was the control offered by private education, particularly desirable for black southerners. The experiences of African Americans confirmed that within unjust and oppressive states, public education could reify rather than challenge inequalities. Blacks looked for alternatives to the overcrowded, underfunded segregated public institutions all too often staffed by overtly racist teachers and administrators.[32] Elite white southerners also preferred private institutions, valuing those that provided a sense of exclusivity and privilege, the "air of refinement" mentioned by the observer of Lucy Cobb.[33]

Both schools analyzed here were founded as private institutions and viewed this status as central to their identity. The Lucy Cobb Institute, educating Georgia's elite, stubbornly fought incorporation by both the city of Athens and the University of Georgia in the 1920s, ultimately leading to its financial failure and closure in 1931. Principal Mildred Rutherford primarily resisted incorporation because she believed that the school's special character came from its history of female (and after 1880, alumnae) leadership, something that would be lost with city or university oversight. Spelman could not have existed as a public school in New South Atlanta. Despite sustained lobbying from local African Americans, the city of Atlanta refused to fund a black high school, and certainly would not have supported an institution with the educational ambition of Spelman.[34] In both cases, the schools' leaders fiercely defended the private status of their institutions, fearing loss of personal control and destruction of the distinctiveness of the institutions that they created.

These southern women's interest in private control of their educational institutions suggests that not all of women's involvement in public activism during the Progressive Era was associated with state building. In recent years, feminist historians have highlighted women's contribution to late-nineteenth and early twentieth-century development of public social policy, especially in policy related to women and children.[35] According to this "maternalist" model, women pushed for new laws benefiting women and children, justifying their public activism as an extension of their role as mothers. The emphasis on "state-building" in feminist historical scholarship has been intended to demonstrate the significance of women's activism. Yet within a restrictive, narrowly defined state such as the turn-of-the-century South, women's work in building private institutions proved equally if not more significant than their efforts to expand government services. By focusing on private, female-headed, and influential schools, this book emphasizes the importance of these extra-governmental institutions in southern society.

For the founders and leaders of the Lucy Cobb Institute of Athens, the subject of the first two chapters, private status was central to the school's character. Founded in 1859 by prominent lawyer and pro-slavery theorist T.R.R. Cobb, the Lucy Cobb Institute remained associated with the Old South planter aristocracy after the war. Cobb's niece, Mildred Rutherford, graduated from Lucy Cobb and then spent nearly fifty years teaching and directing the school. Rutherford had an additional career as a historian and leader of the United Daughters of the Confederacy. Like many contemporary female academies, Lucy Cobb provided young elite white women an education that would mark them as ladies, offering courses in music, art, and French, and a strong emphasis on feminine and sexual modesty. At first glance, the institute appears to be a typical finishing school. But Lucy Cobb, and Rutherford, proved to be much more complex and forward-looking than might be expected.

The pedagogical goals of Spelman Seminary (now College) in Atlanta were also more complicated than they might first appear. White northern female missionaries founded the seminary in 1881 to educate and uplift former slaves and their daughters. Arriving fifteen years after the first postwar northern educators, the school's founders had more experience and dedication than earlier instructors, and just as important, they benefited from the financial backing of John D. Rockefeller. The school combined industrial instruction with academic and religious education. But the intent of Spelman's industrial training was not to keep students as second-class citizens. Indeed, the history of Spelman's first fifty years demonstrates the many meanings of industrial instruction and questions the traditional division of African American education as following either Booker T. Washington's industrial model or W.E.B. Du Bois's support for black intellectual achievement. At Spelman, educators—and many students—viewed industrial and academic education as equally essential in creating a female talented tenth. Those who sought to create race leaders at Spelman viewed not only academic achievement, but also character virtues, including chastity and respectability, as crucial.

By studying Lucy Cobb and Spelman together, I hope to highlight the significance of race in the creation of both white and black women's identities. My analysis focuses on inequalities between women and the complex interaction of race, gender, and class in women's lives. By highlighting intersecting power differences, recent scholarship has examined the ways in which women have benefited from, and sometimes contributed to, the oppression of other women. Comparing these two educational institutions highlights the importance of race in creating the gendered identities of both black and white women, and acknowledges Nell Irvin Painter's call to write history "across the color line."[36]

Differences between these schools are readily apparent. Lucy Cobb and Spelman educated quite distinct student populations with very different material and political resources. Yet the two schools shared a common goal—preparing young women for the changed circumstances of the postwar South. Both black and white women had new opportunities despite the constraints of the postwar South, particularly as teachers. In addition, and importantly, both schools put great emphasis on controlling female sexuality, a goal that links them to Revolutionary-era anxieties about rationality, femininity, and the body, but that also reflects the fragile position of women active in the public sphere in the late nineteenth-early twentieth century South. Both schools put great importance in creating modest and respectable women who would represent their race well in both the private and public sphere.

Yet the meaning of "respectability" varied by race. For white women, respectability meant behavior, deportment, and reputation that signified sexual purity and class status. As was true in the antebellum era, policing white women's sexual purity was a means of ensuring racial purity. In the New South era, it also served as justification for the "reforms" of segregation and disenfranchisement, frequently explained as measures created to protect white women from aggressive black men. White women who acted in ways considered too assertive, bold, or immodest eroded the pretext for these "protections." In sum, respectability for white women was about maintaining whiteness as a marker of privilege and power, by ensuring "pure" bloodlines and justifying legally mandated racial separation. For black women, respectability was about defying and overcoming stereotypes of all black women as sexually aggressive and generally uncouth. Black female respectability was not only a private attribute, but also a way of demonstrating the worthiness of black women as a whole, and the readiness of African Americans as a group for full citizenship rights and privileges. In this way, respectability for black women had political weight, but the pressure to maintain it could be overwhelming. For both white and black women, female respectability was tightly intertwined with sexual reputation and racial ideology, and had political, as well as personal, significance.

Examining schools for girls run and staffed by women allows us to see how women themselves developed new ideas about women's responsibilities and duties for their society and their race in the changed circumstances of the New South. Although both schools stressed motherhood and marriage as central to female identity, they anticipated that graduates would contribute to southern society and racial progress (defined quite differently at each school) as well. In linking education with the reconstruction of women's lives in the postwar era, the following chapters analyze not only region and gender, but also race and class. More broadly, they suggest how women contributed to postwar political and cultural reunification and the redefinition of not only the South, but also the nation as a whole. Education helped women remake their own identities as they strove to create their vision of a just New South within a fully reunified nation.

1 The "Perfection of Sacred Womanhood"

*Educating Young Ladies at the
Lucy Cobb Institute, 1880–1908*

In 1857, the Athens, Georgia, *Watchman* printed a letter pleading for greater attention to female education in the town, home of the nation's first public university. The letter, signed "A Mother," read:

> What now constitutes the education of females in Athens? We answer, some years of instruction in these primary schools, with a few music and French lessons. Our daughters are then sent forth into the world at the age of fifteen or sixteen, with minds undisciplined and uninformed, to buffet with the cares and difficulties of life. . . . Many, feeling the destitution at home, send their daughters abroad—some to Northern schools, where, during their whole course, they have their feelings continually wounded with reflections upon their domestic institutions, or return home with minds half prejudiced against their native state . . . Shame upon classic Athens! Shame upon the wealth and erudition of our citizens.[1]

The author of the letter, Laura Battile Cobb Rutherford, had five daughters of her own at the time; the oldest, eleven-year-old Sarah, would soon complete the highest level of education available for girls in Athens.[2] Laura Rutherford's brother, the nationally known lawyer and pro-slavery writer Thomas Reads Rootes (T. R. R.) Cobb, read the letter in the *Watchman*, and, reportedly unaware that his sister had authored it, was moved to found a school for the young women of Athens, intending to enroll his own thirteen-year-old daughter Lucy. Tragically for the Cobb family, both Sarah Rutherford and Lucy Cobb died before the school opened in 1859. To honor the family's loss, the new school's board of directors named the school after young Lucy. Although Sarah did not live to attend the Lucy Cobb Institute,

Laura Rutherford's four daughters who survived early childhood not only graduated from the school, but also, as principals and teachers, shaped it into one of the leading precollegiate schools for young white women in postwar Georgia.[3]

Although the Lucy Cobb, as it was affectionately known by alumnae, never achieved the financial stability, enrollment numbers, or academic reputation of the best-known southern women's colleges, it was a much more complex institution than the stereotypical "finishing school." At its founding in 1859, Lucy Cobb Institute fit within an antebellum tradition of elite female education emphasizing gentility and social graces. Yet while the school promoted a feminine ideal that in many ways harkened back to a nostalgic version of antebellum southern womanhood, Lucy Cobb Institute also prepared students for diverse public experiences, including clubwork, religious activism, and even employment. The education offered at Lucy Cobb, particularly after 1880 when Laura Rutherford's daughters took over its administration, did more than ready young women for a life of domesticity and motherhood; it shaped women into active participants in the culture, economy, and politics of the New South.

Lucy Cobb Institute offers a window into how elite white women redefined their social role within the context of the economic and social transformations of the New South. Whereas scholars have analyzed the increased public activism of white southern women in the post-Civil War period, less attention has been paid to how education prepared young women for the changed circumstances.[4] Educational institutions, particularly private secondary schools, expressed new expectations for young women. Public high schools remained relatively rare in the post-Civil War South, particularly outside of large urban areas, both because of the limited budgets of the former Confederate states and the preference for private institutions by southern families. But female secondary-level educational opportunities expanded at the end of the century, as many young women enrolled in schools like Lucy Cobb.[5] The increased reliance on the income of and support for the activism of women, even in elite families, combined with a new confidence that education could enhance, rather than destroy, femininity, made secondary education attractive to New South families. As such, it represents a particularly useful arena in which to examine new ideologies about womanhood, race, and sexuality in the postwar era, as expressed by both educators and their students.

Between 1880 and the end of the century, Mildred Lewis Rutherford along with her sister Mary Ann Rutherford Lipscomb, nieces of founder Thomas Cobb, took part in the creation of a new model of southern white womanhood, an ideal that preserved aspects of elite antebellum femininity while also borrowing from the Progressive Era "New Woman." Rutherford and Lipscomb, like other New South educators, attempted to fashion a uniquely southern alternative to both the passive Old South belle and the defiant new woman. Although some hailed from plantations, most Lucy Cobb students lived in towns and cities, and their fathers worked in positions such as agricultural merchants, mill owners, railroad directors, and insurance executives. These young women took advantage of the expanded educational, club, and professional opportunities available to women in the New South period. Yet they retained the propriety, respectability, and modesty associated with antebellum femininity. Indeed, these attributes offered these southern young ladies protection from disrepute even as they took active roles in shaping the character of the New South.

The hope of Lucy Cobb teachers and administrators, especially Mildred Rutherford, was that their graduates would use their new opportunities to defend the ideals of southern womanhood, white supremacy, and upper class hegemony, goals that seemed to be on the mind of her mother when writing the 1857 letter to the *Watchman*. Creation of a "southern" identity, defined as veneration of the Lost Cause, support for racial hierarchy, and adherence to gendered notions of gentility, shaped the schooling offered at Lucy Cobb; students were being educated to become the "southern ladies, new women" analyzed by Joan Marie Johnson.[6] For parents of Lucy Cobb students, the school's association with the antebellum elite and feminine propriety made the school an attractive choice. Not all "Lucies," as they were affectionately known, however, accepted their teachers' views of a properly ordered society, and some created roles for themselves that in some ways fulfilled but also defied the expectations of their teachers. Yet almost all accepted the importance of an honorable public persona—that is, the ideal of respectability—as a prerequisite for public life. This emphasis on propriety attested to the continuing belief that female intellectual achievement could only be achieved by downplaying female sexuality. Additionally, it underlines the importance of the ideal of respectability, defined largely as sexual propriety, for New South women across lines of race and class, especially for those exploring new educational, employment, and activist opportunities in the changing economic and social climate.

In the 1850s, Athens, Georgia, was the major town of Clarke County, situated in the northern edge of the state's plantation belt. Established in 1802 expressly as the site of the first public university charted in the nation, Athens declared the pretensions of its founders in its name. The university, known until 1848 as Franklin College, graduated its first class in 1804. Although the college struggled to maintain adequate funding, retain faculty, and keep up enrollment, it succeeded in drawing settlers into rural north Georgia. The university's Greek Revival buildings, especially its temple-like chapel completed in 1832, signaled what would become the town's architectural ideal. Following this classical style, the elite of Athens built large, stately white homes, with columns, large porches, high ceilings, and plenty of windows.[7] The Lucy Cobb Institute, built in the late 1850s and located about a mile from the university campus, conformed to this grand style. Fronted by columns and an ample porch, the school, a long white building of three stories, faced Milledge Avenue, a street populated by the town's leading families.[8]

Whereas the fortunes of the residents of Athens were closely tied to those of the university, agriculture drove the economy of surrounding Clarke County. In 1840, eighty percent of the county's whites worked the land, some relying on the labor of enslaved people. Although north of Georgia's major cotton growing region, the county was home to a few large plantations, and the area's rate of slaveholding and its concentration in fewer hands increased over time. In 1830, the county reported 4,709 black slaves and 5,467 whites; twenty years later, slaves had a slight majority. Forty-nine planters owned one-third of the county's enslaved people in 1830, but by 1840, 71 owned more than half. Clarke County, however, did not remain entirely dependent on agriculture, and even boasted some industry before the Civil War. Thanks to the presence of local men in its corporate hierarchy, the Georgia Railroad passed through Athens, reaching the town in 1841. The railroad allowed Athens to become a major trade center for the agricultural goods grown in the state, especially cotton. The presence of the railroad also encouraged the development of cotton processing in Athens. By 1840, the county's three cotton factories together had about 220 laborers, both white and black (mostly slaves hired out by their owners), and made Clarke second among Georgia's counties in terms of investment in industry.[9]

Colonel John Addison Cobb, Laura Rutherford's father, profited from Clarke County's opportunities in agriculture, the railroad, and real estate. In the 1820s, attracted by the presence of the university, Cobb settled with his family in Athens. In 1834, he divided up the property he owned within the town's limits and sold the lots to new residents. The area, home to the antebellum elite and now a historic district, is still known as Cobbham. In addition to owning a plantation and 209 slaves by 1840 (only one other man in the county owned more than 200), Cobb served on the board of directors of the Georgia Railroad and of the Athens branch of the Bank of the State of Georgia, and had helped found the Athens Baptist Church.[10]

Cobb may have been a big man in the small town of Athens, but the influence of his sons expanded well beyond the classic city. By the time his younger son Thomas Cobb, a lawyer, founded the Lucy Cobb Institute, he had written the official codification of state law, as well as several widely read defenses of slavery. These included his best-known work, *An Inquiry into the Law of Negro Slavery in the United States of America* (1858), and a series of essays in a Boston paper titled "Letters from an Honest Slaveholder," intended as a rebuttal to Harriet Beecher Stowe's *Uncle Tom's Cabin*. Howell Cobb, Thomas's older brother, made a career as a politician, serving as a congressman for five terms (and briefly as Speaker of the House), as governor of Georgia, and as secretary of the treasury in James Buchanan's cabinet. Although in Congress Howell Cobb was considered a unionist and had been a major supporter of the Compromise of 1850, in 1860 both he and his brother joined the secessionist movement in Georgia and were instrumental in securing the state's vote to leave the Union. The brothers participated in Confederate politics as well, Thomas as part of the committee that wrote the Confederate Constitution and Howell by becoming the first speaker of the Provisional Congress of the Confederate States, and both men served as wartime generals. Thomas Cobb's devotion to the Confederate cause cost him his life; he was killed in 1862 at Fredericksburg. Howell Cobb continued to be active in state Democratic politics until his death in 1868.[11]

Thomas and Howell Cobb's sister Laura married Williams Rutherford, a mathematics professor at the University of Georgia and the owner of a sizable plantation in southern Georgia. The Rutherfords spent the university semester break, then October through December, on the plantation.[12] This arrangement allowed the family to profit from both the wealth and social status provided by the plantation and the sociability and opportunities of town life. In 1859, as war approached, Williams Rutherford sold the family plantation and purchased one just outside of Athens. Both he and his only son who survived infancy served in the Confederate army.[13]

Like other elite southern women, Laura Rutherford faced new challenges during the war, and struggled with the scarcities of food and other goods created by the conflict. After their husbands left for military service, women like Rutherford took on new responsibilities in their homes and on their family plantations. Laura Rutherford also became very active in women's "war work" during the Confederate years. As the cofounder and second president of the Volunteer Aid Society (later the Soldiers' Aid Society), she supervised the collection of clothes and other supplies, and even took wounded Confederate soldiers into her own home. After the Confederate surrender, Laura Rutherford turned the local Soldiers' Aid Society into the Athens chapter of the Ladies' Memorial Association (LMA). Active across the South, LMAs undertook the responsibility of collecting the remains of fallen Confederate soldiers, scattered across the southern countryside, and reburying them in graveyards, a task left to largely female volunteers in the absence of a post-war Confederate state. The work of LMAs represented not only women's interest in honoring the military service of the Confederate dead, but more significantly, attested to the continuing support of elite white women to the ideals of the Confederacy. At the same time, the LMA allowed women an expanded postwar public role and paved the way for women's activism in later organizations. Laura Rutherford viewed her participation as an exten-sion of both her support for the Confederacy and her wartime dedication to aiding ailing soldiers, and she remained president of the Athens chapter until her death in 1888, when her daughter Mildred succeeded her, becoming president for life.[14]

The Rutherfords weathered the war and its aftermath comparatively well. Maj. Gen. William Sherman's "March to the Sea" did not pass through Athens, and throughout the war the family's plantation continued to produce. After emancipation, many of the family's former slaves became sharecroppers on Williams Rutherford's land while he resumed his work teaching at the uni-versity. But the extended family did not escape unscathed. The disruptions of war, economic losses and hardship, and the deaths of family members and of the young soldiers nursed in their home left a deep psychological imprint upon Laura Rutherford's children, especially Mildred, whose later activities attest to her abiding bitterness over wartime loss.[15]

By pushing for better schooling for girls in Athens, Laura Rutherford contributed to the nineteenth century expansion of education for young southern women. In the nineteenth century, separate spheres ideology led to increasing numbers of girls attending post-primary schools in all regions. The nineteenth-century idea of separate spheres viewed women as essentially different from men, but as excelling in their "sphere" of the home and in the sentimental values associated with domesticity. Women, therefore, needed formal education as much as men did, but they needed a particularly feminine education, one fitted to their sphere. Although some scholars have viewed separate spheres as specifically northern and urban, others have identified a southern variant of the ideology that celebrated feminine "values" and viewed women as responsible for family morality and virtue, just like "republican mothers" elsewhere.[16]

Perhaps surprisingly, before the Civil War, the South led the nation in the number of female schools claiming the name of "college" (many of which would have been more accurately described as secondary schools) despite the fact that elite southern women were less likely to work for pay than northern women of their class. Historian Christie Anne Farnham argues that it was *because* women were not expected to work that these female colleges and academies were so popular. In northern towns and cities, middle-class women could seek employment either before or instead of marriage, and retain their respectability. Many of these women worked as teachers, and sought out better education for themselves, encouraging the growth of northern and western schools for girls—schools that also provided them employment. On the other hand, the pseudo-medieval ideas of chivalry and honor that influenced southern gender ideology both stigmatized women's paid labor and encouraged the development of southern schools for daughters of elite families, but their education differed from that of their northern sisters. Female education in the South, especially knowledge of French, music, and art, served as a marker of class status rather than as preparation for work. Nineteenth-century southern schools taught young women how to be "ladies"; they strengthened rather than threatened the gender hierarchy. At the same time, many schools did aspire to be academically rigorous, and offered courses in languages, literature, sciences, and mathematics. In fact, southern women's schools were more likely than northern schools to offer a foundation in the liberal arts, because even academically serious education had little chance of challenging gender subordination.[17]

These schools were, of course, private institutions. Nineteenth-century southerners favored private schools over publicly funded ones for a number of reasons. Public schools, as representatives of state power, suggested a threat to traditional sources of authority—the church, the family, and local elites. Rural white southerners, wary of losing power to distant bureaucracy, resisted the development of public school systems. Yeoman families did not see the value of formal schooling, and although elite families did, they wanted to ensure that the content and method of their children's education met with their approval. Schools for girls, especially, had to reassure parents that they would protect their students from threats to their safety and, as important, their moral and sexual reputations. Many of these schools, as a result, had elaborate rules designed to shield their students and themselves from accusations of sexual impropriety.[18]

In its blending of academic and ornamental subjects, Lucy Cobb resembled antebellum academies for girls. Very involved in the schools earliest years, Thomas Cobb intended that it would teach young women their feminine duties and domestic responsibilities.[19] The school's first director announced the opening of the Lucy Cobb Institute in 1859 with a pamphlet emphasizing the "parental watchfulness" of the institute and the "careful attention" given to the "health . . . manners and morals" of the boarding students rather than academic offerings. The school remained open during the war but lost its original principal, who returned north after the beginning of hostilities.[20] His successor feared overtaxing the minds of his pupils and offered subjects common in southern antebellum female schools such as "Ornamental Needlework" and "Wax Fruit and Flowers," subjects intended to teach students both an eye for beauty and knowledge of botany. But Lucy Cobb also offered instruction in Latin, Greek, and Hebrew.[21] One early principal, the German-born Madame Sophie Sosnowski, also had directed the South Carolina Collegiate Institute, a school with aspirations to college-level education.[22] By the 1870s, Lucy Cobb was given "full power and authority to grant diplomas . . . and to confer all such degrees as are usually conferred by female colleges," but in reality, the education offered was closer to an advanced secondary education, and the institute never renamed itself a "college." Nonetheless, the school had become a source of local pride. Commencements, performances, and other events were routinely reported in the Athens and Atlanta newspapers and enrollment rose steadily.[23]

At the same time, and not unusually for southern female academies both before and after the war, financial uncertainty and unreliable leadership haunted the early years of Lucy Cobb.[24] Several early principals left after very short terms. Madame Sosnowski, the most successful, opened a competing

Figure 1. The Lucy Cobb Institute building. (Georgia photograph file, Hargrett Library, University of Georgia)

school in Athens and brought several Lucy Cobb students with her.[25] In 1880, the Board of Trustees, probably in an effort to create more stability, decided to recruit Laura Rutherford's four daughters, who had all graduated from Lucy Cobb, to direct the school.[26] They first offered Bessie Rutherford, a Lucy Cobb math teacher, a promotion to principal, but she turned it down. So did her widowed sister, Mary Ann Rutherford Lipscomb, at that time teaching in Washington, D.C. The Board finally turned to their sister Mildred who also refused initially, but responding to her parents' pleading eventually agreed to direct her alma mater. Mildred Rutherford's reluctant acceptance of the post of Lucy Cobb principal began nearly fifty years of involvement at the school as director and instructor in the fields of literature, history, and the Bible.[27]

From an early age, Rutherford demonstrated the independence and self-assurance that would mark her career as an educator, author, and activist. Mildred Rutherford was not an especially tall woman, yet she had a commanding presence and inspired admiration among men and women alike. Her most outstanding physical feature may well have been her perfect posture. One alumna remembered that whenever Rutherford passed through a room, people instinctively straightened themselves. Her "queenly bearing" and formal, old-fashioned dress complemented her powerful personality.[28] Although biographies and Lucy Cobb legend claim that Mildred Rutherford had plenty of suitors as a young girl, she neither married nor seemed interested in marriage, a situation not unusual for elite white southern women born in the decade before the Civil War. After graduating from Lucy Cobb in 1867, she left Athens in 1872 to become a public school teacher in Atlanta. She taught there for eight years, including several years at the Girls' High School, until becoming principal of Lucy Cobb in 1880. She did so on her own terms, insisting that she, not the Board of Directors, be given control of the school's budget and of hiring faculty.[29]

Rutherford took on the principalship of the Lucy Cobb during a particularly contentious time in Georgia history as the state's residents continued to struggle with the legacy of secession, war, and emancipation. These economic and political changes had profound impact on the lives of elite white women like Rutherford herself. In her comprehensive study of elite white southern women after the Civil War, Jane Turner Censer found that while the war reshaped the lives of all of her subjects, it was the youngest women, born between 1850 and 1869, that adapted most completely to the new circumstances of the New South. Rutherford, born in 1851, witnessed the disruptions and violence of the war as a young child and the reduction of family fortune that required many families to rely on the income of unmarried daughters.

Figure 2. Mildred Lewis Rutherford in antebellum dress, undated photo. (David Lewis Earnest photograph collection, Hargrett Library, University of Georgia)

Although many of these women began teaching out of financial need, many discovered that they preferred self-support to the alternative of marriage, and consciously decided to remain single. Never married, Rutherford supported herself as a teacher, author, and principal, and like other educators, she clearly valued the respect, independence, and influence teaching and publishing allowed her.[30]

Rutherford, however, although valuing her self-sufficiency, did not advocate for the expansion of women's rights or suffrage. For her, suffrage would destroy rather than enhance women's power by eroding female "influence" in the home and society. Like other anti-suffragists, Rutherford despaired that the vote would destroy women's claim to respectable femininity, and in the process, their source of power and honor. As she argued in 1914 to the Georgia House of Representatives, "the glare of public life" had made modern woman "an unsexed mongrel, shorn of her true power and vainly beating against the air in dissatisfaction with herself" and warned that suffrage would only harm women further, sentiments echoed by other "antis."[31] Anti-suffragists such as Virginia's Emily Bissel, identifying gender difference as a mark of civilization, also argued that suffrage would be a step towards "barbarism" and would erode white supremacy. Southern antis especially worried that racial disenfranchisement would be threatened by increased federal attention to the electoral process. Opposition to suffrage by southern women like Rutherford often signaled support for their privileged class and racial position, one they viewed as dependent on traditional, respectable femininity.[32]

This worldview, both embracing new opportunities for women, but also seeing too much change as a threat, informed the educational philosophy of Lucy Cobb. Rutherford both looked back to the tradition of the education of the "southern belle" and forward to the changed circumstances of elite white women in the New South in creating Lucy Cobb's curriculum.[33] The antebellum southern belle had combined vivaciousness, physical beauty, and sociability with absolute dedication to propriety and chastity. Although she enjoyed the company of young men, the belle understood the limitations of permissible flirtation and realized that premarital sexual experimentation could destroy the honor of an elite white woman's entire family. Like antebellum educators of young women, particularly the male ministers who dominated southern women's education in the 1840s and 1850s, Rutherford stressed the centrality of religious piety and sexual modesty to feminine character, and discouraged the frivolity and coquettishness sometimes associated with the belle.[34] Downplaying these traits, she celebrated the association of antebellum girlhood with the genteel life of the plantation. At the same time, Rutherford also understood that elite women of the New South faced new expectations and opportunities, including clubwork and paid employment, which set them apart from their antebellum counterparts, and Rutherford encouraged students to partake in these new opportunities, as long as they retained their propriety. By retaining the sexual modesty and manners associated with antebellum young women, Lucy Cobb's students could transgress boundaries while appearing respectable, even traditional.

Rutherford could cite herself as an example of a woman who stepped outside of the restraints of traditional southern womanhood, and yet remained unquestionably respectable and widely admired. A leading anti-suffrage activist and advocate for women's domesticity, she nonetheless carved out a public role for herself, writing and speaking on political issues affecting not only Athens, but Georgia and the nation. Although she taught her students to emulate the self-effacement of antebellum young women, she aggressively sought publicity for her own writings and in the 1920s, for an endowment for Lucy Cobb. At Lucy Cobb, Rutherford did not allow students to walk by themselves beyond the front yard's stately magnolia tree, but she introduced them to new cultures and experiences by taking them to Europe, part of the process of becoming "ladies," according to her niece. These contradictions allowed Lucy Cobb students to interpret the meaning or message of their education individually, negotiating their own understandings of the goals and ideology of the school.[35]

During her first tenure as principal, Rutherford worked to improve Lucy Cobb's academic standards while not losing focus on producing respectable young ladies.[36] Rutherford, with the help of her sister, Mary Ann Lipscomb, after her return from Washington in 1881, directed Lucy Cobb Institute's growth in enrollment and reputation over the next fifteen years. In 1880, six boarding and twenty day students attended Lucy Cobb Institute, and eight teachers made up the faculty. Only two years later, 104 students were enrolled, and students were divided into primary, academic (middle school), and collegiate (advanced secondary school) departments, and the number of instructors had risen to twelve. Tuition for Lucy Cobb was on par with other women's schools; in 1883, the school charged $30 a session (semester) for the collegiate department, and $107.50 for board, fuel, tuition, and incidentals.[37] In comparison, Agnes Scott College in Decatur, Georgia, one of the few true colleges for women in the South, charged $127.50 per term for on-campus students in 1888.[38]

Rutherford, like her predecessors, continued to offer courses associated with antebellum schools. Students earned grades for deportment and posture ("shoulders"). A class in elocution, a popular elective, not only developed poise, but also was intended to rid the girls of "even a trace of 'Cracker' accent."[39] Art and music classes, often demanded by southern parents, were thought to bestow students with femininity and gentility, and these classes received special attention in Lucy Cobb catalogues. In 1883, Lucy Cobb employed as many instructors for the art, music, and French programs as it did for its core curriculum. Many nineteenth century institutions relied on fees charged for these extra classes to remain open, and Lucy Cobb was no exception. Fees from electives such as French, music, art, and elocution kept the school solvent. Additionally, they had practical utility; although those subjects seemed most in keeping with the ornamental education of some antebellum schools, in the postwar era, they offered young women of elite families the possibility of respectable employment as teachers or private instructors in these areas. In a nod to elite southern white women's increasing reliance on their own domestic skills rather than those of servants, Lucy Cobb offered optional courses in cooking and dressmaking as well.[40]

Even with these classes, Rutherford's curriculum emphasized traditional academic subjects, and compared favorably to other female academies in the late nineteenth century. She organized the collegiate track into a five-year class system (freshman, sophomore, and so on, with the freshman course spread out over two years) and required five years of Latin, five of mathematics (including algebra, geometry, and trigonometry), and several years of the sciences (botany, chemistry, geology), logic, rhetoric, philosophy, and literature (including history).[41] This plan of study was based on the traditional "male" liberal arts curriculum that emphasized ancient languages and higher mathematics. Despite the fact that educators justified women's education on the basis of sexual difference and women's special instructional needs, most female colleges and academies with serious academic programs followed the liberal arts model. Women's colleges, however, typically either adopted a less rigorous approach to traditional subjects, or substituted modern languages for either Latin or Greek, or both. For example, the Columbia Female College in South Carolina offered English, math, natural science, moral science, and languages.[42] Lucy Cobb followed this pattern; Rutherford included five years of Latin and math, but did not offer Greek and saved more difficult Latin texts for the optional post-graduate year.[43] Although Lucy Cobb did not offer an education comparable with the top northern women's colleges, it did compare favorably with other contemporary southern female academies.

By 1890, the number of faculty, as well as their areas of expertise, had expanded significantly. Rutherford divided Lucy Cobb into "schools" of music, math, languages, and science. Teachers in the academic "schools," almost all of whom were women, included alumnae of colleges such as Wellesley and the College of Music in Cincinnati.[44] An 1893 observer praised the school's

Figure 3. Lucy Cobb library. (Georgia photograph file, Hargrett Library, University of Georgia)

attention to "current literature," or current events, in which students debated issues of political importance such as tariff policy.[45] To further broaden the course offerings, Rutherford created a lecture series given by faculty of the University of Georgia. Professors such as Andrew A. Lipscomb, a leading Shakespeare scholar and later chancellor of the university, and Chancellor P. H. Mell, an expert on law, lectured four or five times a semester at Lucy Cobb.[46] Students also used facilities at the university, such as the chemistry lab. Lucy Cobb's close relationship with the university strengthened its course offerings significantly and gave the school greater prestige than more isolated and rural schools.

Rutherford also improved the buildings and grounds of the school, de-scribed by an alumna as "'run down at the heel,' so to speak."[47] In the 1880s, Rutherford added several new buildings, including an infirmary, a new school-room, and new boarding rooms, and, most significantly, the Seney-Stovall Chapel. Although Lucy Cobb was nondenominational, Rutherford, a devout Baptist, believed that religious instruction ought to be a cornerstone of educa-tion. She wanted a beautiful and architecturally significant building that would symbolize the centrality of religious beliefs to the school, and at the same time announce the importance of the school to the community. Unable to raise funds for a new chapel locally, she assigned members of a composition class to write letters to well-known philanthropists interested in education. The exercise proved successful and had the additional benefit of teaching young Lucies the skill of fund-raising, an essential part of the work of contemporary women's clubs. Student Nellie Stovall's letter caught the attention of George Seney, a New Yorker with ties to Georgia, who agreed to give $10,000 if the town could raise another $4000. Rutherford accepted the challenge, and by 1883, the new chapel was completed and named for Seney and Stovall. The center of religious and social life for the school, it housed performances, commencements, and community events, securing Lucy Cobb's place as an important Athens institution.[48] Students performed in two recitals a year, demonstrating progress in music, elocution, and French, but parents could exempt students from performances for reasons of modesty.[49]

Modesty, in fact, was a chief concern of Rutherford's, and she did her best to make sure that the school cultivated feminine virtue in all students. Like other directors of boarding schools for women, Rutherford needed to protect her school's reputation, and imposed very strict rules on the Luc-ies under her guardianship.[50] Students were not allowed to spend the night away from the school; entertain male visitors other than brothers, fathers, and uncles; receive food other than fruit as gifts; dress "extravagantly" or wear silk or satin; or venture on their own beyond the stately magnolia tree in front of the main building. In 1889 Rutherford also banned student clubs, many of which had secret rituals, exclusive membership, and extravagant entertainments at commencement. The principal cited the impropriety of their mixed-sex commencement parties and the jealousies and rivalries the clubs created among students. Rules like these were justified, Rutherford believed, so "that the school may be protected against criticism as regards to lax discipline."[51] Further, they offered reassurance to families concerned about sending their daughters away from their own watchful eyes during a risky time of their adolescence. Yet as scholar Shira Birnbaum notes, the regulation of young women's dress, behavior, movement, and time at women's schools also functioned to underscore their vulnerability, and emphasized their need for masculine protection, especially against the dangers of the threat of black men.[52]

It was this training in morals and manners, more than differences in curricula, which distinguished Lucy Cobb and other institutions for women from contemporary male colleges. Southern universities had a long reputation for wildness and even violence; antebellum students fought, carried weapons, committed vandalism, and even threatened faculty members.[53] In the New South era, observers feared that university students, including those at Lucy Cobb's neighbor, the University of Georgia, had fallen into a "spirit of dissipation, licentiousness, even lawlessness."[54] Lucy Cobb Institute was the recipient of a particularly flirtatious brand of vandalism—painting the iron and plaster Lucy Cobb goats that sat on the school's front porch red and black, the UGA colors, was an annual ritual for university men. At least once university students snuck a live goat on to Lucy Cobb grounds.[55] Although generally willing to put up with these incidents, Rutherford and her successors did worry about the potential bad influence of university men, one factor in their careful regulation of the movements of Lucies under their care.

Although Rutherford hoped to ensure that rumors of impropriety did not discourage parents from enrolling their children in Lucy Cobb, her chief interest—and that of her pupils' families—lay in creating students who conformed to the social ideal of the sexually, and racially, pure southern lady. Unlike contemporary southern women who ventured north to the Seven Sister colleges, the young women who attended the Lucy Cobb received an education that stressed white female respectability over intellectual challenges.[56] Rutherford's concern with correct and ladylike behavior was not unique to Lucy Cobb; many turn-of-the century southern schools, even those calling themselves "colleges," emphasized propriety and feminine virtue rather than, or at least in addition to, academics.[57] Neither was it new in southern women's education. The tie between sexual reputation and white women's class identity extended back to the antebellum era. Obsession with bloodlines and racial purity created by the fear of miscegenation had made sexual reputation the defining feature of antebellum southern "true womanhood."[58] During and after the war, disruptions such as emancipation and urbanization made sexual propriety even more central to maintaining class identity for women in the New South. Planters like Rutherford's father had lost both wealth and un-questioned political supremacy during Reconstruction. Emancipation and the physical destruction of the war destabilized the plantation system, and "new men" made fortunes in industry. Although conservative Democrats remained powerful, in Georgia, both the Republican and Independent parties threatened Democratic hegemony during the 1870s and 1880s, and the Populists made gains in the state in the 1890s.[59] Because of these changes, families losing income or power sought to maintain their elite status through reputation and behavior. Schools for girls could play a key role in teaching women how to live as New South ladies.[60] As Rutherford's biographer wrote, Lucy Cobb's principal taught her students that "morals and manners," not wealth, indicated "aristocracy."[61]

Further, as early as the Revolutionary period, supporters of schools for women sought to justify the idea of educating women by de-emphasizing feminine sexuality and physicality. The interest in creating a rational, civic-minded citizenry in the wake of the Revolution gave new importance to female schooling and helped redefine the image of learned women. Education would allow women to properly raise future citizens, and to themselves embody the new value given to rationality and restraint. No longer dismissed as a domineering shrew, an educated woman now could be a republican mother—feminine, family-oriented, prudent, and patriotic. The new emphasis on female intelligence led to a de-emphasis or even discomfort with female sexuality and pregnancy in particular as both seemed to link women too closely with their physical bodies rather than their rational minds. In this way, the post-Revolution fertility decline and early nineteenth-century obsession with female chastity reflected new perceptions of pregnancy as a problem rather than a blessing. Indeed the mission of many schools in the early republic was explicitly to impress upon women the importance of sexual abstinence until marriage and restraint within it, in reaction to the high incidence of unwed motherhood in the late eighteenth century. This legacy, of linking female intellectual achievement with a restriction of female sexuality, remained well beyond the formative post-Revolutionary period and continued to shape educators of young women in the later decades of the nineteenth century, including Rutherford and her sister.[62]

Late nineteenth-century administrators of women's colleges and seminaries worried not only about their students engaging in inappropriate behavior with men, but also about overly close friendships with their female classmates. According to Helen Horowitz, whereas in the 1870s the "smash" was seen as a source of amusement by students and a nuisance, but not a moral problem, by faculty and administrators, by the turn of the century the renamed "crush," although still prevalent, increasingly seemed immature in "official student opinion," and alarming to school leaders.[63] These relationships did not seem to trouble Lucy Cobb administrators, however, to any significant degree, and the school had no official policy on them. In their private writings, several Lucies, including Rutherford's niece, referred to emotional attachments between classmates, generally without disapproval.[64] Rutherford herself made no statement that survives, because she either ignored or tolerated these relationships. Instead, she focused her concern on the danger of inappropriate intimacy between Lucies and men.

In addition to reflecting the tradition in female education of emphasizing sexual modesty, Rutherford's concern with personal propriety extended from her Southern Baptist faith. Nineteenth-century Southern Baptists regarded personal morality as key to salvation and to perfecting society, and hence put great emphasis on individual virtue. Southern Baptist faith also supported traditional hierarchies and the ideal of deference to social superiors. Pro-slavery thinkers often utilized evangelical ideology in service of their justification of the "peculiar institution," and religious authorities also declared other forms of social inequality to be sacred, including gender ideology. Although all believers were expected to behave morally, for women sexual modesty was given primary importance.[65] Reflecting her interest in religious training, all Lucy Cobb students took Bible classes taught by Rutherford. Students also were required to attend the church of their parents' choice every Sunday. Rutherford frequently lectured on the Bible in the evenings as students sewed or knitted. These talks emphasized morality, duty, and virtue, as did her literature, history, and religion classes.[66]

By the 1890s, Rutherford sought to expand her educational influence beyond Lucy Cobb by writing and publishing textbooks for precollegiate study. The books became the basis of several of Lucy Cobb's curricular offerings, and were sold around the country. Rutherford's several textbooks, on English, American, French, southern, and biblical literature, published between 1890 and 1906, reflected her deep preoccupation with propriety and morality.[67] All criticized authors who included any allusion to sexuality or appeared to sanction immorality, and authors were judged by the moral, not artistic, content of their work. This was true for both male and female writers, and in this way, the textbooks indicate that Rutherford extended her judgment of appropriate social behavior to men, especially in regard to their treatment of women. Rutherford's rejection of women's political or sexual independence set her apart from feminists of her era. She viewed women's subordinate place as privileged, not subjugated. But Rutherford clearly believed that just as women had a duty to their husbands and fathers to obey, so men had a duty to protect and honor their wives, mothers, and children. Her literature textbooks reprimanded men for acting cruelly towards or neglecting their duty to their families. All testified to her intense sense of moral righteousness and, particularly, of male duty.

Rutherford's first book, *English Authors*, clearly demonstrates these themes. Her essay on each writer combined a two-to-seven page synopsis with excerpts from their work. The major standard, however, by which she judged each writer was moral rather than literary, as she praised or censured authors for the moral implications of their work and for their personal behavior. This emphasis on biography over literary analysis was not unique; other nineteenth-century textbook writers, especially those writing for women, tended to focus on personal details rather than critical analysis.[68] More unusual was her emphasis on male authors' treatment of women in their work and life. She commended Richard Steele, for example, for having "an intense admiration for woman, appreciating her nobler and finer qualities of mind and heart," while she censured Charles Dickens for tending to portray women as "weak, simpering and affectionate." In her sketch on Thomas More, she began, "Sir Thomas More was one of the saintliest men of English virtue" and went on to detail his exemplary marital life and close relationship with his daughter.[69] Rutherford also included several now-forgotten female writers in the textbook, giving particular praise to their domestic lives and womanly virtue.

American Authors, published in 1894, also highlighted personal details and family lives of authors, championed female writers, and clearly favored southern men and women of letters. Rutherford accorded University of Georgia Chancellor Andrew A. Lipscomb (her sister's father-in-law) nine pages whereas Henry James received only two. Southerners such as Edgar Allan Poe, Thomas Nelson Page, and her uncle, T. R. R. Cobb, also received extensive coverage. On the other hand, northerners who she believed unfairly represented the South received her ire. In her essay on Harriet Beecher Stowe, Rutherford blamed the Civil War almost entirely on *Uncle Tom's Cabin* and asked, "Did Mrs. Stowe ever realize what her book had been a factor in bringing about? Did she ever compare the rare and occasional horrors of the slave days with the many brave men of the Blue and the Gray that were

mutilated in the struggle for States Rights?" Throughout the book, Rutherford defended the worthiness of the Confederate cause and of her version
of southern identity. Pointing to political writers such as Thomas Jefferson,
Henry Clay, and John C. Calhoun, she further argued that the South in fact
had led the nation's literary achievements.[70] Unsurprisingly, *American Authors*
received high praise in the Georgian and southern press, but mixed reviews
from northern journals.[71]

Even more influential than her textbooks was her work on behalf of the
United Daughters of the Confederacy (UDC). In 1895, Rutherford resigned as
head of Lucy Cobb, but continued teaching, in order to care for her ailing father;
he died the following year. Rutherford then turned her energy to founding
and leading an Athens branch of the UDC, which she named for her mother.
Remaining president of the Laura Rutherford chapter for ten years, she also
served as Georgia's historian general for life, state president from 1901–03, and
national historian general from 1911 to 1916.[72] The UDC, the most enduring
and influential of the women's organizations formed to honor the Lost Cause,
focused on determining how the South—and the nation—remembered and
understood the Civil War, the Confederacy, and the antebellum South.[73] In
addition to honoring the Confederacy and its soldiers, the UDC celebrated the
sacrifice and heroism of women during the war, and, like other women's clubs,
provided a space for individual women's participation in such untraditional
activities as fund-raising, historical research, and public speaking.[74] Indeed
UDC members often cited the bravery of Confederate women as inspiring
their work on behalf of the Lost Cause. Women of the UDC greatly expanded
women's public visibility and activism around the turn of the twentieth century
by presenting themselves as representatives of a glorious past and southern
tradition.[75]

Rutherford's greatest national influence was as UDC historian general,
and in that capacity, she was given a national stage to articulate her views
about race, sexuality, and social order that had already been evident in her
work as Lucy Cobb director. In her role as historian, Rutherford created an
archive of Confederate memorabilia, set the agenda for the UDC historical
program, and gave an annual speech, often in full antebellum dress.[76] The
titles of her speeches, published as pamphlets, such as *The Civilization of the
Old South: What Made It; What Destroyed It; What Has Replaced It* and *The
South Must Have Her Rightful Place in History*, make clear their messages.[77]
In its first decade, the UDC gave much of its attention to honoring the heroism of southern soldiers; in the twentieth century, activists focused on more
overtly political themes, including idealizing the antebellum plantation and
legitimizing secession.[78] Rutherford defended the legality of Confederate se-

cession and asserted that the true cause of the war had been not slavery but "a different and directly opposite view as to the nature of the government of the United States."[79] Her writings sentimentalized the slave system, and declared that freedom had harmed, not benefited, former slaves.[80] In doing so, she and other UDC members sought to justify the extensive segregation and disenfranchisement laws passed by southern state legislatures in the 1890s and early 1900s. Rutherford further argued that the Reconstruction amendments had been passed in a coercive manner and claimed that, as a result, they were unconstitutional and should not be considered legally binding in the South.[81]

The idea that contemporary southern women benefited from the conservative gender roles associated with the antebellum plantation, although not as prominent in Rutherford's UDC speeches and pamphlets as her attempts to justify secession or prove slavery benign, emerged as a major part of her worldview in her overall activism, teaching, and writing. In one UDC speech, for example, she assured her listeners that antebellum life had been "a picture of contentment, peace and happiness" where ladies received respect and honor. Unfortunately, she lamented, modern women no longer enjoyed the reverence of the belle; "old time chivalry" was fading away.[82] Although she directed some of her criticism against men who had failed their women, leaving them unprotected and vulnerable,[83] her major target was unfeminine behavior on the part of white women, as her restrictions on Lucy Cobb students attested. If women failed to conform to traditional standards of femininity, she believed, they no longer deserved the protection and affection of men. In this way, she seemed in agreement with contemporary male scientists who attacked feminists, warning that if women broke the "contract" of chivalry by behaving in unfeminine ways, men would not feel obligated to uphold their end of the contract and would indulge in violence, even rape.[84] Rutherford was careful not to go so far as to call white men potential rapists, but she did underline that chivalry depended on women's behavior, and fretted about a loss of female virtue. Modern girls had become so much "bolder and less modest," Rutherford lamented, that they allowed boys to address them by their first names, declined to discourage men from smoking in their presence, and, worst of all, pursued men "instead of making the men seek them." Rutherford directly suggested that this familiarity would lead to further sexual misconduct, writing that girls no longer followed the example of antebellum women who "kept their lovers waiting a long time to get the prize well worth the having." By experimenting with new social and sexual behavior, she implied, women acted "so as to not deserve anything better" and therefore endangered their claim to deference and protection.[85] Given this view of sexuality, it is no surprise that Rutherford believed that her students must be closely guarded and taught the importance of feminine respectability.

Rutherford did not restrict her judgment to youthful indulgence in immodest fashion and behavior; she also condemned women's political activism, particularly support for suffrage. Like other female anti-suffragists, Rutherford feared that public life and political participation would negate women's claim to moral superiority, the very quality that had justified their political influence within nineteenth-century gender ideology, and destroy families by making the individual, rather than the family, the basic unit of society.[86] Rutherford never reconciled these views with the fact that she herself was one of the most publicly active and well-known women in Georgia of her time, an unmarried woman who campaigned publicly for many political causes. She was not alone; many leading southern antis, many of whom relied on the language of women's family duties to make their case, never married.[87]

Like other southern "states rights" conservatives, Rutherford also feared that woman suffrage legislation, and especially a national amendment, would create new voting opportunities for African Americans and open the way for more federal civil rights laws. Indeed, Rutherford strongly opposed all proposals for constitutional amendments, including the 1924 proposal to restrict child labor, and Prohibition, despite her anti-alcohol sentiments, on the basis that they were expansions of federal power. A suffrage amendment threatened to create even more profound disruptions in the South's racial, sexual, and political hierarchies. Rutherford recognized the interconnectedness of southern racial and sexual hierarchies, and in calling for a return to chivalry, she reminded both white men and white women of their racial duty to conform to prescriptive gender roles. Too much freedom for women, as well as men's neglect of duty, she believed, actually endangered women and, further, white supremacy. Rejecting feminism, suffrage, and sexual freedom, Rutherford favored instead the protection of feminine privilege within a hierarchy of race, class, and sex.[88]

Not all southern women of Rutherford's background opposed suffrage; both leading suffragists and antis tended to have connections to the antebellum plantation elite, to have obtained some advanced education, and to be active in women's clubwork.[89] Most were committed to white supremacy and defended the "Lost Cause." But women who campaigned for or against the vote viewed their role in protecting women's status, southern interests, and racial hierarchy in different ways. In Georgia, well-known clubwomen, including Rebecca Latimer Felton, Dolly Blount Lamar, and Rutherford, faced off against each other during a 1914 debate over the state's proposed suffrage amendment. Felton, the wife of a congressman, had long supported white women's access to education, employment, and the vote, while at the same time passionately supporting white supremacy, even defending lynching as a means of protecting the virtue of white women. She argued here that suffrage would strengthen, not weaken, racial hierarchy. In contrast, Lamar, who worked with Rutherford in her role as president of the Georgia UDC, joined with Rutherford to successfully campaign against the state's suffrage amendment, arguing that the vote would lead to a decline in women's influence, an increase in black voting, and even a return to the horrors of Reconstruction. Although in disagreement over suffrage, these prominent Georgia clubwomen shared the view that white supremacy, southern autonomy, and women's advancement were essential to the state's progress. As Elizabeth Gillespie McRae has argued, the debate over suffrage "put women at the center of defining the terms of New South politics."[90]

Sexuality factored in here as well. Although Rutherford did not make the connection directly, "ladylike" behavior by white women was essential to the political power of the southern elite and the Democratic Party. Even the appearance of immodesty (a quality often attributed to suffragists) by white women brought into question one of the key justifications for segregation, disenfranchisement, and Democratic hegemony: the protection of white women's virtue.[91] Rutherford's speeches and writings suggest that she understood that white women must prove that they were worthy of the protection offered by disenfranchisement and segregation in order for the racist rhetoric of politicians to resonate with voters. Appeals to protect white women from the "black beast" served as the basis of Democratic Party platforms throughout the South, especially when party hegemony faced internal or external threats.[92] In Georgia, Governor (and later Senator) Hoke Smith freely used anti-black propaganda to win elections in the early 1900s. In 1906, one month after a particularly racist campaign for the Democratic nomination for governor, rumors of rapes of white women by black men ignited a riot in Atlanta that by differing accounts left at least ten and perhaps close to forty blacks dead and over one hundred and fifty people injured. Three years later Governor Smith helped pass a new state constitution that significantly reduced the number of both blacks and whites eligible to vote.[93] Smith, the husband of Lucy Cobb's sister Birdie Cobb and a member of Lucy Cobb's Board of Directors in the 1920s, proved the political success of anti-black appeals.[94]

Rutherford's version of Confederate history and antebellum life had lasting influence. Not only did the "truths" of history she promoted remain southern orthodoxy for almost another half-century, but the hierarchical social and political structure that she favored also remained in place. As chief historian of the UDC, Rutherford was a key architect in the building of what Joan Marie Johnson and Grace Elizabeth Hale call the "culture of segregation" that rooted New South racial policies in a seemingly immutable tradition.[95] Glorifying antebellum life and Confederate heroism in textbooks, monuments, and pamphlets, Rutherford lent legitimacy to economic and social shifts that traditional southern elites used to their advantage. Not the backwards-looking eccentric she sometimes appeared to be, Rutherford's speeches often included New South "booster" language not that different from that of her childhood classmate Henry Grady. Like Grady, Rutherford envisioned a modern South that rested on racial and class hierarchy.[96] By inventing a mythical Old South, Rutherford aided a reinvented elite in asserting its hegemony over New South society and politics and instituting the racial controls of segregation and disenfranchisement.

Similarly, as principal of Lucy Cobb, she emphasized the school's connections to the antebellum plantation elite while educating daughters of the New South. In addition to its emphasis on feminine manners and decorum, Lucy Cobb's link with the Old South elite was attractive to parents of the postwar urban middle class. Part of the appeal of the institution was its association with the prominent Cobb family, a connection advertised by its name. Rutherford's national reputation as an uncompromising Lost Cause advocate also linked the school to a romanticized view of the antebellum past. Yet for the most part its students and faculty were products of the New South. Typically, Lucies were granddaughters of planters but the daughters, and later wives, of businessmen or professionals.[97] Rutherford's own family experienced these changes. Before the Civil War, both of Rutherford's grandfathers owned sizable plantations, and her father had grown cotton while teaching at the University of Georgia. In her own generation, however, her brother became a lawyer and she and her three sisters (all Lucy Cobb educated) taught at Lucy Cobb and were involved in women's clubs and charities.[98] With the rise and fall of family fortunes and contact with strangers in cities, postwar women could no longer rely on those they encountered "knowing who they were," and sought to prove their elite status through personal respectability, demonstrated through proper dress, language, and behavior. Additionally, Rutherford hoped to mold young women who understood the interconnection between southern racial, class, and gender hierarchies, and who would in turn support these hierarchies in their own activism.

Rutherford quite literally enacted these hierarchies at the Lucy Cobb. Alumnae, Lucy Cobb faculty, and family members frequently described Rutherford as having a mischievous sense of humor and a fondness for practical jokes. A favorite was to dress as a beggar, adopt an accent, and beseech a neighbor, fellow teacher, or even her sister for a handout. One time, she disguised herself as a "loud, overbearing, overdressed county woman" planning to enter her daughter in Lucy Cobb. According to these descriptions, Rutherford invariably convinced her targets and made them increasingly uncomfortable until she finally revealed herself, at which point she and everyone else would collapse in laughter.[99] Of course part of the joke was simply her ability to get away with fooling someone who knew her well so completely. But perhaps without quite knowing it, Rutherford was also performing both the distance between and proximity of herself and her students and their less privileged neighbors. The role-playing seemed to underscore the importance of behavior, speech, clothing, and respectability in defining social status.

Lucy Cobb students themselves seemed to value their education in both its academic and social aspects. Rutherford made a strong impression of the students she taught over the course of half a century. Alumnae never failed to note in their reminiscences of the school their deep admiration and respect for her as a teacher, principal, and mentor.[100] As testament to their esteem, former Lucies attending the State Normal School in Athens named their literary club the "Mildred Rutherford Society" in honor of "the strong personality of our beloved Miss Millie."[101] Rutherford once hosted a "Mildred luncheon" for children of alumnae named for her; according to her niece, "there were 26 present and the three colored maids who waited on the table also bore her name."[102] A few evidenced an extremely strong identification with Rutherford. Edna Pope, for example, expressed a sense of nervousness about leaving home to attend Lucy Cobb for a post-graduate year, yet after arriving, loved the "sweet, religious atmosphere my darling Miss Millie sheds through her home."[103] She even favorably contrasted the religious training and sensibility of the institute to that of her home. Pope frequently mentioned loving other students, but her most intense admiration was for Rutherford. She peppered her diary with frequent exclamations of love, writing in one, "How I love her, love her, love her!"[104]

Not all had such strong feelings for Rutherford, but many Lucies created scrapbooks marking their years as students, updating them after graduation with newspaper clippings about their alma mater.[105] For example, Irene Felker, valedictorian of the 1896 class, kept a scrapbook of programs from music performances, postcards of the school, cards of classmates, hair ribbons worn during memorable school projects, descriptions of science experiments, and locks of hair from friends.[106] Sarah A. McElmurray, in her 1903 scrapbook, included photos, postcards, invitations to dances, tickets to University of Georgia football games, as well as clippings from the school's yearbook and her report card.[107] Elizabeth Carither wrote a diary in 1892 detailing personal stories about her family, but also full of descriptions of her classes, noting particularly interesting assignments, and keeping track of her grades.[108] After her graduation, Carither created a scrapbook that she maintained until 1956 honoring Mildred Rutherford, filled with newspaper clippings about Rutherford, Lucy Cobb, school programs, and annual newspaper columns from Athens papers on the anniversary of Rutherford's death.[109] On the whole, students showed very little resistance to the school's strict rules, especially during its early years. Lucies certainly admired classmates who actually managed to speak to a man without getting caught, but for the most part, they understood and respected the rules, and were embarrassed when caught breaking them.[110] In the 1910s, a town student who had attended an off-campus dance remembered her mortification of having to perform the "bunny-hug" in front of Rutherford and her entire class as a rebuke. Indeed shame, more than fear, prevented misbehavior among students, suggesting a strong identification of the students with Rutherford and her goals.[111]

Mary Ann Rutherford Lipscomb, Rutherford's sister, who followed her as Lucy Cobb principal, did not seem to elicit as powerful an emotional attachment as "Miss Millie," but she did earn the respect of her students and of observers in Athens and beyond. In 1895, when Rutherford stepped down from her post as principal, she turned the school's leadership over to her older sister, who would hold the position until 1908. Lipscomb, born in 1848, also graduated from Lucy Cobb and shared her sister's interest in female education, clubwork, and the Lost Cause. Unlike her sister, Lipscomb had married, to Francis Adgate Lipscomb, a Confederate veteran, professor at the University of Georgia, and son of the university's influential chancellor, Andrew Adgate Lipscomb. Professor Lipscomb, however, died in 1874 at the age of twenty-eight, leaving his widow with three young children. After his death, Mary Ann Lipscomb began teaching, first at a private academy in Washington, D.C., and later at Lucy Cobb. She joined the faculty as an instructor in literature in 1881, just after her sister took over its leadership.[112] While retaining Rutherford's general curriculum and her emphasis on molding proper southern ladies, as principal Lipscomb modernized Lucy Cobb by bringing it up to date with recent advances in women's education.

Like her sister, Lipscomb was active in the kinds of women's organizations popular at the turn of the century. A founder and president of the Athens Woman's Club, from 1906 to 1909 she also served as president of the Georgia Federation of Women's Clubs (GFWC). During Lipscomb's presidency, the GFWC supported a compulsory education law, restriction of child labor, Prohibition, and the end of the convict lease system.[113] These issues represented interests broadly shared by Progressive-Era organized women

Figure 4. Lucy Cobb students with Mildred Rutherford (seated, left) and Mary Ann Lipscomb (seated, right), 1895. The young girl next to Rutherford is probably her niece, Mildred Rutherford Mell. (Lucy Cobb Institute Collection, Hargrett Library, University of Georgia)

nationwide active in "social housekeeping" reforms. As GFWC President Lipscomb helped found Tallulah Falls Industrial School in Tallulah Falls, in the northern mountains of Georgia. A frequent visitor to a mountain resort in the area, Lipscomb became concerned about the lack of public education available for children after she learned that a small, poorly maintained room above the city jail served as a school, and that the session only lasted three months of the year. Lipscomb raised money by appealing to other mountain vacationers and the GFWC, and secured enough to open the school in 1909.[114] Her interest in children's issues would seem to conform to the tradition of maternalism identified by scholars as a hallmark of early twentieth century women's reform.[115] Indeed, in her 1908 presidential address to the GFWC, Lipscomb commented favorably on the work of Jane Addams and Florence Kelley on behalf of child welfare measures.[116]

Yet her support for Progressive reform did not preclude a commitment to white supremacy, and indeed, scholars have noted that southern Progressives viewed segregation as of a piece with their reform agenda.[117] For example, support for better education for white women in the South was sometimes directly linked to the maintenance of white supremacy.[118] In the same presidential address in which she praised Addams and Kelley, Lipscomb declared herself "Southern born, Southern bred, Southern to my very heart's core, true to the conditions of the past, loyal to my people and my section."[119] Like her sister, she favored a vision of the Old South and southern Confederacy that painted slaveholders in a favorable light. As Athens chapter president of the UDC, Lipscomb presented a resolution to the state division demanding that the federal government reimburse former slaveholders for their loss of investment in slaves.[120] Lipscomb denounced "higher education for the negro" as a "failure" and "this generation" of African Americans as "dangerous."[121] Even her campaign against the convict lease system could fit into an overall worldview favoring white supremacy. The abolition of the convict lease system in Georgia, a key issue of the sisters' cousin by marriage Governor Hoke Smith, reflected a loss of profitability of the system, and a belief that convicts could be better used for state projects, not moral outrage at the abuses of the system. Smith focused on the reallocation of prisoner labor to public projects in his opposition to the system, and considered codifying disenfranchisement and abolition of convict lease, both achieved in 1908, as his major accomplishments. Both measures could have been seen as a way to rationalize and systemize white supremacy, key southern Progressive goals.[122] Similarly, Lipscomb's support for a day care center for black seamstresses and domestic workers can be seen as way to free black women from childcare in order to make them more efficient servants.[123]

Lipscomb, like her sister, demonstrated her commitment to white supremacy in her sentimental views of slavery and especially of the black "mammy." Lipscomb and Rutherford's childhood nurse, Aunt Dot, who according to Lucy Cobb legend never accepted the notion that she had been freed, worked as a housekeeper and cook at Lucy Cobb.[124] One alumna described Aunt Dot as a "jewel of a darkey" and the embodiment of the "old time Negro," a woman who knew and liked her subservient place. A portrait of Aunt Dot working in the kitchen donated by chapel benefactor George Seney in 1887 compelled many visitors of the school to note, in the words of one, the "kindliness, honesty, and faithfulness" depicted in the portrait.[125] Most obviously, Aunt Dot represented an idealized view of slavery, a symbol of what the South lost in the war, and in that way resembled contemporary portrayals of blacks in advertisements and popular culture.[126] But she also served to remind students of their own racial privilege and the clear division between themselves and the subservient and denigrated former slave. Through conformity to gender subordination, Lucy Cobb students could achieve the racial power symbolized by Aunt Dot's portrait. Perhaps inspired by her view of Dot's faithfulness and subservience, Lipscomb became involved in Athens's proposed Mammy Institute, serving on its advisory board.[127] Although never built, the Mammy Institute, chartered in 1910, was intended to serve as "a living monument" to "these distinctively Southern characters" by training black women as domestic servants and men in manual trades. Like other industrial institutes for southern African Americans, it aimed not only to teach skills, but also industrial values, especially "stability" and "sacredness of contract."[128]

While she identified the "mammy" as the ideal black woman, Lipscomb viewed white women as capable and progressive. Even a short article in the student paper praising the work of Argentinean women in creating the "Christ the Redeemer" statue outside of Buenos Aires became a paean to "Anglo-Saxon civilization," which, Lipscomb believed, had offered women more respect, education, and opportunity than had any other "civilization."[129] If South Americans could create an imposing statue to peace, she argued, "Anglo-Saxon" women must do much more. The principal impressed on her students their special duty to spread Christianity and promote peace, a duty that was meant to inspire within them a sense of racial and class superiority, and of white women's duty to work on behalf of racial privilege.

Lipscomb's commitment to contemporary ideals of both racial difference and white women's and children's progress emphasizes that white southern women often were motivated by a defense of white supremacy as much as by the "maternalism" historians have identified in northern and western clubwomen (who themselves often embraced ideologies of racial and ethnic hierarchy). In the worsening racial climate of the 1890s, characterized by the codification of segregation and increasing racial violence, support for southern white women and children often dovetailed with support for white supremacy. Tallulah Falls, especially, with its focus on Appalachian children, suggested an interest in improving and empowering racially fit but culturally backward whites. In providing "book larnin'" for white mountain children, Lipscomb participated in a movement popular at the turn of the century. Mountain workers, many of them clubwomen like Lipscomb, hoped to both reform white Appalachians and also preserve their distinct culture. Their alleged identity as "100% Anglo Saxon" made this task all the more compelling.[130] Lipscomb's interest in increasing the knowledge, visibility, and influence of white women, and the uplift of white mountain children, were intimately tied to her commitment to racial hierarchy and Jim Crow.

Accordingly, Lipscomb set about raising the standards and reputation of the school, in order to provide the "Anglo-Saxon" women who attended Lucy Cobb a superior education that would fit them for public activism.

Although perhaps not living up to the enthusiastic (if poorly spelled) praise of the observer who believed that Lucy Cobb Institute was "fast becoming to Georgia, what Welsey is to Mass., what Bryn Mawe is to Pennsylvania," Lipscomb did improve Lucy Cobb's facility, faculty, and course offerings.[131] She oversaw the construction of two new buildings and developed a library and hired a librarian. She also sought out faculty with advanced degrees from institutions such as Wellesley College and the North Carolina State Normal and Industrial School for Women.[132] Broadening offerings in music and visual arts, Lucy Cobb's new principal created scholarships for "poor but deserving" Georgia girls sponsored by the United Daughters of the Confederacy, the Daughters of the American Revolution, and the Georgia Federation of Women's Clubs.[133] In order to attract more students, she also introduced a language and literature track for those who did not wish to take Latin or higher math. Lipscomb also created elementary and preparatory departments to make up for the lack of adequate early schooling in Athens. The elementary school later became coeducational and gained its own building. As the public grade schools improved, attendance at the elementary school declined. Even so it outlasted the Lucy Cobb, remaining open until 1941.[134]

But Lipscomb, like her sister, considered the "collegiate" program the core of Lucy Cobb Institute. Historian Amy McCandless notes that catalogues of many New South schools for girls highlighted the beauty of their buildings and grounds over their academic programs, but the Lucy Cobb catalogues consistently emphasized the qualifications of its faculty and the rigor of the course work. During the Lipscomb years, the catalogues listed the courses taken and textbooks used for each semester of the collegiate track, and gave an extensive description of the "departments" of philosophy and criticism; literature; Bible; Latin; English; French; history; science; music; art; and logic, civics, and parliamentary law. Lipscomb saw to it that Lucy Cobb continued to benefit from a close relationship with the University of Georgia, using laboratories of the university for science courses, and hosting professors who lectured on subjects such as "The Latin Poets" and "The Elementary Principles of Law and their Application to Woman."[135]

Lipscomb also introduced modern educational methods associated with John Dewey, favoring questioning and creativity over rote learning. Courses in ethics and psychology encouraged students to think about themselves and their place in and obligations to society. The Lucy Cobb catalogue touted "free classroom discussions" in which "every encouragement is given to the students for the expression of independent thought." Lipscomb's own Shakespeare class used educational methods that sought to engage students in the material. Students read three to five plays closely over the term, made "a personal acquaintance" with the characters, debated questions formally, and

performed one of the plays during commencement.[136] One student, Elizabeth
Carither, recorded particularly interesting assignments in her diary. Just
before the presidential election, Carither noted that Lipscomb required that
all students write their representatives asking for a state normal school, and
then reflected extensively about the policies and chances of each presidential candidate, and expressed her strong preference for Democrat Grover
Cleveland.[137] Although southern schools were known for their emphasis
on memorization over creativity, Lipscomb seemed genuinely interested in
improving students' ability to express themselves orally and in writing, and
to present an analytical argument, as long as they did not lead students to
question the fundamental values of the school.

At the same time, Lipscomb did not loosen the school's careful monitor-
ing of students' behavior, and was willing to crack down on any infractions
of the rules. For example, in 1897, eighteen Lucy Cobb seniors "ran away"
from school on April Fools' Day, leaving campus without permission to visit
a local soda fountain. On the way, several girls spoke a few words to a man
that they met on the street, a severe offense. After the girls were returned to
Lucy Cobb, Lipscomb ordered them to pack their bags for home; although
just a month from graduation, they would not receive their diplomas. The
severity of the punishment chastised the students, and although Lipscomb
eventually relented and allowed the students to finish the school year and
graduate, the girls remembered their embarrassment long after the incident.[138]

Lipscomb was even willing to use her influence to crack down on the behavior of University of Georgia men, generally allowed much greater freedom
than her own students, if they threatened the reputation of Lucies. Also in
1897, three university students walked by the chapel while Lucy Cobb students
practiced for a school recital inside. According to the young men, several
of the Lucies waved and threw notes at them, and they wandered over and
peeked in. A teacher found them and asked them to leave after a "pleasant
conversation." Principal Lipscomb, however, fed up with frequent provoca-
tions by university students, including painting the goats on the front porch
and sneaking onto campus, pressed charges and the men were arrested and
charged $10. The matter did not end there; upon hearing of the incident, the
university chancellor suspended them for the rest of the term. After receiving a heartfelt apology, Lipscomb reconsidered and asked the chancellor
to readmit the students, and he did. Despite the resolution in the students'
favor, the incident underlined how seriously Lucy Cobb's leadership took its
mandate to protect the modesty and virtue of its students.[139]

While continuing to follow the strict moral code begun by her sister, Lipscomb also encouraged independence and accomplishment in her students. A
Lucy was neither a "prim, precise maiden" nor an uneducated woman chained

to the home; she was the sort of "college girl" who did well in her classes, volunteered for clubwork, while also maintaining her modesty, and "fresh, sweet" femininity.[140] The northern women and evangelical ministers who taught antebellum southern women frequently complained about the lack of academic interest and accomplishment of their students—not surprisingly, as intellectual achievement seemed anathema to the image of the antebellum belle.[141] But many postwar students took their studies more seriously. As southern women themselves, Rutherford, Lipscomb, and other faculty offered Lucy Cobb students role models of educated, accomplished, and not incidentally, self-supporting, modern southern women who maintained the respectability of their class position.

Rutherford and Lipscomb's blending of academic rigor with conservative morality at the institute won praise from observers around Georgia and elsewhere in the South well into the first decades of the twentieth century. The Athens and Atlanta newspapers reported annually on Lucy Cobb commencement exercises, praising the graduates on their speeches and singing, as well as their sweet and pretty appearance (one headline proclaimed: "Thirteen blondes and thirteen brunettes graduate from Lucy Cobb Institute").[142] Local businessmen praised the "atmosphere of refinement, of gentle, sweet dignity, of natural and easy culture that has come up through the families for generations" and called the Lucy Cobb ideal a "perfection of sacred womanhood."[143] Others also noted the school's academic excellence. In a letter to the editor of *The Atlanta Constitution*, a "learned gentleman" referred to Lucy Cobb Institute as "the most thorough and ideal [women's seminary] in this country," and observers routinely called Lucy Cobb the leading school for women in the South.[144] Even given the propensity for exaggeration among the press of the period, it is clear that observers believed that Rutherford succeeded in carefully balancing intellectually rigorous education with proper social and moral training for ladies.

Although reluctant to take on the responsibility of running Lucy Cobb, Rutherford's first term as principal, from 1880 to 1895, proved instrumental in shaping the curriculum, goals, and growth of the school, and her sister continued and extended Rutherford's success. Lucy Cobb became a leading secondary school for white young women in the South, priding itself on educating women who would participate in creating a culture of segregation that would justify white elite control. Rutherford hoped that Lucies would contribute as mothers, clubwomen, and teachers, and would follow her into activism but would maintain an appearance of modesty and respectability. Many Lucy Cobb alumnae did fashion themselves as southern ladies after their time at the institution, but some graduates and former students took their education in unexpected directions. As the next chapter will show, alumnae influenced the school itself, clubwork in Athens and Atlanta, and even national politics into the twentieth century. Most Lucies did use their education and activism to support southern hierarchies. Taught to be southern ladies and to uphold racial and class privilege, some Lucies, however, embraced modern roles for women and a few even actively worked against the politics promoted by Rutherford, although even these alumnae tended to remember their time at Lucy Cobb with fondness, and Rutherford with admiration.

2 Clubwomen, Educators, and a Congresswoman

Lucy Cobb Alumnae

Mildred Rutherford decisively shaped Lucy Cobb Institute after assuming the school's leadership in 1880, and she continued to have a significant role in the institution until her death in 1928. To enhance the school's reputation, Rutherford, along with her sister Mary Ann Lipscomb, recruited faculty with advanced degrees from top women's colleges, but Lucy Cobb also represented a major source of employment for its own graduates. Lucies, some of them members of the Rutherford and Cobb families, others not, ran the school until its final years, and made up a significant portion of its faculty, and in this way, passed on the values of the school to younger students. Other alumnae taught elsewhere, including in higher education, or worked in other professions; many took active roles as clubwomen. By doing so, Lucy Cobb alumnae participated in shaping the culture, economy, and politics of the New South. These Lucies invariably cited their education as key in shaping their identity, even those who sought to shape southern society in ways that strongly differed from those imagined by Rutherford.

Despite the conservative moral tone of their education, Lucy Cobb students during the Rutherford and Lipscomb administrations dreamt about exciting lives pursuing artistic, literary, and academic endeavors, although most expected to ultimately become wives and mothers. Yearbook senior prophecies indicated a broad range of ways that students imagined their futures. Possibilities that appeared frequently included marriage and society life, but also clubwork, social work, teaching, nursing, writing, acting, performing music, editing magazines or newspapers, and missionary work. Nearly every year students predicted that one of their peers would become principal of Lucy Cobb. One student planned to become a doctor; another an organist in London's St. Paul's Cathedral.[1] The ambition of Lucy Cobb students suggests that their classroom work in these areas sparked hopes of personal achievement.

Lucies who attended during the principalships of the Rutherford sisters did have diverse and notable accomplishments. Many followed their examples and joined clubs as students, preparing themselves for futures in women's voluntary associations. As enrollment increased by the turn of the century, Lucies had more opportunities to join clubs and student activities. *Nods and Becks*, a yearbook stared in 1899, reported on the activities of a variety of organizations, including the cycling club (about 40 students), the Brush and Palette Club, and the Mendelssohn Club.[2] By 1902, students had added a diverse array of new groups such as the Cicero Club, the Symphony Club, the Glee Club, the Kodak Club, the Tennysonian Society, and the Old Maid Club. The most popular organization was the Young Women's Christian Association (YWCA), joined by faculty and students alike. Almost every year, a few members attended the annual regional conference, and some attended the Training School in Chicago.[3]

Many students remained active in clubs after graduation, especially the YWCA, the UDC, and the Daughters of the American Revolution (DAR), and a few gained positions of prominence.[4] The leadership of the local UDC, in particular, was dominated by Lucy Cobb alumnae.[5] Also popular was the Lucy Cobb Alumnae Association, which had strong chapters in Athens and Atlanta. In 1924, the Atlanta chapter was able to attract eighty Lucies to a luncheon, and three hundred to a bridge tournament that raised funds for the organization.[6] A particularly loyal Lucy, Nellie Stovall, as a student who had helped secure the funding for the school's chapel, remained closely associated with the institution and its alumnae activities, as well as other women's clubs. Married to Billips Phinizy, a wealthy and prominent businessman involved in the Southern Mutual Insurance Company, the Georgia Railroad, and the Athens Railway and Electric Company, she was active in the Athens UDC and the Lucy Cobb Alumnae Association, and served as president of that organization.[7] In 1895, a newspaper reporter described her as idolized by Lucy Cobb students; a young mother, she was beautiful, charming, and modest, but also intelligent and studious, a great reader and "a broad and comprehensive thinker."[8] Mrs. Phinizy remained a dedicated alumna and supporter of Lucy Cobb. She was also the grandmother of both the novelist Walker Percy, whose mother also graduated from Lucy Cobb, and of Phinizy Spalding, a University of Georgia professor of history who spearheaded the effort to restore the Lucy Cobb buildings in the 1970s and 80s.[9]

Several students of this generation used their education to take on paying employment. Many unmarried women from prominent and wealthy families took jobs in the late nineteenth century out of financial necessity, and advanced their education specifically to gain work.[10] With this in mind, Lucy Cobb Institute offered young women training in marketable skills in the respectable female professions. At the same time, the school's emphasis on proper female behavior would allow alumnae to maintain respectability. Lucy Cobb resembled other turn-of-the century female institutions, such as the Florida Female College, that offered an education that prepared women for the New South, by teaching skills but also emphasizing femininity, decorum, and white supremacy.[11]

The 1885 Lucy Cobb commencement address suggested the extent of a new acceptance of elite female employment. John Whitner differentiated between "man with his aggressive spirit, daring, leading, planning, commanding, whilst woman, with her sweet responsive spirit, shrinks, follows, executes, and obeys." Yet Whitner also argued that women should be educated and that "the limits to capacity [of the female mind] is hard, if not impossible, to prescribe." Acknowledging that many women worked, he pointed out the hypocrisy of a chivalry that restricted many women to the backbreaking work of the needle trades. Whitner argued that women ought to be allowed into more professions. Noting that women's waged work had become acceptable and even expected in the South, he clearly saw no conflict between women's "nature" and women's employment.[12] By regulating students' interactions with men, manner of dress, and speech patterns, Lipscomb and Rutherford hoped to mold young women who could be easily distinguished as elite even if they worked for pay.

Education was the most popular career choice for Lucies, and many taught at Lucy Cobb or the elementary school. Teaching represented the major category of employment for educated women in nineteenth and early twentieth centuries, and one that seemed most in keeping with women's duty to care for children, and therefore respectable. State normal schools, founded in many southern states including Georgia in the last decades of the nineteenth century, trained women from less prominent families to become the workforce of the expanding public education system.[13] In contrast, many Lucies took positions in private academies. Private academies offered respectable employment to their own graduates and those of similar schools. Because many of these women presented themselves as upholders of tradition, rather than as pioneers, and because they did not embrace a feminist consciousness or overtly defy gendered expectations, the extent of their wage earning has sometimes been overlooked. Unlike southern women who attended northern colleges and strove to create innovative careers for themselves, such as Sophonisba Breckinridge, these women quietly took positions teaching women

Figure 5. Students on the Lucy Cobb steps, c. 1890. (Lucy Cobb Institute Grade Books, Hargrett Library, University of Georgia)

much like themselves, offering an education that preserved "ladyhood" rather than questioning hierarchies.[14] Private academies offered women from elite families employment, and the connection of these institutions with southern tradition enhanced the respectability of their labor.[15]

Lipscomb hired several Lucy Cobb alumnae to teach in the elementary department and the institute, creating both a sense of tradition and community within the school and respectable work for graduates. This set Lucy Cobb apart from antebellum schools that relied on northern teachers, pointing both to greater acceptance of southern women's paid employment in the postwar era and their stronger academic preparation.[16] Several taught a few years before leaving to marry, earn a college degree, or teach elsewhere (few taught after marriage).[17] Others taught at Lucy Cobb for an extensive time. Most obviously, Rutherford sisters themselves represented influential Lucies with extensive teaching careers. When Mildred Rutherford described herself during her Atlanta years as "very happy in her work" and as "receiving a good salary," her reference to her salary implies that she taught both for the satisfaction it gave her and for income.[18] Attesting to the widespread reliance on the employment of unmarried women of the southern elite, all of the Rutherford sisters taught at Lucy Cobb or elsewhere, and the school continued to represent a major source of employment for its own graduates throughout its history.[19]

One of the best-known alumnae educators not connected with the Rutherford or Cobb families was Rosa Woodberry. In the 1880s, Woodberry travelled to Athens from her home in Savannah to attend Lucy Cobb. After graduating in 1891, she became involved in clubwork and the Episcopal Church, later taking a position teaching science, law, and civics at Lucy Cobb.[20] In 1899, she applied unsuccessfully to enroll in the University of Georgia. Speaking to the Georgia Teachers Association about her rejection, she declared, "in education of the mind there is no sex."[21] Woodberry would persist in her quest to enroll in the university, eventually successfully matriculating and studying chemistry.[22]

In 1908, Woodberry moved to Atlanta, where she founded Woodberry Hall School for Girls, described as "one of the most exclusive and best known finishing schools in the south."[23] Woodberry Hall, like Lucy Cobb, combined academic rigor with moral and religious instruction and was well respected in Atlanta. Woodberry earned recognition outside of Georgia as well; she won a prize from *New York* magazine for the effective teaching of political events.[24] Also like Rutherford, Woodberry combined her work as an educator with significant club activism. A member of the UDC, she "was a firm believer in the Cause of the Confederacy for which her ancestors had fought and believed to be right," according to one obituary.[25] Woodberry held prominent positions in the Atlanta Woman's Club, Atlanta City Federation of Clubs, and the General Federation of Women's Clubs (GFWC), serving during Lipscomb's presidency. Cofounder of All Saints Episcopal Church in Atlanta, she taught Bible classes there and became president of the Christian Council of Churchwomen. As a churchwoman she was also a pioneer, the only woman to serve as a member of the Episcopal Diocesan Board of Georgia.[26] Never married, she remained active in church and educational work until her death in 1932.

Woodberry's career echoes that of Rutherford—the interest in education for young women, the dedication to the Lost Cause, and the commitment to women's clubs and church work. And like Rutherford, despite support for the conservative social values embodied in the Confederate celebration, she chafed against gender conventions that would limit women's educational and professional achievement. This straddling of the line between conservative and progressive values reflects the complexity of the values taught at Lucy Cobb.

Another alumna became a long-time art instructor at the school, fondly remembered by her students as demanding but generous. Oneita Virginia

(Jennie) Smith graduated from Lucy Cobb in 1880, the year after Mildred Rutherford assumed leadership of the school. After graduating she took a job teaching at Lucy Cobb, taking time off to study art in Baltimore, New York, and Paris. She remained on the faculty until the school's closing.[27] Well liked by the students, Smith lived in a cottage next to the campus, and was considered by alumnae an essential part of the Lucy Cobb community. Lucies particularly remembered her insistence on proper diction and distain for a "country" accent.[28] Also unmarried and self-supporting, Smith like Woodberry offers an example of how education, particularly at female institutes, offered respectable employment for Lucy Cobb grads, and other white women of the southern elite as well.

Although not mentioned in any accounts of Smith written by fellow Lucy Cobb alumnae, she is best known today as the person who purchased Harriet Powers's iconic Bible quilt, now owned by the Smithsonian Institution and identified as an "American treasure."[29] In 1886, Harriet Powers, a former slave who after the Civil War lived with her husband on land they had acquired outside of Athens, displayed a remarkable quilt depicting biblical scenes at a cotton fair in town. Attending the fair, Smith, who prided herself in her interest in all kinds of artistic expression, noticed the quilt right away, and asked to purchase it. Powers, however, declined to sell it. But four years later, in difficult financial circumstances, Powers felt she had no choice but to sell her work. Traveling to Smith's cottage next to Lucy Cobb, she asked $10 for the quilt; Smith countered with $5, which Powers, after consulting with her husband, accepted. Smith's own narration of the purchase of the treasured quilt, as poet Jane Wilson Joyce perceptively makes clear, unintentionally echoes the sale of a slave child; Smith described Powers's quilt as "the darling offspring of her brain," and a carefully wrapped "precious burden" that she visited several times after selling.[30] Smith's description of the quilt is equal parts admiring and condescending. She found the colors "gorgeous" and the imagery unique and compelling, but described the religious symbolism as primitive, even whimsical. In keeping with a romantic, nostalgic idea of black womanhood that would have associated Powers with the "mammy" ideal, in her recounting of the purchase Smith never acknowledged that Powers was literate, a church member, and a property owner, and subsequent accounts of Powers and her quilt often describe her as illiterate and impoverished.[31]

In 1895, Smith arraigned to display the quilt in the Negro Building of the Atlanta Exposition, where it received considerable attention. Best remembered today as the site of Booker T. Washington's "Atlanta Compromise" speech, the well-attended exposition dramatized contemporary beliefs of racial hierarchy, but also provided some room for competing interpretations of racial identity. In the racially charged exhibition, held during the decade that witnessed the implementation of segregation and disenfranchisement laws and an increase of lynching and violence, the Negro Building, designed by black clubwomen and educators, sought to tell the story of black progress. The exhibit began with a representation of a Dehomey village, meant to demonstrate African savagery, and ended with displays of black uplift and accomplishments in business, science, and art. Powers's work was placed at a midpoint, demonstrating a primitive and naïve interpretation of Christianity, and simple if striking handiwork.[32] Smith also helped create a Lucy Cobb room in the exposition's Women's Building (reserved for demonstrations of white women's achievements), full of art and decorations meant to evoke the refined atmosphere of the school. In November, nearly all currently enrolled students traveled to Atlanta to participate in a performance of music and poetry directed by Lipscomb that lasted nearly three hours. Discussions of the Lucy Cobb room in the press and alumnae reports emphasized the beauty of the room, the remarkable collection of art, and the student recital, but do not mention the Powers quilt at all. Instead they emphasize the school's work in creating ideal white femininity, intelligent but not overbearing, refined and modest but accomplished. Smith was particularly proud to display paintings donated by George Seney to the school, especially one rumored to be the work of French artist William-Adolphe Bouguereau.[33] Jennie Smith's portrayal of Powers's lovely but "primitive" quilt contrasted quite sharply with her commitment to associating elegance and high culture with Lucy Cobb students.

Like Smith and Woodberry, graduate Moina Michael also began her career as an educator, but unlike them did not teach at her alma mater, instead finding a position at the University of Georgia. Although still unusual, increasingly in the twentieth century southern women obtained graduate degrees and then faculty positions, although most at women's colleges, not coeducational universities.[34] Michael attended the Georgia State Teachers College in Athens and Columbia University after her time at Lucy Cobb. She began her career teaching in the public schools in Athens and then taught at the University of Georgia for over twenty-five years. She became widely admired not for her work at the university, but for her support of wartime veterans. When the United States entered the First World War, she took a leave of absence from the university to train YWCA workers going abroad. According to later accounts, while working for the Y in New York, she read John McCrae's iconic poem "In Flanders Fields," and, moved by his description of poppies growing next to fallen soldiers, began wearing a silk poppy in remembrance of those killed in battle. Returning to Athens after the war, Michael continued to promote the wearing of red poppies as a way to commemorate the war dead, and the selling of silk or paper poppies as a means of raising money to aid veterans and their families. Both the American Legion and British Legion endorsed the idea in the 1920s. She became internationally known as "the Poppy Lady" and her likeness was commemorated on a U.S. stamp in 1948. Although the tradition of wearing poppies to commemorate the war dead has mostly disappeared in the United States, it remains popular in Canada and the United Kingdom.[35]

Michael was not the only Lucy with a position at the University of Georgia. Other women, including Mary Lyndon, the first woman to earn a graduate degree from the university (before women were admitted as undergraduates) and its first Dean of Women, made their mark in higher education.[36] Lyndon taught at Lucy Cobb before her appointment at the university.[37] Lyndon's successor as dean, Anne Brumby, also had graduated from Lucy Cobb. Prior to her appointment, Brumby, and along with another alumna, Susan Gerdine, had directed the school for nine years after Lipscomb stepped down as principal in 1908. Gerdine, along with Rosa Woodberry, had been a pioneer in advocating for the acceptance of women into the University of Georgia, a top goal of many activist women in the state. The two women, with the support of the Georgia Federation of Women's Clubs, had filed separate unsuccessful petitions in 1897 for their admission into the university. As Athens residents and educators, they were frustrated by the university's refusal to provide them with advanced education and additional training.[38] Gerdine, Brumby, and especially Woodberry did not give up, and supported other women's efforts for university coeducation. In 1918, the university finally relented, allowing female students in selected majors. Brumby and Gerdine earned their B.A.s in 1920, after .stepping down as co-principals but while still teaching at Lucy Cobb, and after Lyndon's early death in 1924 from pneumonia, Brumby replaced her as dean of women, having earned a masters degree in education, writing her thesis on women's education. Her major focus as dean was securing adequate dormitory space for the increasing numbers of female students. By this time living in Atlanta and running her own institute, the determined Woodberry nonetheless earned her degree in 1927.[39] The proximity of Lucy Cobb to the university, and its close ties, helps explain the remarkable representation of Lucies among early women students and faculty.

Like Woodberry and Smith, Brumby and Gerdine combined their work on behalf of educational and professional opportunities for white women with New South racial ideologies. All three held leadership positions in the UDC (Brumby and Gerdine were officers in the Athens branch, working with branch president Rutherford), and apparently accepted the racial beliefs of that organization.[40] In this way, they exemplified the new ideal of elite white womanhood taught at Lucy Cobb—one that would engage in public life, bound by but also empowered by female respectability, on behalf of class, and especially racial, privilege.

Whereas women like Woodberry, Smith, and Brumby balanced conservative and progressive aspects of New South womanhood, another nineteenth century Lucy Cobb graduate crossed that line to become a full-fledged twentieth century progressive. Caroline Love Goodwin was born in 1869 on a plantation south of Macon, Georgia, but grew up in Savannah, where her father was a successful businessman. Her background thus resembled that of other Lucies of her generation. Goodwin graduated from Lucy Cobb Institute in 1886, the highest degree she would earn. Interested in pursuing a career as an artist, she moved to New York City, where she took art classes at Cooper Union, and eventually traveled to Paris to continue her training. She remained in Europe for eight years, studying painting and etching with Raphael Collin, a French painter in the academic style, and James McNeill Whistler. She had some success selling her paintings and working as a fashion illustrator, and had a few pieces exhibited at the prestigious Paris Salon in 1899 and 1900.[41]

While in Paris, Goodwin met Daniel O'Day, an oil industrialist and son of a powerful Standard Oil executive. O'Day expressed romantic interest in the artist, but she was at first unreceptive, reluctant to give up the independence of her life in Paris. In 1902, however, the couple married and returned to the United States, eventually settling in Rye, New York. Now in her early 30s, O'Day raised her three children in the suburban town outside of New York City.[42] According to an oft-repeated story, it was Dan O'Day who prompted Caroline's interest in woman suffrage, by turning to his wife as they watched a New York suffrage parade and asking pointedly why she was not herself participating.[43] This incident, if true, may have occurred during the failed state referendum of 1915. In any case, Mrs. O'Day did begin to become more active in the state-level suffrage campaign in the mid-teens, especially after her husband's untimely death in 1916.[44]

O'Day's involvement in New York State's second, and successful, suffrage referendum in 1917 launched her into a full-fledged political career. Like other women of the "female dominion" in American reform, O'Day joined groups such as the National Consumer's League, founded by Florence Kelley, the Women's Trade Union League, and the board of Lillian Wald's Henry Street Settlement. Through her work in the Women's Division of New York's Democratic Party, she began life-long close friendships with reformers Nancy Cook, Marion Dickerman, and Eleanor Roosevelt. By 1923, O'Day was head of the state Women's Division and chair of the New York State Board of Charities (later the State Board of Social Welfare) and one of the most prominent female activists in the state.[45]

Her record of activism and Democratic Party service led to her run for Congress in 1934 as representative-at-large for New York. Running very much as a supporter of President Franklin D. Roosevelt's New Deal and a progressive, and with active campaigning by First Lady Eleanor Roosevelt, O'Day won the seat, and held it for four terms. O'Day, described as one of the two most influential female congresswomen of the time, clearly was a Roosevelt ally, but also was willing to break ranks with the president, especially on issues of racial justice and pacifism. O'Day not only supported New Deal initiatives such as labor protections, but also vocally supported less popular measures such as protecting immigrants from deportation, allowing Jewish refugees into the United States, and creating federal anti-lynching legislation. In 1939, when Eleanor Roosevelt invited renowned African American opera singer Marion Anderson to perform at the Lincoln Memorial after the DAR refused to allow her to sing at Constitutional Hall, O'Day chaired a congressional committee sponsoring the concert, and personally accompanied Anderson to the event. Up for her fourth election in 1940, O'Day again won comfortably, despite an illness that left her "an invalid," unable to campaign. She did not return to Washington, and in January 1943, just days after her final term ended, she died at her home in Rye.[46]

Figure 6. Congresswoman Caroline O'Day (Library of Congress)

O'Day's political opinions would seem to suggest that she put behind her the values taught by Rutherford and others at Lucy Cobb. Her progressive views on race, labor, and immigration did not at all conform to the southern conservatism of Rutherford. Yet in several articles published in Georgian newspapers, O'Day embraced Lucy Cobb and the education she received there.[47] In a 1934 profile written just after her election, O'Day spoke highly of the school, declaring, "I am always running across someone who went there. We have grand times talking about the old days, and about the great personality of Miss Milly Rutherford."[48] In a visit to her home state in 1936, after attending events in Atlanta, she made a point of visiting Athens, hosted by Lamar Rutherford Lipscomb (niece of Mildred Rutherford and Mary Ann Lipscomb), a classmate and friend from her years at Lucy Cobb (and herself a strong Roosevelt supporter). Newspaper coverage emphasized O'Day's "love for her Alma Mater" and her desire "to come back to the old institution where as Carrie Love she received the background training for the job she holds today."[49] Even given that this "love" of Lucy Cobb may have been exaggerated for the Athens and Atlanta audiences, it is worth noting that her diploma from Lucy Cobb was the highest degree O'Day received, and that she did not distance herself from the school or from Rutherford. In a private note to Lamar Lipscomb, she noted looking forward to seeing the "girls" from Lucy Cobb and asked Lipscomb to arraign a meeting with Jennie Smith during her visit to Athens.[50] Although not a typical Lucy, O'Day's career demonstrates that Rutherford's students might internalize her lessons of female achievement and social activism, and at the same time, actively work to overturn the racial controls advocated by Rutherford's adulation of the Old South and the Confederacy. A Lucy Cobb education had the potential to shape its graduates in unexpected ways.

The extent of employment and activism among the Lucy Cobb nineteenth-century alumnae, including those profiled here, may at first seem surprising, given the school's emphasis on socializing southern ladies. Yet Rutherford and Lipscomb, along with the school's other teachers, offered students a model of prominent and active women. Despite her emphasis on feminine decorum and ladylike behavior, Rutherford herself was an accomplished educator, historian, author, and activist. Further, her textbooks and lectures promoted the achievements of women in literature, art, and even the Bible. Lipscomb, a well-respected teacher, principal, and clubwoman, stressed independent thinking and creativity in the classroom. Many of the faculty, especially in art and music, had received external recognition for their creative work. Their achievements sparked ambition in students, as did the curriculum itself. Writing essays and poems, performing music, acting in plays, and debating current events encouraged students to consider themselves poets, pianists, or social workers. Just as importantly, in the new circumstances of the urban New South, families might depend on the income of women, particularly unmarried daughters or "maiden aunts," to help maintain trappings of their class. That is, elite women might violate the gender expectations of their class in order to maintain their families' income and class status. They would do so while conforming to expectations of feminine behavior. In teaching students marketable skills as well as genteel decorum and dress that would negate the stigma attached to seeking employment, Lucy Cobb contributed to a broader re-imagining of New South womanhood.

In the spring of 1908, Lucy Cobb celebrated its "Golden Jubilee" with a well-attended all-alumnae reunion. Birdie Cobb Smith, Lucy's sister and Governor Hoke Smith's wife, donated a thousand dollars towards a new library, and other graduates and alumnae reminisced about their years at the school. That fall, Lipscomb handed over leadership of the school to alumnae Anne Brumby and Susan Gerdine, who served as co-principals until 1917.[51] The letter nominating Brumby and Gerdine to the board emphasized that both women were not only intelligent and experienced teachers, but also from prestigious, well-known families.[52]

Gerdine and Brumby strove to shape Lucy Cobb into a college preparatory school, but continued to incorporate courses viewed as particularly suitable for women. During these years, in keeping with trends among northern and southern women's schools and colleges, Lucy Cobb's "domestic department" became a more rigorous four-year domestic science course.[53] As elsewhere, the new attention to training young middle class and elite women in domestic skills signified the trend towards housewives actually performing, rather than supervising, housework in their homes.[54] All students took two years of the course, studying cooking, sewing, household management, and household chemistry. Completing an optional additional two years provided students with a diploma in domestic science.[55]

The school continued to receive commendation locally and even nationally. Elizabeth Avery Colton of the Association of College Women, after publishing an extensive report on southern higher education for women, gave a speech in which she declared, "a diploma from Lucy Cobb Institute, which does not pretend to be a college, is preferable to a degree from any of the nominal nine colleges [in Georgia]."[56] Despite the praise, co-principals could not prevent the school's extreme financial problems that they identified as resulting from the domestic effects of the First World War. Overwhelmed by the financial difficulties, and pursuing their own advanced degrees, they stepped down as co-principals in 1917, but remained on the faculty.

Knowing of the institute's continued financial difficulties, both the University of Georgia and the city of Athens had approached the Lucy Cobb board in the 1910s about taking control of the school. Anticipating the enrollment of female students, the university hoped to use the building as sort of a women's college with its campus. Although there was some interest on the board, Mildred Rutherford strongly opposed the idea, and spent the next ten years working to maintain the independence of Lucy Cobb.[57]

Resuming her position as head of the Lucy Cobb in 1917, Mildred Rutherford borrowed $15,000 in order to lease the school for the next five years to prevent its takeover by the city of Athens. This time she took on the title "president," a title used by women's colleges, rather than "principal" used by academies and elementary schools. In the catalogues from these years, Rutherford emphasized the degrees of the faculty, the content of courses, and the preparation Lucy Cobb offered for college education.[58] Rutherford managed to raise enough money from alumnae and the Athens community to pay off the Lucy Cobb debt, and energetically continued fund-raising hoping to create an endowment that would end permanently Lucy Cobb's financial woes. Fund-raising was a major focus of her second term as head of the Lucy Cobb.[59]

In 1922, again planning to relinquish her position as president of Lucy Cobb, Rutherford recommended her niece and namesake, Mildred Rutherford Mell, for the position. Mell was the daughter of Mildred Rutherford's younger sister Bessie Mell. Before her marriage Bessie Mell had taught mathematics and law at the Lucy Cobb, and later founded the Bessie Mell Industrial Home for "poor but deserving" women in Athens.[60] Her husband, George Mell, a banker, was prominent in business, civic, and philanthropic organizations.[61] Five years after giving birth to Mildred, Bessie Mell died, leaving three young children. Mildred Rutherford and her sister Mary Ann Lipscomb shared the responsibility for their young niece until her father's remarriage in 1901.

Mildred Mell entered Lucy Cobb at age six and continued her primary and secondary education there.[62] As a "collegiate" student she was a star pupil, but her name appeared infrequently in students' sketches for the school newsletter or yearbook, and she did not participate in drama or other activities.[63] Perhaps her status as Rutherford's niece set her apart, or perhaps this was indication of a reserved personality. In any case, she shone academically, and in 1907 Mell graduated from Lucy Cobb as valedictorian and winner of the best essay prize.[64] After graduating, Mell earned a certificate from the Carnegie Library School of Atlanta. She then returned to Athens in 1908 to work in the University of Georgia library, remaining there for ten years. That same year, at age 20, Mell accompanied her aunt Mildred and a group of Lucy Cobb students on a summer tour of Europe. Her letters home from that trip reveal a witty young woman full of intellectual curiosity and marvel, impressed by the grandeur of European cities. The young Mell also clearly admired her aunt and shared her conservative views on race and sexuality. The letters express shock at viewing an interracial couple in Paris, and approval of a ship steward with the deference of "an old Plantation Negro" (despite the fact that Mell was born twenty-five years after emancipation, she nearly "clapped her hands" with pleasure with his manners). In another letter she asks if "the negroes at home are behaving themselves or not after the Johnson-Jeffries fight" and implies that blacks were to blame for the Atlanta race riot of 1906. The correspondence also suggests that money problems haunted the family and caused them considerable stress, a theme that appears in numerous letters.[65]

While working at the library, Mell took summer classes at the university towards her B.A. (before women could enroll as regular students), then spent two years at the University of Wisconsin, graduating with honors from one of the nation's most-respected departments of sociology in 1920.[66] Her interest in sociology and social problems fit with a general pattern of college women of the time. Indeed, women's enrollment in these fields helped expand the number of women in higher education, whose numbers reached forty percent of all undergraduates in the first decades of the twentieth century.[67] Many of these women studied sociology and social work, fields viewed as closely connected and particularly appropriate for women.[68] As a southern woman, however, her decision to attend a midwestern coeducational university was unusual. Few southern women attended large coeducational universities such as Wisconsin, and Mell's choice to do so attests to her academic commitment and willingness to not conform to expectations.

Mell returned to Athens to teach mathematics at Lucy Cobb, and after two years, Rutherford, her health failing, asked her niece to take over the school's administration. Mell did not feel confident that she had either the charisma or experience to take her aunt's place, but reluctantly agreed to serve as president, holding that position from 1922 to 1925.[69] Mell took the position during a particularly difficult time for the school. By the 1920s, Lucy Cobb suffered from declining enrollment as well as continuing financial strain. The growth in educational opportunities for women and girls in Athens and across Georgia meant that the school had more difficulty attracting students, and the agricultural depression and boll weevil outbreaks of the 1920s led to problems in retaining them.[70]

In order to encourage enrollment, Mell advertised the academic rigor of Lucy Cobb and the diversity of its course offerings in the catalogue. The school continued to offer extensive music and art courses, as well as classes in stenography, typewriting, and journalism. All of Mell's almost entirely female faculty had attended college, and eight held A.B. or M.A. degrees.[71] Mell promoted the school as a steppingstone towards a college degree. In 1918, once the University of Georgia began accepting female students in some departments, Lucy Cobb graduates were eligible to transfer in with two years of course credit. Within a few years a diploma from Lucy Cobb guaranteed acceptance into the university as a junior.[72] Attending Lucy Cobb prepared students both academically and emotionally for university life, Mell wrote in the 1923 catalogue, as "a student in a large college must sink or swim for herself, and the average girl finds this much easier to do if she has had the advantage of gaining both knowledge and maturity where she is not lost in a crowd." Mell emphasized that Lucy Cobb followed the university's curriculum, but in a more protective, nurturing environment.[73] Many Lucies who graduated from the institute in the 1920s did go on to attend the University of Georgia or other universities.[74]

Other courses prepared Lucies for employment. A Lucy Cobb graduate noted in 1922 that alumnae included "[l]ibrarians, teachers, authors, business women of all kinds."[75] She continued, "[i]t is certainly desirable, and we might almost say essential, for every woman to prepare herself for some vocation," and praised Lucy Cobb's efforts in doing just that.[76] Teaching remained a popular option for these later Lucies, and the school made a special

Figure 7. Mildred Mell with honors students, 1925. (Lucy Cobb Institute Collection, Hargrett Library, University of Georgia)

effort to prepare future educators. For example, completion of courses in music rewarded students with teachers' certificates. A child psychology class prepared students to train children "whether in home or at school." Many Lucies became educators after earning advanced degrees, such as Carrie Walden, who attended the University of Chicago and Columbia, and then took a teaching position at the Lucy Cobb elementary school, or Eugenia Preston Brooks, who earned both a B.A. and a M.A. from UGA after finishing her Lucy Cobb degree, and taught in France before returning to Georgia to teach high school French.[77] The school also offered an optional business course that included bookkeeping, stenography, and typing, preparing them for a job market that by the 1920s employed large numbers of young single women as secretaries and clerks.[78] Several Lucies entered the law, including sisters Marie Lumpkin Upson and Mathilde Lumpkin Upson. The Upson sisters each earned a B.A. in law from the University of Georgia Law Lumpkin School, founded by their great grandfather, Joseph Henry Lumpkin, the first Chief Justice of the Georgia Supreme Court.[79]

Several later Lucy Cobb graduates entered the field of journalism. Journalism and other kinds of writing were viewed as appropriate kinds of labor for southern ladies, and many southern women entered these fields.[80] In the early 1920s, Lucy Cobb created a "School of Journalism," directed by University of Georgia professor John E. Drewry. Drewry enthusiastically proposed creating extensive training in the field at Lucy Cobb, hoping it would join Wesleyan University and become one of only two southern institutions training women for newspaper and magazine writing and editing.[81] Although just beginning his career at the time, Drewry would become one of the most influential journalists and journalism professors in the state as the first dean of the University of Georgia's Henry W. Grady School of Journalism, known for his view that journalism students should be deeply educated in the liberal arts, and that writers should be a force for social change (within limits—Drewry would later strongly oppose UGA student editors who questioned segregation in the mid-1950s, leading to the student editors' resignations).[82] During his time teaching at Lucy Cobb, Drewry supported journalism as a career for women, believing women to be particularly suited as "feature writers, fiction writers, and editors of Sunday supplements and of magazines."[83] He also married one of his students, Kathleen Merry, who had been voted "most intellectual and the best all around girl" of her class.[84]

Perhaps because of the presence of the journalism department, several Lucies worked in that field. Keeping with traditions of the day, most found themselves writing for the "society" or "women's" departments. Erskine

(Richmond) Jarnagin, for example, worked as a society reporter for the At-
lanta *Journal*, then in 1920 directed the society department of the Atlanta
Georgian and the *Sunday American* and wrote a gossip column under the
name "Polly Peachtree."[85] Lamar Rutherford Lipscomb, Rutherford and Mary
Ann Lipscomb's niece, edited *The Mountain Star*, promoting Tallulah Falls
School, and Lucy Cobb's *Lightning Bug*, and wrote a column for the *Athens
Banner-Herald*, which she later collected in a book.[86] Not all Lucies stayed
in the "women's section" of newspapers. The best-known journalist to have
graduated from Lucy Cobb was Mildred Rutherford Woolley, later Seydel,
Mildred Ruthford's grandniece, and another namesake. Under the name
Mildred Seydell (she added an "l" as her penname), she had a long and extensive career as a journalist, first becoming prominent with her coverage
of the 1925 Scopes Trial. Her syndicated column covered everything from
politics (she interviewed Benito Mussolini, for example) to Hollywood and
was widely read.[87]

Lucies of the 1920s had a more rigorous education and more exposure
to career diversity than younger women had, but as they continued to be
strictly supervised. Despite her emphasis on academics, Mell did not alter
rules regulating behavior or dress, and the 1923 announcement included an
article first published in 1917 in the *Athens Banner*, extolling the school's
"atmosphere of refinement, of gentle sweet dignity, of natural and easy culture" that shaped students into "the acme of Southern womanliness and the
perfection of sacred womanhood." Students who attended the Lucy Cobb
in the 1920s remembered both the continuing strictness of the rules gov-
erning behavior and their efforts to evade them. The 1925–26 Handbook of
Regulation reminded students of its sixty-seven-year-long "honorable and
enviable place in the educational world of the South" and entreated students
to uphold its alumnae's "high ideals of truth, of honor, of courage, of purity."
Chaperones were required whenever a student left campus, and "talking out
of windows" was still considered a "very serious offense."[88] A student who
ran past the magnolia tree in the front yard, still outside the boundary of
permissible space, to retrieve some oranges tossed by admirers was confined
inside for two weeks.[89] Rutherford continued to teach at the Lucy Cobb and
to try to impose proper standards of behavior. For example, when asked
how she handled students experimenting with flapper fashion, Rutherford
replied, "we have no flappers at the Lucy Cobb."[90] Watching a few students
demonstrate the "shimmy," an "appalled" Rutherford warned them, "to shake
the hips aroused the passions of men." One of the dancers remembered,
"At that stage of my life I had no idea what the passions of men were, but it
sounded terrible."[91]

Figure 8. Students in a life drawing class, c. 1924. Note the bobbed hair and exposed ankles. (Photo by Tracy Mathewson. Lucy Cobb Institute Collection, Hargrett Library, University of Georgia)

In other ways, however, the school loosened its rules. Students were permitted to invite dates to sit with them in the supervised living room.[92] Although Rutherford continued to measure dress lengths and to check faces for any hint of makeup, some of the other teachers looked away as girls surreptitiously applied rouge and hiked up their skirts. Lucies of the 1920s were willing to accept a few demerits in exchange for the thrill of waving to boys out of their windows, and risked being caught smiling at university students they encountered on their weekly chaperoned walks downtown. Mildred Mell's niece Bessie Lane recalled bobbing her hair while at Lucy Cobb during her aunt's years as director. Although her grandfather had given her $25 in exchange for keeping her hair long, once she arrived at the school she felt so "wretched" with "all these older and more sophisticated girls" that he gave in. Lane also remembered sneaking under the Lucy Cobb porch to talk with Athens High School boys, adding "I don't know whether anyone [on the faculty] knew it or whether they just didn't want to make a hullaballoo out of it, but they ignored us."[93] By 1926, students could attend up to three dances at the university if accompanied by their mothers and if they left from a hotel or home in town (not from the campus).[94] Although Lucy Cobb remained quite strict by today's standards, by the 1920s enforcement of some of its most restrictive rules had loosened.

Mell put most of her effort not into supervising students' behavior but into trying to keep the school afloat financially. Most of her correspondence with the school's board of directors concerned its unstable finances, and she complained that she could not "make both ends meet" for the 1922–23 school year, partially because twenty boarding students withdrew in September "on account of the deplorable financial condition of Georgia at that time." These problems were due mostly to the state's boll weevil epidemic, the harbinger of the agricultural depression that affected the South in the early 1920s. Students from rural areas in particular could no longer afford tuition and board. Despite Mell's best efforts, Lucy Cobb continued to experience financial difficulties.[95] At a loss over how to pay the school's $5000 debt, Mell resigned in 1923, only to be talked into staying two more years after the city Chamber of Commerce offered to help.[96] These problems set the stage for her aunt's return in 1925 as principal, despite her faltering health, and the aggressive campaign that Rutherford then launched for an endowment, something she had worked towards for more than twenty years.[97]

Again head of the Lucy Cobb, Rutherford set about gaining the school's accreditation as a junior college and attempting to secure an endowment for it. Both the city of Athens and the University of Georgia hoped to take over the school, and the issue divided the board and alumnae. Andrew Cobb, Rutherford's cousin, supported the university's move to incorporate the school as a dorm for female students, as did some alumnae, especially those with husbands affiliated with the university. Cobb and others believed that with coeducation at the University of Georgia, Athens no longer needed a women's institution, and that the school's chronic financial instability limited its effectiveness. Rutherford, however, remained convinced that Lucies benefited from an all-female educational environment. She adamantly opposed giving up the school's independence and volunteered to create a self-perpetuating endowment herself.[98]

The Board of Trustees gave Rutherford sixty days to raise $500,000, a nearly impossible task at a time when Georgia was burdened by statewide decline in agricultural income. With her niece, Lamar Rutherford Lipscomb, Rutherford created a newsletter, the *Lightning Bug*, to raise money and encourage alumnae donations. Rutherford along with alumnae supporters hosted fundraising lunches and teas, and networked with local businessmen and politicians. Despite her strenuous efforts, Rutherford did not succeed in raising the funds, and the endowment campaign failed. By 1926, she had fallen into poor health and depression, caused partially from the difficulties of keeping the school financially afloat. That year Lucy Cobb Institute did earn the distinction of becoming an accredited junior college, but financial insecurity continued to haunt the school.[99] Beginning in 1926, for the first time since the school's early years, a nonalumnae—and man—took on the leadership of the Lucy Cobb. Dr. W. F. Hollingworth, who many hoped would save the school, instead drove it deeper into debt.[100]

Rutherford became seriously ill while attending a Children of the Confederacy convention in June 1927 and was hospitalized. On Christmas night that year a fire in her home destroyed most of her personal collection of Confederate artifacts.[101] She never fully recovered from the illness and the shock of the fire and died August 15, 1928. Lucy Cobb struggled on a few more years, finally closing in 1931.

The complex legacy of Lucy Cobb can be seen in the career of Mildred Rutheford Mell after her years there. In 1925, she left Lucy Cobb to take a position as the first dean of women and later academic dean at Shorter College in Rome, Georgia, where she won praise for her administrative skills.[102] Mell's choice to pursue an academic career and forgo marriage resembles that of older Lucies like Woodberry, Smith, and her aunt, unmarried, self-supporting southern women from elite backgrounds. Although as a young woman Mell daydreamed about a future husband and European honeymoon, she, like her aunt, never married. As she moved through her thirties and marriage seemed increasingly improbable, her family, rather than expressing disappointment with this choice, wrote of her accomplishments with clear pride.[103]

While still working at Shorter, Mell entered the doctoral program in sociology with Howard Odum at the University of North Carolina. Mell had first met Odum while he was teaching at the University of Georgia and she was working in the university's library. Although no direct evidence remains that Odum encouraged Mell to continue her education, her decision to later enroll in his Ph.D. program suggests that this meeting was pivotal. She finished her degree in 1938, at the age of forty-nine.[104] Her dissertation, "A Definitive Study of Poor Whites in the South"sought to define "poor whites," identify the cause of their poverty, and determine if they still existed in the South of the 1930s.[105]

After completing her degree in 1938, Mell taught sociology and economics at Agnes Scott College in Decatur, Georgia, for over twenty years. In general, Mell strove to make her fields both accessible and socially relevant.[106] Mell became active in the 1940s in social welfare groups in Atlanta, such as the Social Planning Council (SPC), the Community Fund of Atlanta, and the YWCA.[107] Mell hoped her academic perspective would improve the quality of life in her own community. In this way her work reflects the legacy of early twentieth century female social scientists and social reformers.[108] However, Mell in her academic and social reform work never really grappled with the fundamental issue of racial inequality. Like other southern liberal organizations, the SPC did not directly challenge segregation, instead advocating for better funding for segregated institutions as a way to make "separate" closer to "equal."[109] By focusing on southern poor whites in her scholarly work and by working within groups like the SPC, Mell was able to support issues such as progressive taxation, stronger state welfare measures, and improvements in education, but at the same time elide the issue of segregation and racial discrimination. Significantly, although she remained active in sociological associations and on campus until her retirement in 1960, Mell did not directly address the effects of the civil rights movement on Atlanta or the South in any surviving writings.[110]

In 1978, Mell wrote University of Georgia professor Phinizy Spalding, thanking him for his efforts to preserve the Lucy Cobb building and acknowledging the importance of the school to her.[111] Her affection for the Lucy Cobb Institute and her aunt was fitting, because while Mell seemingly went against everything Rutherford espoused, by leaving Athens to attend a northern coeducational school, earning a doctorate with a scholar known for his relatively liberal views on race, and eschewing marriage in favor of an intellectually and socially active life, in many ways Mell followed her aunt's example. Rutherford, while a critic of female political participation and public activism, led several women's clubs and spoke widely on a variety of issues. In spite of her support for "female influence" in the home, like her niece she never married. Rutherford's interest in benevolence, mostly through the YWCA, may have interested Mell in the plight of the poor. And, most importantly, Rutherford spent fifty years educating girls and championing the intellectual accomplishments of women, a legacy Mell continued at Lucy Cobb, Shorter, and Agnes Scott. That Mell viewed her aunt's legacy of one of female achievement testifies to the complexity of Rutherford's career and the contradictions of women's anti-feminist activism.

After the Lucy Cobb closed, the University of Georgia leased the building, using it as a women's dorm for several years, but later allowed it to fall into disrepair. Once considered one of the city's architectural gems, the Seney-Stovall Chapel was condemned and closed. In 1970, however, the school building won nomination to the National Register of Historic Places, and over the next decade received renewed attention from the community. In 1978 concerned local citizens, headed by Nellie Stovall's grandson and University of Georgia professor of history Phinizy Spalding, created the Friends of Lucy

Cobb and the Seney-Stovall Chapel as part of the Historic Cobbham Foundation. The group raised money and helped obtain congressional funding for an extensive restoration of the entire campus. Today, the main Lucy Cobb building houses offices for the university's Carl Vinson Institute of Government, and the chapel is used for university and community events.[112]

The history of the Lucy Cobb Institute complicates historical understanding of the purpose and legacy of southern women's education. On the surface, the school's concern with behavior and its inclusion of decorative subjects in the curriculum seems backward looking, even an anachronism in the urban New South. But a closer examination reveals a school that took academics seriously, and a faculty of independent and assertive women whose own lives belied their idealization of the antebellum belle and plantation life. Rutherford and Lipscomb did not train women for seclusion in the home. Rather, they provided students with genteel manners and a mandate to publicly defend the interests of their class.

3 Training "Leaders of Their Own Race"

The Educational Mission of Spelman Seminary

Only a few months after Mildred Rutherford returned to Athens from Atlanta to assume the leadership of the Lucy Cobb Institute, two white northern missionaries founded an educational institution in the Georgia capital serving a very different female population. Sophia Packard and Harriet Giles, both of Massachusetts, opened their school in the basement of western Atlanta's Friendship Baptist Church with the intention of providing religious, academic, and moral instruction to African American women. Their first group of students, eleven adult women, most of them former slaves, learned basic literacy and studied the Bible. From these modest beginnings the school would become Spelman Seminary, with stately buildings, tree-lined walkways, and a significant endowment. By the 1920s, the institution achieved the status of a college, contributing to Atlanta's reputation as a leader in black higher education.

Whereas Lucy Cobb prepared young white women whose activism and ladylike appearance would help maintain their family's economic and political power within the industrializing New South, the founders of Spelman Seminary set out to train African American young women who in turn would aid in uplifting and educating rural black southern communities. Students of the two schools differed not only in racial and class background but also in their educational goals and their vision of the South's future. Yet both of these private institutions viewed secondary schooling for young women as key to the region's future and development, and both offered an education that combined academics with training in Christianity and morality. In particular, the schools shared a preoccupation with feminine sexual modesty, viewing it as a crucial part of young women's education, and as key to defining racial and class identities. At Lucy Cobb, Mildred Rutherford and other alumnae refashioned antebellum femininity to protect the reputations of white women active in the public sphere. For black women, proper behavior was even more essential. Stereotypes of black women's sexual aggressiveness obscured the problem of rape of African American women by white men, and denied them a public voice to protest lynching, disenfranchisement, and segregation—themselves justified by white supremacists as means of controlling black lasciviousness.

Scholars have stressed the importance of "the politics of respectability"— the adoption of respectable behavior as a means of protection against racist stereotypes of black women as sexually aggressive, uncouth, and generally lacking in self-control. Respectability, African American women hoped, would shield them from attacks against their character and allow them greater access to the public sphere. Scholars have generally identified education as a key marker of respectability, along with sexual restraint, proper manners and dress, and contemplative worship.[1] An analysis of the content of the education offered at Spelman and the goals of administrators, board members, faculty, and supporters provides an understanding of how secondary schools for girls would teach the attributes of respectability. To a surprising degree, industrial education was viewed as essential to the curriculum of a school for "striving" black young women. In contrast to traditional interpretations of black education that oppose industrial and academic education, Spelman faculty, board members, and many students and alumnae viewed industrial and academic education as mutually reinforcing rather than at odds with each other.

This chapter analyzes the ideological assumptions behind, and the content of, education for black female respectability. The seminary sought to create educated, sexually pure, community minded, Christian women whose behavior would be always above reproach. Spelman's emphasis on morality, modesty, discipline, and hard work indicated the somewhat accommodationist nature of its agenda for social progress through character reform. Yet within the school's message of self-improvement lay a challenge to southern racial ideology and an endorsement of African American economic and political progress. The complexity of the Spelman educational mission allowed diverse groups, including the northern white female missionary founders and faculty, northern white male educational reformers, white southern progressives, and African American educational and religious leaders, to highlight aspects that favored their own agenda. All viewed Spelman's blend of industrial and academic education as beneficial to black women and essential to racial progress, yet they differed widely in what the legacy of the benefit would be. Industrial education could be understood as a way to maintain racial control, as a means to racial progress within a hierarchical social order, or as a chance to create racial equality. The seminary's ability to appeal to diverse groups and to balance their interests contributed to its survival and growth, long after many schools for African Americans founded during the post-Civil War era shut their doors.

When Sophia B. Packard and Harriet Giles founded what they at first called the Atlanta Baptist Female Seminary, Giles was nearing fifty and Packard was close to sixty. Packard and Giles both hailed from New Salem, Massachusetts, an agricultural town west of Boston.[2] Packard, born in 1824 to a large and prosperous farm family, gained a powerful sense of Christian faith and duty from her father. An admiring student remembered Packard as strong-willed, decisive, hardworking, and inspirational. Yet her religious sensibility and seriousness of purpose did not interfere with a mischievous sense of humor; as another former student put it, Packard tended to find the "droll side of a subject." The younger Giles, born 1833, was more reserved, described by students and colleagues as unassuming, thoughtful, gentle, and sympathetic.[3] Her journals reveal a woman of steadfast commitment and deep religious faith but also someone full of self-doubt and uncomfortable with attention.[4]

Packard attended the prestigious New Salem Academy, a coeducational boarding school, for several years and then graduated in 1850 from the Charlestown Female Academy. She taught for four years elsewhere before returning to New Salem Academy as "Preceptress." While directing the academy Packard met Giles, then a student in the school's classical, or pre-collegiate, program. The two became close friends and after graduating, Giles began teaching at New Salem.[5] The two would continue working and living together until Packard's death.[6]

In 1869, after teaching in various New England academies, Packard accepted an appointment in Boston as the pastor's assistant at a Baptist church, a job not normally given to women.[7] Packard used her influential church position to help found the Woman's American Baptist Home Missionary Society (WABHMS) as an auxiliary organization to the venerable American Baptist Home Missionary Society (ABHMS).[8] The ABHMS hoped to bring both white and black southerners into the Northern Baptist organization after the Civil War, but had little success among whites outside of wartime Unionist areas. Northern and Southern Baptists had split in 1844 over the issue of slavery, partially because the ABHMS, already active in working among free blacks in the South, refused to give up its antislavery stance. Resentment of the organization by whites in the former Confederate states remained high during the Reconstruction period.[9] The group therefore de-

Figure 9. Sophia Packard and Harriet Giles, founders of Spelman Seminary. (Courtesy of the Spelman College Archives)

voted most of its attention to African Americans. Befitting its role as part of the postwar "abolitionist legacy," the ABHMS viewed Christian training for freedmen and women as the logical extension of its antebellum ideology.[10] The ABHMS's primary goal in its work among the former slaves was to create a trained black ministry to rid the freedmen and women of what is identified as their "ignorance, superstition, and groveling sensuality." The organization also sought to provide laypeople with a broad education that would include religious, academic, industrial, and moral instruction.[11] Towards these goals, the ABHMS founded schools for freedmen and women throughout the South, including the male-only Augusta Baptist Institute, which later moved to Atlanta and became Atlanta Baptist Seminary and ultimately Morehouse College.

As corresponding secretary for the WABHMS, in 1880 Packard traveled throughout the South observing the state of missionary and educational work among African Americans. She returned to Boston determined to found a school for black women in Atlanta with Giles and asked for the financial support of the WABHMS. Their interest in the education of girls fit a general pattern of turn-of-the century reform. Progressive-Era social workers and educators often targeted poor or immigrant girls and young women, believing that they in turn would instruct both their parents and their future children in "American" ways of life.[12] Just as female settlement house workers, missionaries, and public school teachers viewed the instruction of girls as their best hope in assimilating immigrants, Packard and Giles believed educating young black women represented the best hope for racial uplift. At first the society's board, citing lack of money, refused Packard's entreaties, but after ten months of lobbying gave in. Although balking at funding a school, the WABHMS eventually agreed to sponsor Packard and Giles as independent teachers to the freedwomen. In the spring of 1881, full of excitement and anticipation, the pair set out for the three-day train ride to the Georgia capital.[13]

A railroad hub linking northern cities to southern farmers, Atlanta by the 1880s was on its way towards surpassing the port city of Savannah as the state's commercial and financial center. Named state capital in Georgia's 1867 constitution, by 1910 it also could claim to be the regional leader of banking, insurance, and finance. When Giles and Packard arrived, the city was witnessing only the beginning of its population explosion; over the next thirty years, the number of Atlantans would quadruple to reach 150,000. Both blacks and whites flocked to the state capital. In 1880 blacks represented 43 percent of the city's population, although that number would shrink to 33 percent by 1910 as white migration increased. The city's famously aggressive "New South" boosters could claim some credit for its rapid development, as northern investors looked to the "Gate City" for investment opportunities and migrants escaping rural poverty rushed in from the countryside.[14]

Race played a major role in determining the opportunities for these recent migrants. African Americans faced restrictions on voting rights as early as 1868, restrictions that were tightened by the imposition of a poll tax in 1877 and the creation of a white primary in the 1890s, and limited further still in amendments to the state constitution in 1908. In the early years, the fast pace of growth discouraged the maintenance of sharply segregated neighborhoods, but by 1900, Atlanta's western, eastern, and southern areas were primarily African American, while the city's center and north side contained majority white communities. Most of the predominantly black areas were located in undesirable, often industrial, areas and lacked basic city services such as sewer lines, paved roads, and sanitation services. African Americans received inadequate health services and overcrowded, poorly financed public schools in segregated facilities. In September of 1906 Atlanta endured one of the most violent race riots of the New South era, a four-day assault on the city's African American citizens.[15]

Because of exclusion and discrimination in public life, private institutions, including schools, represented key focal points for building community in postwar Atlanta. An ethic of racial solidarity, developed in slavery and extending beyond emancipation, served as the basis of black community support in the Gate City. As a few African Americans gained status and income, they used their resources to aid others in the community. Central to this process was the creation of black-owned institutions. Through the purchase of real estate, a few black Atlantans of means "created autonomous social spaces, owned and controlled by African Americans"—places such as churches, banks (which helped support other businesses), schools, clubs, and charities. These institutions both provided a sense of independence from whites and also allowed some African Americans to form a small but influential black middle class.[16]

Private schools represented a key institution in community building and filled a void left by the inadequate funding given to black public schools, a problem throughout Georgia and the South generally. Public schools for blacks in Atlanta in the late nineteenth century were depressingly inadequate. The city created its first public school system in 1872 for white children only. Two schools for African American children founded by missionary organizations were soon incorporated into the public school system, bringing the total number of elementary schools to five for white students and two for blacks, despite the fact that African Americans made up 45 percent of the city's population in 1870. Building of schools for whites continued to outpace that for black students, and in the 1880s, almost three-quarters of white children attended school, but just over 40 percent of black children did so. After 1889, Georgia required racial segregation in education by law. The schools that black students attended received less funding, fewer teachers, poorer buildings, and fewer classroom supplies. The city refused to provide a high school for black students, despite pressure from African Americans, until 1924.[17] The lack of public educational services for African American children made private institutions such as the school created by Giles and Packard essential to black educational, social, and economic progress in southern cities like Atlanta.

The pair built on an educational foundation created by a diverse group of Reconstruction-era educators that included freedmen and women, earlier northern missionaries, and white southerners. According to scholar James Anderson, southern African Americans themselves founded the first schools for newly freedmen and women after the end of the Civil War and blacks became the first southerners to campaign for universal public education.

The origins of their deep-rooted desire for education and literacy lay in their exclusion from any sort of learning during slavery; for former slaves, literacy represented "a means to liberation and freedom."[18] Northern African Americans, too, became teachers in the Reconstruction-era South in remarkable numbers considering their small proportion of the northern population. As Ron E. Butchart found, African Americans made up one-third of the teaching force in postwar southern black schools. Butchart also stresses that although historians have portrayed the archetypical Reconstruction-era teacher as white, single, young, well off, female, and motivated by abolitionist convictions, few fit that description. He paints a diverse portrait of postwar educators that included former slaveholders, former abolitionists, and former slaves; northern blacks and southern whites; married women and single men; teachers motivated sometimes by ideological or religious conviction; and others by merely a need for self-support.[19] Together they started the process of beginning an educational system for black southerners. Although most Reconstruction-era teachers did not fit the stereotype of the "Yankee schoolmarm," the examples of earlier northern women who traveled south did serve as a precedent for the work of Giles and Packard.[20]

In April 1881 the missionaries arrived in Atlanta, supported by the WABHMS as "independent teachers." Immediately after their arrival, however, they met with black pastors interested in founding schools, including the influential Father Frank Quarles of Friendship Baptist Church located in Jenningstown, a predominantly African American area in the western part of the city.[21] Religious institutions frequently housed schools in the postwar black community, both because missionaries funded church schools hoping they would produce ministers who would promulgate their views, and because of the deeply meaningful association between literacy and liberation. In this way, African American evangelical Baptists "merged salvation with educational uplift and social reform."[22] Friendship Baptist Church participated in this tradition. African American members of Atlanta's primarily white First Baptist Church had founded Friendship Baptist in 1848, winning permission for a separate worship for slaves under the supervision of a white member. In 1864 Quarles became pastor of Friendship Baptist, and after the war the two churches officially separated. Hoping for financial security, a new physical space, and the means to fund a school, Quarles turned to the American Missionary Association (AMA) for support, with success. The resources provided by the AMA gave Friendship Baptist a degree of stability and in particular the ability to support a school that smaller, more independent black churches lacked, but at the cost of reliance on northern white institutions that expected to have influence in exchange for funding.[23]

Because of his tireless support for black education, and his willingness to work with white missionaries, Quarles seemed a natural ally for Packard and Giles. By all accounts, Quarles welcomed Giles and Packard after their arrival in Atlanta in April 1881. Further, he lent his support and resources to the missionaries to help them expand their work beyond the limited role assigned to them by the WABHMS and create their original plan of a school for women. Father Quarles allowed the missionaries to use the church's basement for instruction, and within ten days of their arrival, Packard and Giles began classes. Along with influential African American minister William J. White, a cofounder of Augusta Baptist Institute (precursor to Morehouse College), Quarles helped raise interest in and financial support for the missionaries' project among black Atlantans. Attesting to his commitment, Quarles even engaged on a fund-raising tour of New England for the fledgling school later that year. This dedication cost him his life; while in Boston, Quarles contracted pneumonia and died.[24]

Atlanta's new "basement school" began with eleven adults; by the end of the term in July, eighty pupils attended. Although the 1881 catalogue boasted two tracks, a normal department and an ambitious "academic" department based on the contemporary secondary school curriculum and offering algebra, philosophy, and Latin, most students focused on mastering basic literacy.[25] A student from these first years described the basement as cramped, with a floor made of "boards, dirt, and coal, and in the Spring months, a little grass."[26] In addition to their teaching, Packard and Giles participated in or founded Sunday schools in local black churches, and visited members at home.[27]

The basement school attracted enough students that the Massachusetts educators sought to create a more permanent, more ambitious school.[28] In late 1882, the ABHMS purchased several former Union army barracks and nine acres of land in west Atlanta, and the following January the women's seminary moved in. A fund-raising tour of Northern Baptist churches that same year provided the money necessary to construct more substantial buildings. While traveling, Packard and Giles made a special trip to the Cleveland church of the Rev. George King, a former student of theirs. King could boast oil magnate John D. Rockefeller as one of his parishioners. Knowing Rockefeller's interest in education and that his wife, Laura Spelman Rockefeller, had attended one of the seminaries where the two had taught, Packard and Giles believed that their school had a chance of attracting his interest. That Sunday, Rockefeller gave only $250, but he soon followed this initial gift with more substantial donations, totaling $94,000 over eleven years. Rockefeller also served on the seminary's board from 1888 to 1907, at the request of the school's founders. In appreciation,

Figure 10. Spelman Seminary in 1883 on the new West End campus. (Courtesy of the Spelman College Archives)

Giles and Packard named the school Spelman Seminary, in honor of Laura Rockefeller's father, an outspoken abolitionist.[29]

Rockefeller's donations allowed the campus to witness considerable development over the next forty years. Rockefeller Hall was completed in May 1886, followed by Packard Hall in 1888, Giles Hall in 1893, MacVicar Hospital in 1901, and Morgan and Morehouse Halls in 1902.[30] Rockefeller also donated quite a bit of land, some of which the school sold to developers, contributing to Atlanta's unusual geography of predominantly black suburbs extending west from the city, rather than the typical white suburbs ringing a mostly black inner city.[31] Land ownership allowed Packard and Giles to close off streets and smooth out hills to create a compact but beautiful campus.[32] Like New England's "seven sister" colleges, Spelman strove to create a cloister-like campus separated from the city providing, in Giles's words, "undisturbed privacy, to our untold relief and advantage."[33] Boarding students lived in dorms with teachers expected to "take the place of mother."[34] In 1917 Spelman received more funds from Rockefeller and constructed two new buildings, one used as a dormitory for nurses and the other for home economics courses.[35] Along with Atlanta University, Atlanta Baptist, Morris Brown and Clark Colleges, and Gammon Theological Seminary, Spelman formed part of a unique center of higher education for African Americans.[36] Because of Rockefeller's funding, Spelman became the "prettiest and richest" of the Atlanta schools.[37]

Students in the school's first few years often were adults, some formerly enslaved. One early student, for example, born into slavery in 1849, traveled to Atlanta after the war. Once there she joined the Friendship Baptist Church and when Packard and Giles began classes in its basement, the woman, married, employed, and in her early thirties, began attending, an experience she cited as life-changing twenty years later.[38] A student graduating in 1892 remembered the taunting she received when she first enrolled, including white boys laughing, "Just look at them old women sitting in school."[39] Some early students attended classes with their daughters.[40] As late as 1894, an observer noted "some of the students have themselves been slaves" and "there are mature women, mothers of families, who even now are learning to read."[41] In addition to illiteracy, many Spelman students, especially in the early years, shared the lack of material resources of the overwhelming majority of black southerners, and made significant sacrifices to attend the school. In a private letter in 1884 Giles described early students as hardworking but very poor, and noted that many boarding students were orphaned. The poverty of many early students cut short their education, such as one who wrote with regret that she was unable to afford the bus fare to return to Atlanta.[42]

The seminary's motto, "Our whole school for Christ," indicated the centrality of religion to Spelman.[43] Baptist faith motivated Giles, Packard, and other faculty, and religious education formed the heart of their mission. As Giles confided in her journal, "I do want to be a power for Christ in this school."[44] This religious emphasis shaped the Spelman curriculum. Every student attended Bible classes and religious services daily.[45] Even students already part of a church, Giles and Packard believed, would benefit from religious education. The founders stressed that Spelman taught an orderly, quiet, and contemplative faith and discouraged the emotional worship they associated with southern African American churches.[46] Northern missionaries to the postwar South tended to view this expressive religious style as backward and even superstitious and linked it with the corruption and degradation of slavery.[47] Attesting to the importance they placed in what they viewed as proper worship, the principals proudly listed the number of students "converted" each year in statistics documenting enrollment and graduation rates.[48] In her private diary, Giles made little note of academic matters but kept careful track of the number of conversions.[49] Other faculty encouraged students' religious faith and often cited their own as the basis of their decision to teach at Spelman. Like Packard and Giles, most of the women who taught at Spelman were single white women from the Northeast, joined by the mid-1890s by a few Spelman graduates. In the school's first years, most of the faculty had been educated at seminaries, although by 1905, several had advanced degrees. Their own student experience in single-sex institutions that combined academic rigor with Christian training in morals and self-discipline shaped faculty members' thinking about proper education for young women.[50]

Figure 11. Graduates of the high school, 1887. (Courtesy of the Spelman College Archives)

At least some students welcomed the school's religious emphasis. The regimented schedule of Spelman left little time for extracurricular activities, but students participated in Christian clubs such as the YWCA, temperance groups, the Christian Endeavor Society, and the Social Purity Society, and remained active in church-based organizations after graduation.[51] Many students cited their better understanding and acceptance of Christianity as their major accomplishment while at Spelman, and wrote articles with titles like "Prayer" for the school paper, the *Messenger*.[52] Obituaries and other alumnae notices often highlighted religious commitment of former students.

Packard and Giles continued to lead the school together until Packard's death in the summer of 1891. Lucy Upton of Salem, Massachusetts, replaced her as co-principal. Highly intelligent, methodical, serious, and disciplined, Upton assisted Giles during twenty years of remarkable physical and academic growth at the seminary.[53] That same year, only ten years after the founding of the "basement school," Spelman's enrollment reached 830, although it dropped sharply over the course of the 1890s. Economic hardship resulting from the depression of the 1890s may have prompted families to withdraw their children from school. Additionally, the expansion of public schools, limited as they were, probably contributed, as much of the loss occurred in the lower grades, and the more advanced classes actually grew in proportion to the rest of the school. Whereas after the turn of the century many missionary schools faced dire shortages that led them to close their doors, Spelman, benefiting from the Rockefeller donations, grew after 1900. Enrollment reached 664 by 1911, and 744 by 1923. At the same time, the average age of students dropped, bringing the school more in line with contemporary secondary schools. By 1907 ninety-three percent of the student body was under the age of twenty-five. With greater numbers hoping to enroll, the seminary became more selective, favoring boarding students and those in higher grades.[54] Most students came from Georgia, a few from surrounding states, and a handful hailed from northern and western states and from foreign countries, including Honduras, Columbia, and the Congo.[55]

Although religious instruction remained at the center of the Spelman mission, over time, the school put increasing emphasis on creating an academic program with rigorous and pedagogically up-to-date classes. In its first few years, Spelman offered a normal course divided into six grades, including classes in critical reading, elocution, grammar, math, geography, history, botany, and hygiene, as well as instruction in "good morals and gentle manners." With a year of additional study a student could earn a "higher or scientific normal" diploma. To educate younger students and to provide classroom training for potential teachers, Spelman offered a "model school" for the elementary grades.[56] As elsewhere in the South, primary schools attached to seminaries attracted African American parents, who frequently viewed them as better than the public schools taught by white southerners.[57]

In 1891, ABHMS Superintendent of Education Malcolm MacVicar reviewed Spelman and submitted a list of recommendations on ways the school might strengthen its educational offerings to Giles and Packard. The two readily accepted the suggestions, viewing them in keeping with their own goals.[58] By the early 1890s, Giles and Upton had created an "academic" or high school course emphasizing English language and literature, natural science, math, and art, with Latin optional.[59] Teachers observed that by then, students entered the seminary better prepared, and consequently raised requirements for graduation. The school also began a college preparatory course that included classes in Latin, German, French, Greek, and advanced algebra and geometry.[60] In many ways, especially in its emphasis on languages, science, and math, the Spelman curriculum closely matched that of Lucy Cobb. Yet in 1900, reflecting the continuing limited public education for African Americans in Georgia, seventy-five percent of students took the "English preparatory," or pre-high school course, and even in 1920, more than half of the total number of students were enrolled in the elementary grades of the "practice school."[61] The concentration of students in the lower grades was typical for black institutions of higher education at this time; in 1915, 79 percent of students attending black colleges enrolled in precollegiate classes.[62] But Spelman, like other schools founded by northern missionaries, did strive to offer a college degree, and in 1897, two students entered the seminary's first college class, adding economics, sociology, psychology, and other subjects to their course load.[63] Spelman was not yet able to truly offer a college-level curriculum on its own; collegiate and precollegiate students took many of their advanced courses at Atlanta Baptist. Nonetheless, the seminary was extremely proud to offer a college degree. Both women graduated in 1901, and eight more Spelman students earned B.A.s by 1911.[64] Over the course of the school's first thirty years, Spelman granted 350 diplomas (to students graduating from the high school, college, or professional programs) and 576 certificates (for domestic arts, printmaking, and music).[65]

Despite the heavy concentration in the lower grades, by the 1890s Spelman's faculty and board believed the seminary's advanced academic offerings ranked among those of the nation's top women's schools.[66] Visitors to Spelman frequently compared the school to Mount Holyoke or Vassar, and the seminary self-consciously looked to these schools as models.[67] Mount Holyoke had begun in the 1830s as a seminary preparing rural women of limited means to become self-disciplined, modest, Christian teachers. Like

Figure 12. Students at study hall inside Packard Hall, 1889. (Courtesy of the Spelman College Archives)

Spelman, the Massachusetts school required students to perform daily domestic work to defray costs and keep tuition low.[68] Vassar, on the other hand, was founded in 1865 as the first true college for women and aspired to offer a curriculum on par with Harvard or Yale.[69] In truth, during its first years, Spelman resembled Mount Holyoke much more than Vassar. Still, the seminary aspired to become the "Vassar of the South," as the *Messenger* referred to it after an 1895 visit from Vassar's Lucy Salmon and A. M. Ely.[70] In doing so, the paper indicated that Spelman hoped to prove the appropriateness of a college-level liberal arts education for southern African American women.

By the 1920s, Lucy Tapley had instituted changes that brought Spelman closer to its aspirations. Tapley had assumed the school's leadership in 1911 after several years on the faculty.[71] Like her predecessors, she hailed from a New England Baptist family. In contrast to Giles, described by alumna Claudia White Harreld as "diffident to what was sometimes a trying degree," Tapley was strong-willed, efficient, confident, and physically imposing. One faculty member remarked that Tapley had a brother who was a sea captain but looked like a schoolteacher, whereas she was a schoolteacher but looked like a sea captain. During her tenure, Tapley especially focused on teacher training and believed Spelman's major mission to be providing instructors for rural Southern schools. In keeping with current trends in women's education, she also added more physical education and home economics courses. Although very concerned with rules about proper behavior and dress, Tapley also allowed more social activities, including events with Morehouse students.[72]

Tapley also pushed for a college program that would gain recognition from the state department of education. Towards this end, in 1922 she rehired former dean Edna Lamson, who rejoined the Spelman faculty after spending a year at Columbia's Teachers College. There, Lamson studied standardized testing and intelligence testing, and after her return she introduced these to Spelman to track students and to, in her view, document the potential of students interested in the college program.[73] In 1923, the seminary obtained a grant from the General Education Board to build a science building, allowing the school to offer a complete college course independent of Morehouse. The following year it became formally incorporated as Spelman College, and by 1927 received first-rank recognition from the Georgia Department of Education. Fifteen of the eighteen college-level faculty members had earned B.A.s, one from Spelman, and seven also had M.A.s. Students could major in elementary education, high school education, or home economics education for a B.S. (or spend two years to earn a junior college diploma in these subjects), or in literature or music and literature for a B.A. All college students took classes in English literature (Elizabethan to Victorian), modern languages, the Bible, history (general European, English, and American), science, economics, sociology, and household arts. Negro history, a semester-long course, was part of the standard curriculum, and courses in American literature and sociology promised particular attention to African Americans. Students majoring in education studied educational methodology, history, and psychology, and engaged in extensive practice teaching.[74] By 1926, nearly 15,000 students had attended the school, and over one thousand had graduated, several earning more than one degree. Almost one-quarter had completed their degrees between 1921 and 1925, indicating the increasing expansion of the college and high school.[75] According to Tapley, as a college the school would improve academic standards without altering its founding mission, as "the original aim of the school, that of training for Christian womanhood, is still kept uppermost."[76]

Spelman's leaders believed that helping students achieve an ideal of educated Christian womanhood required not only religious and academic instruction, but also industrial training. This emphasis on industrial education mostly clearly distinguishes the curriculum of Spelman from that of Lucy Cobb. Although not absent in white southern education, industrial education was not part of Athens institute's formal or informal curriculum, reflecting the status of its student population. Historians of African American education often have viewed industrial training, associated most closely with Booker T. Washington's Tuskeegee Institute, as incompatible with liberal arts education. James Anderson wrote that industrial training "had no major role in the missionaries' philosophy and program of training a leadership class to guide the ex-slaves in their social, economic, and moral development."[77] Scholars such as Anderson who see a division between industrial and academic education view "industrial" as indicating vocational training in manual labor. Yet other historians have argued that its primary purpose was moral education and the creation of good character.[78] These scholars and others argue that nineteenth-century educators often used "industry" to mean disciplined hard work.

Creating "habits of industry" represented as central a goal to Spelman as "train[ing] the intellect" according to the 1883–84 catalogue, which also deemed the industrial department a *prominent feature of this Institution*."[79] Industrial training was part of both the school's curriculum and of daily life, especially for boarding students, about half of the school population. Although by the 1890s white women's colleges like Mount Holyoke and Wellesley had reduced or gotten rid of their work requirements and raised tuition, Spelman continued to require one hour of housework daily through the 1920s.[80] Students unable to afford tuition could do extra cafeteria or laundry chores.[81] In 1909, about half of boarders paid their tuition and room and board in full, one-third paid part and worked for part, and one-fifth exchanged work for the entire amount. Some students alternated years working full time with attending school full time.[82] Campus work served both a practical and pedagogical purpose. In 1912 President Lucy Hale Tapley noted that labor taught self-reliance by requiring students to earn, rather simply be given, scholarships.[83] The system also allowed the seminary to avoid the kind of tuition increases that followed the end of the work requirement at Vassar and Mount Holyoke.[84]

In addition to the mandatory chores, students took classes in cooking, housework, laundry, and simple sewing.[85] Progressive-Era schools for urban immigrant or rural white women and girls offered courses like these to provide models of "proper" households to working-class families.[86] Similarly, at Spelman, these classes were intended primarily to improve African American home life. Knowing how to properly cook, clean, and sew, Spelman students would become "economical" and "useful" wives and mothers, and proper housekeeping would help their families obtain "higher ideas of true living."[87] The "ideal home," as one student wrote, was owned by the family, as home ownership would promote frugality, cleanliness, order, and intelligence.[88] Clean, well-maintained homes reflected not only good character but also respect for God; as one student wrote, "We should make our homes a symbol of the home above."[89] This emphasis on domestic life fit with broader trends in black thought that emphasized the cultivation of proper homes as an expression of activism. In the wake of disenfranchisement, some early-twentieth-century African American authors, perceiving political involvement as dangerous or even deadly and ultimately futile, advocated that blacks give up trying to secure the vote and instead focus on strengthening family life. In this way, they viewed domesticity as "a surrogate for electoral politics in their quest for self-determination."[90] The frequent discussions of clean and orderly homes in Spelman publications fit with the heightened importance given to domestic life as a symbol and achievable goal beginning in the 1890s.

Although Spelman emphasized that education in the domestic arts would benefit black families, the school also acknowledged the limited options for educated black women by obliquely suggesting that that their training might also prepare them for work as domestics. References to students' work in domestic service, although notably infrequent, occasionally did appear in the school's publicity literature. Giles asserted in the 1896 annual report that industrial training would aid students to "preside intelligently over her own household, or to do good service in any family."[91] That same year, the *Messenger*, a monthly newsletter read by students and potential donors, reprinted a short article from *The Atlanta Journal* by a white woman who had hired a Spelman student as a cook. The employer, at first skeptical of what she termed "the educated darkey," was pleased with what she described as the woman's thorough work and scrupulous honesty, and the newspaper praised Spelman for its exemplary "training of colored women."[92] John Hope, the first African American president of Atlanta Baptist College, declared that when Atlantans "want intelligent helpers in their home, they telephone Spelman."[93] And indeed, until the early 1920s students could earn certificates for industrial training if they had attended the school for at least two years, showed "good moral character," and learned sewing, cooking, and housekeeping skills.[94] The school's willingness to promote students as potential domestics, even ones who might earn additional pay because of their training, would seem to support the interpretation of industrial education as nothing more than training for menial labor, a way to keep southern African Americans in low-status, low-paid jobs.

Yet Spelman's industrial program extended beyond domestic chores and included professional programs. Unlike many industrial schools, the seminary offered training that provided real opportunities for work other than the domestic and personal service positions that employed 92 percent of Atlanta's African American women in the workforce.[95] Some of the criticism of Tuskegee Institute, both during Booker T. Washington's lifetime and by historians, has focused on the school's preparation of students for artisanal trades no longer part of the industrializing economy.[96] Graduates of Spelman's professional programs, however, found work in the respectable female professions, as teachers, nurses, and missionaries. Contemporary schools for black women run by African Americans, such as Lucy Craft Laney, Mary McLeod Bethune, and Charlotte Hawkins Brown also focused on teacher training.[97] Segregation laws that required separate black schools, hospitals, and other facilities gave black women professional opportunities in these areas.[98] Although a small proportion of the overall student body took the professional courses, the school took pride in them and viewed them as a central part of their overall mission.

The earliest professional department, printing, began in 1884, and by the following year students printed the school's monthly, the *Messenger*. Printers also made stationery and other "fancy work" for sale.[99] A grant from the Slater Fund, a northern-based organization that was the primary supporter of vocational training for southern African Americans in the 1880s, helped finance the department.[100] Printing represented the most traditionally "industrial" aspect of the professional program. In a glowing review, a white northern visitor noted that training in printing not only provided its graduates with a marketable skill, but with "habits of close observation," attention to detail, and discipline, work habits associated with Tuskegee-style industrial education.[101] Still, it did provide training for future work; several graduates reported finding jobs as printers, and some edited their own papers as well.[102]

The nursing program, founded in 1888 by African American physician Sophia Jones, a University of Michigan medical school graduate, offered students a well-respected and financially stable career, and Jones herself represented black female achievement in the medical profession.[103] Spelman began its nurse-training program just as nursing began to shed its association with domestic service and establish itself as a trained profession. Black nurses in particular had struggled to separate their work from domestic service, and were sometimes expected to do janitorial work both in homes and hospitals. Their exclusion from nurse-training programs in many hospitals and the contempt they received by white physicians and nurses made professionalization especially difficult. In response, the 1890s witnessed the founding of several training programs for nurses in black colleges and hospitals.[104]

Before 1896, Spelman students could take the nursing course as part of their general education, and many students took the course intending to use their skills in their work as missionaries, teachers, or mothers. Beginning that year, however, the program became more professionally oriented.[105] A survey done in 1899 of the sixty-four nursing graduates showed that one-half had done some nursing, and that one-third currently worked in the field. Those working in the South made on average $10 a week. By means of comparison, at that time domestic workers in Atlanta made $1-$2 a week.[106] Indeed, observers considered nursing to be the best-paying work available to black women.[107] In 1901, after a long fund-raising effort, Spelman opened its own MacVicar hospital on campus. The hospital aided nurse training and also provided much-needed care, often free of charge, to Atlanta's black community.[108] Still, the hospital reflected racial mores of the time. In keeping with Georgia law, although reportedly against the wishes of Giles, only white doctors were hired, and only white doctors could admit black patients to MacVicar.[109]

The missionary training department, inaugurated during the 1891–92 school year, included courses in the Bible, temperance and social purity, and family organization.[110] Like the nursing program, it too was at first an emphasis within the high school course, and later became a post-graduate program.[111] Most of its graduates did "home missionary" work in their own communities, but a few traveled to the Congo, Burma, and Oklahoma Territory.[112] Faculty especially encouraged students to travel to the Congo and follow the example of other African American missionaries such as the celebrated William Shepard, nicknamed the "Black Livingstone," who spent nearly twenty years in the country.[113] Although the school did its best to impress upon students their duty to their African "brothers and sisters," including publishing extensive letters from Spelman missionaries stationed there almost monthly in the *Messenger*, only four students traveled to the Congo. In recognition that most graduates would become home missionaries, the program was renamed the Christian Workers' Course in 1900, and enrolled adult women interested in becoming active in church work and religious outreach.[114]

The seminary heavily promoted the missionary, nursing, and printing courses, but the training of teachers remained its primary goal.[115] After 1892, the "higher" or "scientific" normal program was renamed the "teachers' professional," and required completion of the high school course. The program attracted students from Atlanta University, Atlanta Baptist, and other institutions.[116] Instruction lasted one or two years, depending on a student's preparation, and course work included a "thorough review" of elementary branches; psychology and its relationship to teaching; history and philosophy of education; and methodologies of teaching.[117] Normal students also taught in Spelman's elementary school.[118] The program had an unusually high rate of retention; in 1904, nineteen of twenty students remained for the entire year, compared to only 38 percent of students enrolled that year in the State Normal School for whites in Athens.[119]

Although graduates of the high school and even non-graduates might pass teachers' certification exams, Spelman continued to develop and refine its specialized training for educators, and to heavily promote its teachers' professional department. To recruit students into the program, the *Messenger* published former students' essays containing sentiments such as: "I am so glad I was permitted to take the Teachers' Professional Course. I needed just that training in order to be a successful teacher."[120] Faculty and board members even encouraged the state of Georgia to make the teachers' exam harder so that their students would need the normal course to pass, and noted with approval when the state did raise its standards.[121] Spelman hoped to inspire future teachers to strive, in the words of one, to "bring variety, life, and nature into the schoolroom." They learned to emphasize "the thought of the writer" over pronouncing words correctly, and to teach learning by doing, pedagogical goals consistent with Progressive ideals.[122]

Faculty hoped alumnae, with the training they received at Spelman, would spread the ideal of respectable Christian womanhood to African American children. Teaching not only was one of the most respected professions for women at the turn of the century, it also represented a way to reshape society through the transmission of values and beliefs to the next generation.

Fund-raisers for Spelman who spoke in northern cities made the case that the seminary educated women who would uplift the black poor.[123] Particularly in rural communities, teachers, sometimes without fully realizing it themselves, introduced modern ideas, challenging the authority of traditional institutions such as the family, church, and local elites. As historian Ann Short Chirhart argues, educators "undermined the roles of family, church and community by redirecting authority to the state and to educators." Students were encouraged to define themselves by modern ideas of material success and self-invention rather than traditional local and familial hierarchies. In this way teachers, particularly female teachers who represented a new claim of power by women, served as agents of modernization and state bureaucratization. By training black female educators, Spelman faculty hoped to aid in the modernization and uplift of rural black Georgians and to undermine what they viewed as superstitious worship, poor parenting, and destructive behavior of their communities.[124]

After 1911, Lucy Tapley updated the school's academic and industrial curricula. Training teachers remained the school's major goal, but Tapley broadened the normal program by introducing new emphases. She introduced agricultural classes, along with a small working garden to encourage graduates working in rural areas to combine practical courses in scientific farming with religious, moral, and academic instruction. Home economics became available as a high school major and a two-year post-graduate course in 1918. Most who graduated with this major took positions teaching home economics themselves or became county demonstrators, women who traveled to rural areas to instruct homemaking skills.[125] In addition, recognizing the beginning of new employment opportunities for black women in office work, the seminary also began teaching classes in bookkeeping and stenography.[126]

Proud as the school was of its normal, nursing, and other specialized programs, the major rationale for Spelman's industrial curriculum went beyond training women for work. For Spelman faculty, as for educators at similar schools, the chief purpose of industrial training was the creation of good moral character in black women, and through them, both as mothers and teachers, the next generation of African Americans.[127] In this way, industrial training would reinforce the school's faith in the Protestant values of self-discipline, hard work, thrift, temperance, and responsibility. As the 1887–88 catalogue stated, the school's "aim is to build character," and words such as "morality" and "discipline" appeared throughout teachers' and board members' descriptions of the goals of the school.[128] In a typical example, a board member asserted that the school championed "thorough work" and "discipline" over "superficial feminine accomplishments."[129] Spelman faculty maintained that the sort of industrial training it offered would improve, not detract from, academic study; as one teacher wrote, "moral culture and intellectual culture go hand in hand."[130] By instilling in students a sense of personal responsibility, Christian self-sacrifice, and dedication to work, faculty and administrators hoped that students and alumnae, no matter whether they became college teachers or domestic servants, would work with diligence and discipline. This emphasis on respectability, however, held a dual message. Although faculty hoped to inspire student success, the constant emphasis on improving moral character and providing the tools for uplift underlined their belief in their own moral and behavioral superiority. In private writings, for example, Giles mixed condensation with affection and pride in student accomplishments.[131] Although Spelman's leadership did not voice the explicit and extreme racism common at the time, the implication was clear—their African American students needed the help of Christian white women like themselves.

Spelman's interest in "broad, thorough, practical education," not confined only to books, linked it to educational trends of the time.[132] Most black schools combined industrial and liberal arts education. Partially this resulted from the fact that the major philanthropic organizations supporting black education expected or even required industrial instruction.[133] In addition, vocational training was part of white high school education in many states, north and south. Although Atlanta had no purely vocational public white schools, its white high schools did incorporate manual training and teach work skills.[134] In rural areas, white southerners received instruction in new agricultural methods along with their academic lessons.[135] Industrial training was commonly part of preparation for teachers. For example, North Carolina educational reformer Charles MacIver sought, in his words, to "combine . . . industrial and normal features" with college work at the North Carolina State Normal and Industrial School for white women.[136]

Many of these schools and programs provided students with job skills, but the major purpose for industrial training for groups such as immigrants, Native Americans, and African Americans was moral training. Social settlements, for example, taught cooking and other domestic work to girls to improve the homes of immigrant and poor families as well as the character of their students. The purpose of education for all of these groups was assimilation or "Americanization." Moral training would bring outsider groups into the American mainstream, providing social order. The mostly northern, Protestant, elite men and women who created these schools feared that industrialization and immigration threatened to destroy their values and erode their moral system, a system, they believed, that ensured stability.[137]

At the same time, these reformers sought to include these groups in the American community. With assimilation, activists hoped, immigrants and others outside of the American mainstream could achieve the full duties and responsibilities of citizenship. Reformers believed that their modern, Progressive values gave individuals more true freedom than did the cultures they viewed as backward and immoral. Further, they maintained, the health of the nation mandated the education of immigrants and outsiders into the American mainstream.[138] Spelman teachers and board members self-consciously viewed their own work as Americanization and viewed acculturation of southern blacks as part of saving and improving the nation as a whole.[139] Board member T. J. Morgan wrote that by uplifting black women Spelman aided in the "the progress of civilization" and that its work must be considered "an expression of patriotism."[140]

Additionally, the values taught at Spelman resembled those of black southern female educators. They shared a commitment to female achievement, conservative morality, Christian values, and the work ethic. As Stephanie Shaw, Sharon Harley, Audrey Thomas McCluskey, and others have argued, black female educational leaders of the New South era incorporated industrial training partially to please northern funders, but also because they reinterpreted industrial education to reflect their own values. To educators such as Lucy Craft Laney, Mary McLeod Bethune, Nannie Burroughs, and Charlotte Hawkins Brown, teaching students the dignity of work, self-discipline, propriety, and sexual modesty would allow them individually and collectively to resist white supremacy.[141] Using "Christian morality, self-sufficiency, and achievement," these black educators "destabilized the narrative of black inferiority," in the words of McCluskey.[142] Schools like that of Burroughs', designed to train domestic workers, as well as that of Brown's, targeting the black elite, employed the politics of respectability not only to gain financial support, but because black respectability functioned as a challenge to white supremacy.

Where perhaps Spelman most differed from schools such as those run by Burroughs, Laney, Bethune, and others was in its relationship with northern philanthropists and southern whites. The overwhelming struggle for funding was a major source of anxiety for black-run schools in the New South era. Accounts of the leaders of four of the most prominent schools for black women emphasize how exhausting fund-raising and trying to stretch budgets was for leaders and educators. A constant theme in writing by black female school administrators was the unrelenting stress of inadequate funds. Bethune and

Burroughs commiserated through letters, and corresponded about their hope to secure endowments for their institutions. Brown named her school for a white Bostonian she had met once, Alice Palmer, in order to court Palmer's friends as donors, and carefully constructed a persona meant to appeal to these women.[143]

Spelman's original founders, Giles and Packard, unlike these other educators, were able to secure a long-running financial commitment from the wealthiest man of his time that far exceeded his initial gift of $250. Rockefeller himself, and later his General Education Board (GEB), provided ongoing contributions to the seminary.[144] Rockefeller founded the GEB in 1902 as a way to systematize his charitable giving in education at the urging of his son, John D. Rockefeller Jr. Giles and Packard developed a close relationship with the oil magnate, to the extent that he gave both women money for personal use. By 1906, Rockefeller and the GEB had together donated nearly $70,000 to Spelman, and he served on the school's board of directors from its incorporation in 1888 to 1907. During this time he also provided funds for buildings and land, allowing the school's growth, as noted earlier.[145]

Rockefeller's support, however, was not an unmixed blessing. Other potential donors sometimes disregarded requests from Spelman, believing that the seminary was well taken care of by their benefactor. Additionally, Rockefeller's real estate contributions meant that in the early decades of the twentieth century the school had impressive buildings, but little means to maintain them, an ongoing frustration. Scholar Johnetta Brazzell suggests that the founders' dependency on Rockefeller and the money required to keep up their physical plant, in addition to their gender-conditioned reticence to aggressively fund-raise, meant an oddly precarious financial situation for the school in its formative years, despite benefitting from funding well beyond its peer institutions.[146]

After 1900, when the GEB became the primary way the Rockefeller family funded education, and when the younger John Rockefeller became more prominent in managing the family's charitable giving, the school's relationship with the family changed somewhat. Like other clients of the GEB, Spelman was expected to apply through the foundation for funding, and to reflect the commitment of the organization to industrial education for southern blacks. However, school leaders continued to correspond privately with both Rockefellers, to the annoyance of GEB officials. Giles maintained a good relationship with the GEB and leaders such as Wallace Buttrick (general agent from 1902 to 1917), and Frederick Gates (board chairman, 1907–17), who approved of Spelman because of the school's emphasis on industrial education, its exclusively female student body, and the lack of pretense to be a college. Yet

Buttrick, Gates, and other GEB members believed that the ABHMS should increase its funding for the school, and worried that the founder's reliance on Rockefeller set a bad precedent and would encourage other schools to become dependent on his personal generosity. In a turning point decision, in 1906 the GEB rejected a request by Spelman's board for money towards an endowment. The GEB wanted to see more financial commitment from the ABHMS; the Baptist society believed that Rockefeller's donations relieved them from responsibility; and other donors thought the school was well supported by these two institutions. As a result, the school's finances continued to be uncertain until President Florence Read finally succeeded in creating an endowment for the then Spelman College in 1929.[147]

White northern philanthropists, including Rockefeller, Gates, and Buttrick, supported Spelman with the hope that the school would create black women who would contribute to social and racial stability. Rockefeller was, in some ways, a surprising benefactor for a school that became a symbol of black female educational and professional success. The corporate philanthropist had little interest in challenging white supremacy; rather, he supported black education as a means of creating social harmony in the South, and ultimately the nation. Believing that education would create a more efficient, productive workforce, he viewed education generally, and southern black education in particular, as part of national progress and sectional reunification. Education, he hoped, would modernize the South economically, while also reifying racial hierarchy.[148] Spelman, like other black schools, relied on funders who did not always entirely share the educational goals of administrators, faculty, and students.

Racial and national uplift through moral and cultural education mixed with academic instruction also represented the goal of the northern educational philanthropists who represented the most vocal members of Spelman's board of directors.[149] From its inception in 1888, the board included male and female members of the ABHMS and WABHMS as well as representatives of southern African American Baptist groups.[150] Most members, however, were white northern men, and two, Henry Morehouse and Thomas Jefferson Morgan, visited Spelman frequently and spoke publicly about their expectations of the school. Morehouse, president of Spelman's board during the 1890s and the executive secretary of the American Baptist Education Society, was the first to use the term "talented tenth" to refer to the men and women the mission schools hoped to educate. His work for Atlanta Baptist prompted the renaming of the school in his honor in 1913.[151] Morgan had served as a Union colonel, seminary principal, and commissioner of Indian affairs, and during his tenure on Spelman's board held the positions of executive secretary of

ABHMS and editor of *Home Mission Monthly*.[152] He spoke on behalf of the seminary in northern cities as a means of raising support and funding for the school.[153]

Like Giles and other members of Spelman's faculty, these men believed that Spelman prepared black women to become "leaders of their own race." "The talented tenth man or woman of this type," Morehouse argued, served a greater need than did "nine others with some knowledge of the use of the jack-plane, the saw and the blacksmith's forge, and very little else," referring to outdated skills particularly associated with Tuskegee.[154] In another speech Morehouse dismissed the view that "the Negro cannot be educated, or should be educated for his sphere, as if he were fore-ordained to everlasting intellectual inferiority," as "antiquated nonsense." Disparaging the "bread-and-butter theory of education," he insisted that education must develop "intelligent, thoughtful, refined, and better men and women."[155] Yet Morehouse did support industrial training, "especially for the Negroes," and lauded Spelman's balance of academic and industrial education.[156]

Similarly, Morgan believed that missionary schools ought to provide African Americans with a true college education and cautioned southern schools away from giving up their academic offerings in favor of purely industrial curricula.[157] He commended southern African Americans for the "phenomenal progress" they had made in education since emancipation. "Not a few," he wrote, were "showing rare aptness as scholars," and many men and women had become "preachers, teachers, lawyers, physicians, editors."[158] Notably, he called for equal treatment under the law for blacks and an end to lynching, which he called "hideous," "anarchy," and "a return to barbarism and savagery." He argued that black women deserved the same "protection" as given to white women, and despised the use of "opprobrious epithets."[159] Although Morgan suggested that since emancipation some blacks had become lazy and criminal, and deserved contempt and punishment, "the industrious, thrifty, honest, intelligent, faithful man and upright citizen," he argued, deserved "respect and power" and the rights of citizenship, including the vote. In Morgan's view, Spelman and other schools like it were creating "a new type of Negro character" that would make significant social, economic, and political progress.[160]

The speeches of Morgan and Morehouse revealed a positive perception of African American ability, as well as confidence that blacks who became educated and industrious would earn the respect of whites. Yet like other white northern "paternalists," Morgan and Morehouse believed that only with the help of schools like Spelman, run by northern Christian whites like themselves, could blacks turn away from a backward past.[161]

A key aspect of Spelman's success was its ability to appeal to men like Rockefeller and Buttrick, as well as to Morgan and Morehouse. White male philanthropists, whether openly supportive of white supremacy, like Buttrick, or optimistic about black progress, like Morehouse, agreed that white leadership was necessary to improve and educate southern blacks. Major donors felt more comfortable with white northern female leadership than with southern black female leadership. Although Spelman was quite similar to schools run by Burroughs, Laney, and other black women in terms of curriculum and ideology (and did not conform to the racial etiquette of the South, by, for example, addressing students with titles and eating in interracial groups), Spelman seemed more benign, less threatening because of its white leadership. The cover of an early catalogue picturing a white woman in white robes reading the Bible in the jungle, with a pair of clasped black hands in the corner beseeching her for help, illustrated the idea that white leadership would uplift the seminary's black students, an idea in keeping with the thinking of the school's funders.[162]

Further, in emphasizing the development of character, Spelman board members and faculty placed the burden of responsibility for overcoming racial prejudice on blacks themselves, underplaying the racist social and economic structures that limited their progress.[163] Morgan's and Morehouse's emphasis on black progress and a "new Negro character" reinforced the idea of an "old" Negro character that had kept blacks from progressing. Both men occasionally remarked on blacks' tendency towards laziness or passion without instruction and guidance.[164] President George Sale of Atlanta Baptist, another advisor to Spelman, came close to Washington-style "accommodationism" in a 1895 speech at the seminary. Acknowledging that "there is not equality of opportunity for you yet in this country," President Sale implored his audience not to "wrap your talent in a napkin" in discouragement and instead keep striving.[165] Spelman's publications tended to de-emphasize segregation, disenfranchisement, and lynching and other violence, generally ignoring evidence of increasing racial hostility in Atlanta in favor of emphasizing the school's mission of individual uplift. Early leaders never pushed for legal challenges against segregation and disenfranchisement, and little attention was given to incidences of violence.[166] The horrific race riot of September 1906 and its aftermath, for example, were ignored in the school's newsletter and other publications. In part this was because the seminary was not yet in session for the academic year during the violence and no students were on campus. In addition, Spelman's campus was not harmed, thanks to the efforts of Atlanta Baptist president John Hope and other black faculty in guarding the Spelman, Atlanta Baptist, and Atlanta University campuses armed with guns. Yet the riot was a major event in the city's history, and it is notable that even in her private diary, Giles barely mentioned the violence or the work of Hope and his colleagues in patrolling the campus. Giles and other faculty chose to minimize, or were not fully sensitive to, the oppressiveness of the racial climate in which they worked.[167]

Further, board members and faculty viewed "assimilated" black leaders as responsible for mitigating racial tension by controlling the unruliness and potential violence of the black masses. In Morgan's words, the educated elite would act as "a restraining force" on the lower classes during "any time of racial disturbance or public excitement."[168] The school leadership's interest in outward appearance and behavior downplayed the legal and economic restrictions on southern blacks and shifted the responsibility of containing violence from whites to blacks themselves. At the same time, while they minimized the oppressiveness of white supremacy in their society, they displayed a confidence in black advancement. Unlike contemporary views of African Americans as unredeemable "black beasts," the beliefs held by Giles, Morgan, and Morehouse provided room for black progress and accomplishment.[169]

The complexity and contradictions within the agenda of Spelman teachers and board members allowed diverse groups to interpret the meaning of a Spelman education in ways that served their own purposes. Some prominent white southern educational reformers, for example, gave their support to the school. Georgia-born educator Jabez L. M. Curry proved essential in securing financial assistance for Spelman beginning in the 1880s as a representative of the Peabody Fund and later the Slater Fund.[170] New York banker George Foster Peabody represented a significant figure in a network of mostly northern philanthropists active in southern education, and his organization, closely connected with the Southern Educational Board and the General Educational Board, favored industrial education for southern African Americans.[171] Curry, a former planter and a lawyer who had served in both the U.S. and Confederate Congresses, was a key southern representative of this network and a vocal supporter of southern educational expansion and the development of public school systems. In 1890 Curry became the agent of the northern-financed John F. Slater Fund. Created in 1881 to support industrial training for southern African Americans, the Slater Fund became a major financial backer of the seminary. During its first decade the fund supported a variety of schools, but after 1890 it chose to finance a few schools generously rather than spread its money among many. By 1894, under Curry's leadership, it gave more money to Spelman than any other school other than Hampton.[172]

Notably, the money was earmarked not for cooking, laundry, or other domestic training but for the normal department and its practice school.[173] Although the printing department had received Slater money throughout the 1880s, it was teacher training that netted the larger donations of the 1890s and after. Perhaps to court Slater funds, teachers called the normal department a "trades school" that produced "skilled workmen in the teaching art."[174] Scholars have suggested that the school's leadership may have intentionally misled Curry by accepting generous grants for industrial training even though no more than two or three students a year enrolled exclusively in industrial courses.[175] Curry, however, fully expected that the money would go towards teacher training, and indeed, teacher training, along with training in values, represented a major funding priority for the Slater Fund.[176] In this way, Spelman's program was a perfect fit.

In fact, creating better African American teachers represented a central goal of white southern educational reformers like Curry who believed that universal education would aid in modernizing the South and help make it more economically competitive, while at the same time help maintain white supremacy by teaching blacks their "place."[177] Curry endorsed both black education and the prevailing southern racial and social order, and saw no contradiction between the two. Indeed, he viewed black education, sectional reconciliation, and national progress as dependent on each other. Curry was instrumental in both advancing black education and entrenching educational segregation.[178] In an 1899 speech to other southern educators he declared, "The white people are to be the leaders, to take the initiative, and have the directive control in all matters pertaining to civilization and the highest interests of our beloved land" but insisted that this did not indicate "hostility to the negro, but friendship for him."[179]

Although some conservative southern whites opposed any education other than basic manual training for African Americans, other openly racist white southern leaders agreed with Curry in supporting black education as a more enlightened, less violent means of social control.[180] Other white southern racial conservatives who supported Spelman included Henry Grady of *The Atlanta Constitution*, one of the New South's best-known economic boosters, and G. R. Glenn, Georgia's state commissioner of education.[181] Sidney Root, a Massachusetts native who became a Georgia plantation owner, slaveholder, and loyal Confederate, was a charter member of the Spelman board of trustees, serving until his death in 1897.[182] A racial conservative his entire life, he maintained that blacks respected him because he always denounced "social equality."[183] Additionally, Hoke Smith, whose stridently white supremacist campaign for governor in 1906 helped provoke Atlanta's racial violence of that year, advocated black education.[184] These supportive white southern observers tended to emphasize the school's goal of training mothers and teachers. Spelman graduates' work in homes and schools would help "redeem the race," as Glenn put it, and thereby benefit the entire region.[185] Educating African Americans, men such as these believed, would reduce crime and other social ills while creating a more efficient and disciplined workforce. The interest of men like Root and Smith in black education and uplift underscores the conservatism of Spelman's self-help message when uncoupled from a larger critique of southern society and politics.[186]

African American leaders of Atlanta, in sharp contrast, understood the potential of education to challenge white supremacy and viewed schools like Spelman as a vehicle for racial progress rather than control. Unlike cities such as New Orleans and Charleston, Atlanta lacked a sizable free antebellum African American elite, but by 1890 the city housed a small but influential leadership class of businessmen, artisans, and professionals. Most had been educated at Atlanta University, attended the First Congregational Church, and lived on or near Auburn Avenue in the Shermantown region on the east side of the city. After 1910, a new group of entrepreneurs and professionals, spurred both by an ethic of self-help and by heightened racial distrust in the aftermath of the 1906 race riot, rose to economic and social prominence catering to an exclusively African American clientele. "Sweet" Auburn became the major black business district of Atlanta and a national symbol of African American economic success. Increasingly in the early twentieth century, the black bourgeoisie lived in the West Side, near the colleges, in mixed-class areas. Yet status distinctions within the black community were often fluid and people might rise or fall in prestige over their lifetime. High- and low-status people often shared social and family ties. Further, achievement, profession, and education meant more than income in defining one's place on the social hierarchy, especially because some highly respected professions, like teachers and ministers, paid little. In "degree-conscious Atlanta" especially, higher education represented an important indicator of status.[187]

The short-lived publication *Voice of the Negro* published in Atlanta between 1903 and 1907 offers a window into the politics and ideology of the city's contemporary black leaders and their views on education.[188] Articles condemning lynching, disenfranchisement, and segregation appeared regularly, reflecting the views of its editor, J. Max Barber. Barber, a member of the Niagara Movement, spoke out strongly against white supremacy, and even took on such taboo subjects as "social equality" and the rape of black women by white men.[189] Barber professed that he intended the paper to be truly a "voice" for a diversity of black opinion, and published writings by a wide range of black leaders, including Booker T. Washington, W. E. B. Du Bois, and Mary Church Terrell.[190] The paper's frequent articles on education by Atlanta residents and others generally endorsed a combined industrial-academic approach.[191] One contributor, for example, wrote that teachers in particular benefited from both industrial and academic instruction as the two "mutually dignify each other and make teachers more able to increase social and economic efficiency of the community."[192] Other writers argued that education would improve morality as well as intellectual culture, especially for women.[193] The paper frequently gave positive attention to Spelman, reporting for example on its twenty-fifth anniversary and calling it a "great school," and the seminary advertised in the publication.[194]

As this suggests, many black leaders, even those opposed to accomodationism, accepted the idea of moral uplift, both as a Christian value and a political tool.[195] In this way, reform-minded black Americans engaged in a politics of respectability. By proving their morality, intellectual attainments, and public virtue, black leaders hoped to convince whites of their worthiness for full citizenship. Respectability included gentility, dress, education, worship style, and personal accomplishments. But sexual behavior was the defining feature of black respectability.[196] Especially after the turn of the century, African Americans concerned with racial progress believed that "the race's destiny and sexual practices were intertwined." Like education, and often linked closely with it, sexual restraint indicated class status, much more so than the attainment of wealth, and linked the aspiring classes to the middle class and truly elite. Black reformers, influenced by the eugenic ideology of their day, made direct links between sexual control, healthy reproduction, and racial uplift. For these men and women, sexual practices outside of a reproductive marital context led to racial decline.[197] Popular stereotypes about black women's aggressive sexuality made the pressure on black women to appear sexually pure particularly intense. They shouldered the burden of proving their own personal respectability and worthiness as modest and properly behaved mothers, teachers, and church members, and they were aware that deviance would implicate the entire race. In the worsening racial climate of Atlanta at the turn of the century, and especially after the race riot of 1906, local African Americans increasingly stressed personal uplift as central to racial progress.[198]

Given this concern with respectability and sexuality, moral and industrial education proved attractive to many black educational and religious leaders and reinforced messages taught in churches and other black-run institutions, publications, and homes.[199] African American visitors to Spelman praised its combination of industrial and academic education and linked moral, intellectual, material, and political progress.[200] As one wrote, "Make a man feel that you are his equal and you thereby compel him to respect you."[201] Even as late as 1921, a visiting minister lectured Spelman students on the importance of education, economic success, land ownership, and a sense of self-worth.[202] Other, less prominent African Americans supported the seminary through donations, usually giving small amounts that nonetheless represented significant sacrifices.[203] Both for leaders and community members, the belief that education would improve black character held a defiant message, one that challenged the idea of inherent black inferiority.

Even the more outspoken of Atlanta's black leaders looked to self-improvement through Christian character as an answer to racial tension. The Rev. P. J. Bryant, pastor of Auburn Avenue's prestigious Wheat Street Baptist Church, strongly rejected both segregation and the belief of black racial inferiority in a speech at Spelman on Emancipation Day in 1902. Critiquing the idea of a "Negro problem," he wrote that "the race problem" was "as much, or more, the white man's problem as . . . the Negro's." Bryant's solutions, however, were the usual ones—education, wealth, and Christianity for African Americans—again attesting to the widespread faith in the importance of "improving" character.[204]

Spelman earned the support of two of the most prominent African American activists in Georgia, John Hope and William J. White. White, a strong advocate for advanced black education and an ally of W. E. B. Du Bois, had been instrumental in founding the Augusta Baptist Institute in 1867, the institution that later moved to Atlanta and became known as Morehouse College. A minister, White also published the influential *Georgia Baptist*, described by Du Bois as "probably the most universally read Negro paper in the South." In the weekly, White spoke out against disenfranchisement, lack of educational opportunity for African Americans, and racially motivated violence, leading to threats against his life that temporarily caused him to leave Augusta in the wake of the 1906 Atlanta riot. White strongly supported the work of Spelman; he was a charter member and vice-president of its board of directors, and sent both of his daughters to the seminary.[205]

John Hope, the first African American president of Morehouse College (and later president of Atlanta University), along with his wife Lugenia Burns Hope, viewed Spelman as contributing significantly to Atlanta's place as a leading center of black higher education. Before founding the Neighborhood Union in 1908, Lugenia Hope taught occasional classes Spelman, and after she devoted her attention to the social settlement, she actively recruited Spelman students and alumnae to participate. John Hope spoke frequently at the seminary and praised the work done by its faculty, students, and alumnae. Most dramatically, he personally helped save the campus during the 1906 riot. Hope, as head of Morehouse and after 1929 of AU, created close ties with Spelman presidents, especially the long-serving Florence Read.[206]

The two best-known African American leaders of the era, Booker T. Washington and W. E. B. Du Bois, both visited Spelman, and both used the language of uplift in speaking to students. Increasingly, scholars have been questioning the stark polarization of the political and educational philosophies and legacies of these two men. In particular, several have questioned the traditional view of Washington's Tuskegee as "schooling for the new slavery" and Du Bois as rejecting out of hand the idea that schools offer anything other than classical education, finding that both men were more open to diversity in black education than previously thought. Washington did not preclude the possibility that some African Americans could benefit from advanced college education; he, however, did not find it appropriate for the majority. Similarly, Du Bois did not dismiss completely industrial education, seeing some justification for industrial education for the ninety percent outside of the talented tenth. Before 1905, much of his work stressed self-help, respectability, and racial solidarity.[207] And significantly, many schools for African Americans, including Spelman, rather than aligning themselves with one view or the other, blended industrial and academic education, and perceived them not as incompatible, but as mutually beneficial, especially because many of these schools, such as Spelman, stressed the moral training aspects of industrial education.[208]

Washington spoke at Spelman several times, as did his wife, and a teacher praised him as "eminently practical in all he says and does."[209] Members of the faculty attended the annual conferences held at Tuskegee for educators and others active in racial issues.[210] Du Bois also visited occasionally, especially during his Atlanta years. In 1902, while teaching at Atlanta University, he gave an address at the seminary on "the role of women in society."[211] This speech was notably conservative in both its gender and racial politics, embracing the idea of racial "uplift" through improved home life. Echoing other turn-of-the century African American leaders who linked racial progress to domestic reform, Du Bois declared women's highest duty their physical work of bearing children and the cultural aspects of homemaking.[212] Acknowledging that "house-keeping of all careers seems to hold the fewest attractions to many women," Du Bois also declared that proper family life would do more than education, organized religion, material progress, or political opportunity to advance the race. Housekeeping, he argued, was women's "spiritual function."[213]

The belief that educated women would uplift African Americans was shared by Du Bois, Curry, Morgan, and Morehouse, as well as by Spelman's faculty. Each understood Spelman as providing a useful service for the race and the nation. Yet they sharply differed as to the meaning of racial uplift and racial progress. In attempting to lift its students out of second-class citizenship, Spelman emphasized an industrial morality of individual character, including the traditional bourgeois values of frugality, discipline, and the "habits of industry." Yet Spelman students and alumnae created their own understanding of their education and of their post-graduation duties, fashioning a community ethos out of the individualist moral reform emphasized in their studies. The following chapter focuses on Spelman students and alumnae, analyzing how they interpreted their education and used it towards their own ends. With the "habits of industry," they believed, they would themselves create a female "talented tenth."

4 Respectability and Reform

Spelman Alumnae

In 1957 a woman wrote to Selena Sloan Butler, an 1888 Spelman graduate, after reading about her accomplishments in the school newspaper, the *Messenger*. Butler's admirer wrote, "I entered Spelman in 1899 a girl of 13—but on account of ill health I returned home in 1901 and was very sorry that I could not complete my studies but God does all things well but I can say this much that Spelman had made me the woman that I am and as the chorus we used to sing at Spelman—'Well we love our Alma Mater—Mother kind and true.'"[1] Although the author spent only two years at the school, she cited her experience there as transformative fifty-six years later. This chapter will focus on the relationship of Spelman women to their education as students and alumnae. The women who attended Spelman incorporated the message of the seminary with values they learned from their families, churches, and community to fashion their own definition of respectable Christian womanhood. Although accepting the school's message of moral improvement, alumnae perceived it as a means to attain leadership and an opportunity to work for social justice. Spelman graduates viewed their cultivation of personal respectability, their work as homemakers and professionals, and their participation in church and club organizations as their responsibility as educated women and as part of their quest for social and racial justice. Like Lucies, Spelman women fashioned themselves as "leaders of their own race"—educated, refined, well-mannered, sexually pure, and race-conscious women who would take an active part in reshaping the New South.

The majority of Spelman students took their studies seriously and appreciated the seminary's academic rigor. For the first generation of black women to receive a formal education, achievement of even basic literacy was a life-changing experience. Education boosted self-confidence, agency, and autonomy, allowing women to take political and social action. Further, the advanced academic programs offered at Spelman provided students access to the cultural knowledge of elite Americans and developed their rhetorical and critical skills. In addition, an advanced degree conferred status.[2] Indicating the value they placed on higher education, graduates of Spelman went on to do post-graduate work at the University of Chicago, Harvard, Columbia, Howard, Hampton, Meharry, Oberlin, Pratt, Tuskegee, and New England Conservatory of Music, among other institutions, earning advanced degrees in diverse fields including music, medicine, sociology, and education.[3]

At the same time, most students also valued the emphasis the seminary placed on moral training. Reflecting the importance they placed on character, morality, and self-discipline, Spelman students frequently referred to these themes in essays written for classroom assignments for publication in the school paper, the *Messenger*. Similarly, they praised the school's emphasis on Christian training, usefulness, and lessons in "habits of industry, personal neatness, cleanliness and daintiness . . . and . . . piety and true godliness."[4] Many wrote about the evils of idleness and the necessity for self-reliance. Others cited a need for better schools offering Christian education for African Americans, portraying these institutions as a cure for racial strife and black poverty.[5] Some connected moral education and racial progress, such as the student who declared, "Races, like nations, become strong, not in a day, not by political offices, not by undue independence, but by individual industry and honesty, and by united effort and eternal vigilance."[6] Like contemporary African American leaders, Spelman women pointed to good homes, clean neighborhoods, and hard work as evidence of blacks' fitness for full citizenship rights.[7]

Perhaps students were merely trying to please their teachers in these essays. Indeed, much evidence about the attitudes of Spelman students and alumnae towards the seminary comes from school-sanctioned sources such as the classroom essays, reports, and letters printed in the monthly newsletter that may have been fashioned to meet the approval of white faculty. But these sources also can be read as a space in which Spelman women contributed to the definition of ideal black femininity. By helping to shape a model of black womanhood themselves through these essays and writings, Spelman students and alumnae directly participated in its construction, and these sources therefore offer valuable insight into how these women perceived themselves and the meaning of their education.

Other forms of student and alumnae support attest to their dedication to the school. Alumnae kept in touch, sending letters, filling out annual surveys, and attending special events, and many remained in contact with the faculty for several decades. Several reported attempting, as one wrote, to "put into practice all the good teachings gained" at the seminary.[8] Many returned for additional degrees, such as Sallie Adams, who finished the nurse training course in 1892, the high school in 1898, the teachers' professional in 1900, and in 1901 enrolled in the college preparatory course. In the 1923–24 academic year, half of the former year's high school graduates returned for college work.[9] Alumnae encouraged their sisters and daughters to attend Spelman. By 1910, enough second generation students attended to found a "Granddaughters' Club."[10]

Alumnae showed their support for the seminary off-campus as well. In cities including Atlanta, Chicago, and Cleveland, clubs promoted social activities and local "good works."[11] Alumnae also aided the seminary financially, often sending small donations along with their letters. On its thirtieth anniversary, Spelman created an annual "Founders' Day Rally" designed to encourage consistent giving by students, alumnae, teachers, and "friends." Most gave anywhere from 25 cents to $2, although by the 1920s several gave five or ten dollars. One alumna left Spelman $100 in her will. Both graduates and non-graduating former students consistently donated to their alma mater.[12]

Indeed, many of the students who left the seminary before graduating, such as the alumna who wrote Butler, showed the same loyalty and continuing interest in Spelman as did graduates. One wrote that she had been "blessed to attend a part of two terms" at Spelman, and was teaching; another used her training to become the head nurse of a hospital.[13] Others reported teaching in rural schools, marrying ministers, and engaging in church activities. Several non-graduates promised to send their daughters to Spelman.[14]

Not all Spelman alumnae enjoyed their time at the school or conformed to its expectations. In her diary Giles expressed frustration with students who were "naughty" or "disobedient."[15] Instructors, especially Lucy Tapley, also lamented that several students felt "the lure of the north" and chose to live in Chicago, New York, Detroit, or western cities rather than working in rural southern communities.[16] A minority of students seemed to have not even come close to the faculty's hopes. In 1911, ten of the 309 living graduates were listed as "unworthy of record."[17]

In the late 1910s and 1920s, students evinced less willingness to conform to their teachers' expectation of obedience than they had earlier. During this time campus unrest swept through many black colleges and students protested restrictive rules on behavior and freedom of movement, a narrow curriculum, and condescension from white faculty and administrations.[18] Spelman students did not take part in the overt unrest that occurred on campuses such as Fisk and Howard, but they did in quieter ways begin to question some rules and expectations. For example, like other college women, by the later 1910s, some students experimented with modern, less modest clothing, to the chagrin of faculty, and some alumnae, who feared that students indulging in the more sexual styles of the time would harm the reputation of the school and its students. But after the school became a true college, the dress code loosened, partially in response to students and partially because the student body became more typically college-age as the school shed its elementary and high school. By the later 1920s, the student-founded paper the *Campus Mirror* discussed dating, fashion, and other once-taboo subjects.[19]

In the 1920s, especially in the later years of Lucy Tapley's leadership, students and alumnae voiced discontent with some in the school administration. Tapley favored a more vocational approach to education than either the founders or later administrators, and stressed efficiency and practicality over liberal arts education. According to her successor, Florence Read, Tapley valued order and rules, even those that became outdated or made little sense. Read recounted that Tapley would set the dates when students were required to begin wearing woolen underclothes in the winter, and stop wearing them in the spring, regardless of the temperature, and would check to make sure students were in compliance.[20] Students, however, figured out how to evade this and similar regulations, and laughed among themselves at Tapley's rigidity. Tapley's dean, Edna Lamson, became a particular target of student displeasure. Perhaps because of her old-fashioned piety, her new-fashioned enthusiasm for intelligence tests, or perceived lack of courtesy towards students, students quietly mocked or even openly spoke out against her.[21] One alumna and recruiter for the school reported to Tapley in 1925 that she had overheard current students "talking down" the school. Their major complaints seemed to be that "students are not looked upon as women capable of thinking for themselves" and "rudeness" on the part of some white faculty, including Lamson.[22] Tapley sought to assure her by blaming the rumors on rival schools. Although she acknowledged that "we have waves of unrest among the young people of our schools from time to time and during the year just passed some of the schools have been having a hard time," she added, "we had not felt it during the year."[23] Spelman did not encounter open dissent or protest, and even during these less conformist times, on the whole the majority of alumnae highly regarded the education they received at Spelman.

For most students, the combined academic-moral education offered by the seminary seemed valuable because of the importance they themselves placed on cultivating respectable black femininity and the centrality of education, including moral education, to respectability. In Atlanta as well as other southern cities, "status" rather than "class" divided African Americans, as very few postwar blacks had substantial income or material resources. Rather, attributes like education, religious affiliation, and personal conduct determined degree of status. Professions such as teaching might be recognized as high status, but earn little income. Additionally, status was fluid and might vary across lifetimes and among family members. This, along with the shared experience of exclusion and second-class citizenship, encouraged an ethic of responsibility and community.[24] Not until the turn of the century did a handful of black Atlantans achieve substantial wealth, and even then, they tended to continue to feel a sense of responsibility towards the less successful in their community.[25] Although over time Spelman attracted young women from the developing black middle class, many of its students, particularly in its first twenty years, were from modest or even poor backgrounds.[26] It was their Spelman education and respectable behavior, rather than family wealth, which improved their social standing.

Further, Spelman students and alumnae believed that education and proper conduct would give them the authority to speak and act in the public sphere. Reform-minded blacks strove to counter destructive stereotypes by presenting themselves as industrious, educated, temperate, thrifty, and responsible. For black women, respectability and sexual purity were inseparable, as the myth of the aggressively sexual black woman restricted their public activity. Much like white women who sought to keep their reputations intact while entering the public sphere but with even higher stakes, activist black women used respectability as a means of protection against sexual slander meant to silence their voices of protest.

Some scholars have argued that the ideal of respectability failed to actually empower African Americans at all. Instead, they argue, it led black elites to shift their focus from combating racial prejudice to regulating individual behavior. Further, by downplaying or ignoring the material circumstances that made the attainment of respectability impossible for most blacks, the middle class gave support to racist assumptions of black inferiority, thereby actually strengthening white supremacy.[27] Yet many historians, sensitive to these criticisms, conclude that respectability represented a powerful, if flawed, tool in the fight for racial equality, particularly because successful blacks relied on it to legitimize social welfare and social justice activism.[28] Elite African Americans, while not unconcerned with maintaining their own elevated social status, had a strong sense of obligation to the less privileged of the race, a legacy of slavery and white racism. White supremacy's economic, social, and political consequences, including the shared reality of second class citizenship and the physical proximity of blacks of all classes in racially segregated urban neighborhoods, gave elites a sense of shared destiny with and duty to the working class and poor.[29]

In Atlanta, respectability and interracial elite cooperation became a major strategy of the black leadership class after the race riot of 1906. David Fort Godshalk argued that in the wake of the riot, the black male elite created a "New Black Man" image to counter the stereotype that all African Americans were vicious and uncivilized. By stressing their own accomplishments and respectability, however, they created greater social distance between themselves and the working class, and reinforced stereotypes of nonelite blacks as lazy and violent. It also led some leaders to downplay the very real problems of underemployment, labor exploitation, and the convict lease. Notably, Godshalk finds that elite black women were much more successful than men in creating cross-class social movements, as feminine respectability, with its emphasis on uplift, allowed greater identification with the needs of other women than did masculine respectability, which emphasized individual achievement.[30]

For men and women, physical appearance demonstrated respectability. At Spelman, faculty attempted to create respectable women by teaching students to control the body, emphasizing cleanliness and modesty in dress and manner and distrust of all appetites. In contrast to white collegiate women, who wrote home proudly about their weight gains on campus, Spelman women were expected to eat daintily and to carefully observe table manners, reflecting their achievement of physical self-control.[31] In addition, the fashionable but modest outfits worn by Spelman students and graduates, including tight bodices, long, full sleeves, and trimmed skirts in sober colors set them apart from the domestic servant's mob cap and apron, as well as the worn, yet often flamboyantly colorful, clothing of less affluent black women.[32]

Although it might appear that the school's interest in enforcing modesty and sexual morality reflected the faculty's unthinking acceptance of stereotypes about black women's sexuality, the school's emphasis on decorum and modesty reinforced what many students had been taught in African American churches, publications, and material culture. Churches that attracted the striving class often advocated the kind of less emotional, more reserved worship style favored by Spelman faculty, and many prominent African Americans supported this more contemplative approach. Reformer Ida B. Wells-Barnett, for example, connected her religious faith with her social activism, but frowned on what she viewed as excessively emotional worship. The *Atlanta Independent* praised Spelman highly, giving particular attention to the school's teaching of an intellectual worship style. Additionally, black newspapers and magazines exhorted readers to maintain clean, well-regulated homes, and African American businesses designed children's toys, especially dolls, meant to instill race pride and domestic respectability.[33]

Spelman parents sought to teach their daughters modest and chaste personal behavior.[34] As alumna Selena Sloan Butler noted, "the foundation for character building is laid before the student enters the school," often "by the mother under adverse circumstances."[35] Sue Bailey's mother expressed her concern for her daughter's spiritual growth and personal conduct in letters, entreating her to "be a consistent Christian" and "guard your reputation." "A young girl's name is like a clean white sheet until it is spotted with ink," she warned.[36] Parents like those of Bailey looked to Spelman to keep their children's behavior in line with their own expectations. Rather than faculty imposing new values on their students, teachers and parents were united in their wish to train pure and virtuous young women, and parents actively sought out schools that would emphasize moral training.

Although seemingly a private virtue, the real significance of respectability was its use as a political tool. Using the idea of feminine respectability, Spelman faculty, students, and alumnae argued for recognition of racial equality among women, claims potentially too dangerous if made by men in the violent racial climate of the New South. President of the board Henry Morehouse, declaring that Spelman encouraged "the recognition of worth in the colored woman as well as the white," asserted, "true womanhood everywhere is entitled to respect."[37] Students and alumnae were addressed and referred to with the titles "Miss" and "Mrs.," a courtesy that whites did not usually extend to blacks in the South.[38] The idea that black women deserved respect equal to that given to whites and that they were included in the ideal of "true womanhood" was quite radical in turn-of-the-century Atlanta. As historians of southern women have made clear, race and class are key components of gender ideology, and most white southerners would not have accepted that black women could ever deserve the same respect given to white "ladies."[39] By demanding respect for their students as African American women, Spelman's faculty challenged a key component of late-nineteenth-century white supremacy.

Yet, perhaps because the ideal of true womanhood suggested racial equality but underlined gender difference, it was less controversial than a similar insistence on full masculine privilege for black men would have been. The feminine ideal's emphasis on duty, self-sacrifice, and loyalty perhaps made it appear less threatening than black men's demand for full citizenship rights, including the vote. Similarly, training women for "feminine" professions seemed less disruptive than educating men for more prestigious, powerful positions. Exploiting gendered ideas that obscured the significance of their social and political activism, black women staked out space for themselves in the public sphere.

Indeed, for black women, individual achievement and respectability could not be separated from racial progress. Historian Stephanie Shaw labeled the relationship between black women's personal achievement and racial uplift "socially responsible individualism." Individual success aided the black community both because it signaled the capabilities of African Americans, and because women often chose employment in fields that aided others. Striving for personal achievement, therefore, also benefited African Americans as a group.[40] The motto of both the National Association of Colored Women and the Spelman Graduates Club of Atlanta, "lifting as we climb," highlighted the connection between black women's individual success and racial progress.[41]

One of women's most important social and racial obligations, Spelman alumnae believed, was to become good wives and mothers. Like the prominent black clubwomen studied by Linda Gordon, most Spelman students married and had children.[42] Many alumnae viewed their primary role as that of homemaker, and several reported "trying to make a Spelman ideal home" or implementing the cooking and housekeeping lessons learned at the seminary.[43] Even college graduates justified higher education as a means of improving homemaking and child raising skills.[44] Spelman graduates and former students married men of all occupations, including farmers, but a large number wed professionals, especially teachers, ministers, and doctors—men who comprised Atlanta's and other southern cities' growing middle class.[45] Many of those who became teachers continued to work after their wedding vows, and a few founded schools with their husbands.[46] Others stopped working for wages after marrying, but remained active in religious or community activities.[47] Those married to church leaders usually made a career of serving as a minister's wife.[48]

For Spelman alumnae, black domesticity carried political symbolism. Through creating respectable Christian homes, they would build nurturing communities that offered a haven from the violence and degradation of white supremacy. In addition, stable and successful communities would counter stereotypes of the disorderly black neighborhood.[49] Domesticity also could represent a refusal for black women to accept white claims to black women's labor, and at the same time allowed them protection from violent or sexually predatory white male employers. In this way, viewing themselves as primarily wives and mothers symbolized black women's resistance to white expectations and an assertion of independence.[50]

Many students and alumnae, however, believed that women's duty also called for work outside of the home, as good "teachers, missionaries, and physicians are needed" and women "must do her part in earning and saving."[51] As early as 1890, one student wrote, "every woman should have a trade" as it is "truly Christian to be able to support oneself.[52] After 1910, and especially as a result of World War I, Spelman women increasingly wrote about the importance of black women working after marriage and about new opportunities for women in politics and law, industry, journalism, literature, and medicine. Graduates applauded these opportunities as well as attempts to standardize wages between the sexes and races.[53]

At a time when over three-quarters of Atlanta's wage-earning black women worked in domestic service, Spelman alumnae managed to find more desirable kinds of work.[54] A few practiced medicine.[55] Several became businesswomen, like Ezella Mathia Carter, who owned and operated a successful beauty shop in Chicago and founded a national trade group.[56] Others took jobs as stenographers, accountants, and office clerks, positions in which black women in general remained underrepresented.[57] But the majority worked in the "helping professions," especially nursing and teaching, making the connection between black women's professional work, individual achievement, and community betterment even more direct.[58]

By far the largest number of graduates, over 80 percent worked as teachers for at least part of their lives. This number remained remarkably consistent over time; in 1906, 83 percent had done some teaching, and in 1921, the number was also 83 percent.[59] Most graduates of the teachers' professional course, not surprisingly, taught at least a few years, but graduates of all of the programs, and non-graduates as well, spent time in front of classrooms.[60] Spelman alumnae viewed teaching as both honorable employment and as a duty. By becoming teachers, they demonstrated their appreciation for their own education and helped contribute to community betterment.[61]

Spelman women taught in all levels of schools in urban and rural areas across the country. Several graduates, especially those who completed the teachers' professional course, spent a few years teaching at the seminary.[62] Others taught in public schools around the South or in state normal schools for blacks.[63] In Atlanta, African American leaders and Atlanta University graduates had successfully pressured the city to hire black public school teachers in the 1870s, paving the way for the later employment of many Spelman graduates.[64] Some alumnae founded private or church-based schools. Sylvia Jenkins Bryant, for example, the wife of the pastor of Atlanta's prestigious Wheat Street Baptist Church, opened a school at the church offering literary, industrial, and religious training to kindergarten and elementary school students.[65]

Many alumnae taught at schools that shared the seminary's philosophy, such as the graduate who wrote that she "aims to make her school as near like Spelman as possible."[66] By this, alumnae usually meant replicating its blend of academics with religious and industrial instruction.[67] Spelman women particularly influenced two Georgia schools created on this model, Jeruel Academy in Athens and Americus Institute in Americus. Jeruel, like Spelman, began

Figure 13. High school class of 1920. (Courtesy of the Spelman College Archives)

in a black Baptist church, but with southern African American leadership. Considering itself "a branch" of Atlanta Baptist and Spelman, the academy blended religious, industrial, and academic instruction in a way that resembled the curriculum of the seminary, and its directors declared that they hired only Spelman and Morehouse alumni as faculty.[68] Several Spelman graduates also taught at Americus Institute, another Baptist school stressing both academic and industrial education.[69] After earning both a high school and teachers' professional degree at Spelman, Hannah Howell taught at her alma mater for three years before marrying an Atlanta Baptist graduate and together directing Americus. After attending Columbia University for a year, Howell became active in social work, including mothers' meetings, the YWCA, and sanitation campaigns.[70] On the Howells' retirement in 1923, another Spelman-Morehouse couple took over the school.[71]

Spelman faculty especially encouraged students to teach in rural schools, as remote areas were regarded as the most backward and in need of social improvement. Spelman alumnae, faculty hoped, would begin a cycle of uplift by educating young women in isolated, poor areas who would then create their own schools in similar communities.[72] Lucy Tapley especially believed the mission of Spelman should be to provide teachers to rural schools. According to one account, she was particularly interested in recruiting "average or even below average students" to rural schools because she saw them as more likely to stay in these demanding situations.[73] Tapley correctly sensed that many Spelman grads were uncomfortable in isolated rural areas. Alumnae teaching in rural schools sometimes expressed shock and dismay about the poverty and poor conditions they encountered, such as the graduate who viewed her students as "an almost barbarous people" with whom she could barely communicate. Alumnae educated into the "Spelman ideal" of Christian respectability found it difficult to relate to their pupils, many of whom came from families that evidenced the kind of behavior that Spelman students rejected. In turn, rural students and parents often regarded Spelman-trained teachers with skepticism or even hostility. Unsurprisingly, most Spelman teachers favored positions in cities or even the North. Those that did teach in rural communities tended to do so for only a short period of time.[74] This caused much hand-wringing on the part of faculty, who viewed grads as ambassadors for the Spelman ideal into what they viewed as the most needy and backward areas of the state.

Some teachers in these rural areas, however, proudly reported improving the industriousness, manners, morals, and even kindness of their pupils.[75] Others looked beyond moral uplift to community revitalization. Several rural teachers also served as county supervisors, demonstrating scientific agriculture and modern housekeeping designed to make farming and housework easier and more efficient.[76] A few graduates became Jeanes Fund teachers.[77] The Anna T. Jeanes Foundation, funded by Rockefeller's General Education Board, sponsored African American women to teach industrial skills in rural areas. Contemporaries and historians alike have credited Jeanes teachers for their responsiveness to local needs and their work to aid, educate, and empower poor communities.[78]

Both rural and urban Spelman-educated teachers included industrial training in their curricula because they viewed moral and practical education as useful in black education. Partly the choice was strategic; adding "industrial" to the name of a school helped win donations from white philanthropic funds.[79] Yet black teachers had their own reasons to include industrial training. Like the well-known African American female educators Nannie Burroughs and Charlotte Hawkins Brown, these teachers believed that industrial education would help to destroy harmful stereotypes of black female immorality and extend to their students the protection of respectability. Also like Burroughs and Brown, Spelman alumnae did not view their interest in improving the morals and manners of their students and a wide-ranging agenda of social betterment as mutually exclusive. Rather, reformers and educators often viewed moral education as part of their work for social welfare, community uplift, and ultimately, social justice.[80]

Since the 1890s, Spelman had offered special training in nursing and missionary work as well as teaching, and graduates of these programs also viewed their work as part of community uplift. Although black nurses faced discrimination and resentment from their white counterparts and white physicians, the African American community held them in high esteem. Like teachers, nurses were regarded as race leaders and social welfare activists who would provide lessons by example of "moral rectitude, cleanliness, order, proper diet, and deference to and respect for authority."[81] In her study of black nurses, Darlene Clark Hine labeled Spelman's nursing training "conventional" compared to the best-funded and most-prominent programs, and noted that many graduates worked privately for white families.[82] Perhaps the more limited opportunity for community service helped explain the relatively small numbers of students enrolled in the nursing, as compared to the teaching, program.

Still, many Spelman-trained nurses worked in public health and in hospitals, and frequently achieved positions of leadership.[83] Indeed, one of the most influential black nurses in Georgia received her education from Spelman. Ludie Clay Andrews, a 1906 Spelman nurse training graduate, founded a program to train African American nurses at Atlanta's Grady Hospital in 1917, extending to the city's black women the advantages of an education in a large, well-equipped hospital for the first time. Andrews later ran MacIver Hospital at Spelman and taught both there and at Morehouse. She herself considered her greatest achievement to be the state of Georgia's agreement, after her ten-year lobbying effort, to apply the same standards for certification to black and white nurses. In her work for improved black health care and her outreach work through local black schools and churches, the YWCA, and the Neighborhood Union, Andrews exemplified the ideal of the black nurse—socially active and racially conscious.[84]

Spelman-trained missionaries to Africa, like nurses and teachers, viewed their work as contributing to racial progress. Although fewer than ten alumnae actually traveled to Africa (mostly to the Congo), many believed that they had a duty, as Christians of African heritage, to extend what they perceived as the benefits of their own culture to Africans.[85] As one student wrote, Africa ought hold particular interest for her classmates because "it is the home of the Negro." Spelman students, she continued, should "try to do all we can to help them to read as we can, to sing like we can, to talk like we can, and, above all, to love Jesus."[86]

Spelman alumnae joined a growing number of missionaries to the Congo in the 1880s and 1890s. In the last decades of the nineteenth century, Protestant missionaries, many from Britain, Sweden, and the United States, poured into the country. Spelman missionaries were not the first black Americans to work in the area; African American missionaries had traveled to the region by the 1820s, and two of the most notable late nineteenth-century missionaries were African Americans, George Washington Williams, a Baptist (in the Congo from 1890–91), and William Shepard of the Southern Presbyterian Church, who spent over twenty years in the country, beginning in 1890.[87]

Spelman graduate Nora A. Gordon traveled to the Congo earlier than either of these better-known men, in the spring of 1889, to teach English, homemaking, sewing, and Sunday school.[88] Gordon and later Spelman missionaries settled in Ikoko Station on Lake Tumba, not far from the Congo River in the western area of the country. The missionaries created churches and prayed with the natives. Although their work in many ways resembled that of male missionaries, Spelman alumnae made a special effort to reach out to women and children. Female missionaries seemed to particularly emphasize "cultural transformation," and believed education, particularly of girls, to be the quickest and most dramatic way to, in their view, reform and uplift African womanhood and thereby society generally.[89] In this spirit, Gordon and others set up schools, recruiting converted natives to teach in them, as well as homes for orphans and churches in the Congolese missions. They modeled their schools on Spelman, teaching practical or industrial subjects such as gardening, carpentry, and house construction for boys and cooking, sewing, and cleaning for girls.[90]

The missionaries entered the Congo during a time of considerable turmoil. African, Arab, and European groups struggled for control of the area in the mid-nineteenth century. Beginning in the 1870s, the Belgian King Leopold II began colonizing the area, and in 1885, other European leaders acknowledged his claim in the Conference of Berlin. That year Leopold declared his control over the area, which he termed the Congo Free State, although other factions (Arab and African) continued to resist. During the years between 1885 and 1908 Leopold treated the area as his private estate, supporting forced labor in mining camps and agricultural centers that became infamous for their brutality. Workers who did not produce enough ivory, rubber or other products were routinely killed and their hands taken as evidence of this "discipline" to the Belgian authorities. Missionaries and other observers began to publicize these and other atrocities. In response, the Belgium Parliament annexed the Congo in 1908, taking direct control away from the king. It is estimated that 10 million Congolese died during Leopold's reign.[91]

Spelman missionaries condemned the political violence and economic exploitation of the region. Nora Gordon wrote about the Belgian officials: "They force the natives into their service, whip, kill, and oppress them in every way, burn their towns, take away their sheep, goats, fowls, and pigs, and keep their daughters for their unholy purposes."[92] In one letter of 1899, another missionary (and Congolese native), Lena Clark, reported from Ikoko Station witnessing the murder of three children, two women, and a man. She also noted a soldier demanding that a woman throw her baby over the side of a boat in order to free both her hands to paddle him across a river, but added, "His orders were not carried out, because we were at the beach, too."[93] Clark and others heard constant rumors of atrocities and expressed horror at the brutality of the occupying force.

Although the Spelman women condemned the violence of the colonial powers, they shared with other missionaries the view that the Congolese were backward and in desperate need of their help. Congolese, they wrote, were "heathen," living in "sin and ignorance."[94] Gordon, for example, wrote that, "people born in a Christian country can form no conception of the moral ruin, awful misery, and degradation of heathenism."[95] Missionaries described the natives as naked, loud, and indolent.[96] Lacking medical knowledge, they engaged in gruesome practices associated with witchcraft.[97] Worse, missionaries wrote, many were cannibals or took part in vicious warfare.[98] Even two native Congolese girls who attended Spelman and then returned as missionaries described their countrymen and women as lazy, primitive, and exotic. Margaret Rattray, described as a former "Congo slave girl," spent several years at Spelman before returning to Ikoko as a missionary in 1901. She, too, remarked on her students' laziness. After four years at Spelman, Lena Clark asserted that "I am going back to help my dying friends in Africa."[99]

Spelman alumnae especially criticized what they viewed as the hard lot of women, who did the majority of field labor, and commented frequently on the strain of their physical work. They also expressed dismay that women married young and often polygamously, and sometimes suffered physical abuse. Lena Clark described a very young girl dragged on the ground kicking and screaming to be sold to an old man to satisfy a debt, and another missionary declared that kindness towards wives was rare enough to be remarkable.[100] The overwork and abuse of women has long been a way of marking a culture as uncivilized, and the missionaries, consciously or not, might have been influenced by this trope. But they also objected as black women to what they perceived as abuse of other black women, identifying with African women while at the same time viewing local culture as backward.[101] Black missionaries also disapproved of women's open display of sexuality and minimal clothing, affronts to the value they themselves placed on modesty.[102]

To some extent, reports emphasizing the backwardnesss or "darkness" of Africans reflected the need of all missionaries to justify their work and raise contributions.[103] But additionally, Spelman missionaries' dismay with the behavior and culture of the Congolese reflected their attempt to define themselves by distancing their own identity from that of the African natives. In this way, Spelman missionaries, like other late nineteenth-century missionaries, participated in the creation of a view of the Congo as a "heart of darkness"—an area of barbarity, cannibalism, and depravity.[104] On the other hand, although the Congolese represented an extreme example of cultural and religious backwardness to these missionaries, they believed that the Africans could be rescued by using the same approach—education, Christianity, and industrial training—used by other Spelman alumnae as teachers in the American South. Just as Spelman graduates would uplift the rural poor through moral and industrial instruction, graduates of the seminary would "save" their brothers and sisters in Africa through Christian moral training, a hallmark of their own education at Spelman.

Their faith that the Congolese could be saved through moral, religious, and industrial instruction pointed to a belief central to Spelman: that behavior and culture, not race, accounted for the perception of inferiority of the Africans—and themselves. Their project to educate and convert the Congolese pointed to their hope that just as schooling and respectability—coupled with social uplift and political action—could tear down discrimination and segregation at home, it would allow the Congolese greater control of their homeland abroad. Missionary Emma Delaney, reporting that her ship to Africa contained three missionaries and "two hundred and sixty-seven who are going to South Africa for the purpose of oppressing the natives and taking the country," suggested a solution that combined condensation towards Africans with hope that they would actively resist exploitation: "I am impressed as never before that if Africa is to be redeemed for God and in part retained for the Negroes, they had better bestir themselves."[105] Missionaries' willingness to include the Congolese in their beliefs about reform and respectability is most clear in their interest in sending the most promising pupils to Atlanta to further their education. Despite the rather conservative bent of their message of self-help and personal discipline, Spelman missionaries ultimately believed that Christianity and "civilized" culture would provide the Congolese the tools for greater autonomy and even a means of resisting Belgian exploitation and violence, just as respectability would allow them to resist segregation, disenfranchisement, and racial violence at home.

Spelman women's faith in respectability is evident in their voluntary social service and social justice work in the South as well. In addition to professional employment, Spelman graduates participated in women's clubs, social welfare groups, and church organizations also designed to improve the lives of other African Americans. Precedents for black women's organization for social welfare dated back to mutual aid groups of the Reconstruction era and even to networks of assistance on slave plantations. Both working- and middle-class women created community aid and self-help organizations after emancipation, often with the sponsorship of black churches. In the wake of the turn-of-the-century disenfranchisement campaigns and violence directed primarily at black men, black women's seemingly nonpolitical religious and benevolent clubs took on a more public, activist role. Although in some ways the social service networks established by African American women resembled the "female dominion" identified among northern white social workers, black women had their own tradition of organization and responded to the specific needs of the black community.[106]

Religious and church-based groups represented a significant focus of black women's social welfare organization. Local church associations attracted women of all classes, in rural as well as urban areas. Among Spelman alumnae, both homemakers and professional women volunteered in church-based work.[107] Many, including 96 percent of teachers, taught Sunday school.[108] Graduates also became involved in missionary outreach in their communities, including church-sponsored academic and religious instruction.[109]

In addition, Spelman graduates joined national black Christian groups, especially the YWCA. Many of these organizations viewed helping the poor, orphaned, elderly, or ill as part of their Christian duty, and created church-affiliated groups to provide care for these groups. The YWCA, one of the largest women's organizations of the early twentieth century, remained segregated at this time but allowed for interracial communication and created a forum for discussion of race relations.[110] The student Y, particularly after 1920, went beyond the "cooperation" that characterized the more conservative traditional organization, and sought something closer to racial understanding and even the tearing down of racial difference. Spelman had a particularly robust student Y, and one of its graduates, Sue Bailey, became prominent in efforts by the student organization to combat segregation and inequality within the organization and society more generally.[111]

The church-based nature of social welfare work may have also represented a response to the exclusion of African Americans from many state-funded services. Until the 1920s, the city of Atlanta did little to aid either the black or white poor, and most social welfare was provided by private charities. Public agencies serving African Americans received especially inadequate funding, and black welfare workers did not enjoy even the modest successes their white counterparts won working with the courts and legislature.[112] In Atlanta as in other cities, children's needs especially claimed the attention of black women in both religious and independent organizations, and they created kindergartens, day nurseries, and orphanages, as well as homes for the elderly, health care clinics, and community centers. Women's clubs also raised money to supplement the meager funding given to black public schools, and indeed, fundraising represented a major focus of much of black women's organizational work across the South.[113] Spelman students aided in this effort, donating to the seminary's "Christmas offering," which supported the Gate City Free Kindergarten, the Leonard Street Orphans' Home, and other local groups.[114] After graduating, many local alumnae joined these and similar organizations.[115]

Atlanta's best known and most influential African American social welfare organization, the Neighborhood Union (NU), attracted many of the seminary's students and alumnae. Lugenia Burns Hope, wife of Atlanta Baptist president John Hope, founded the NU in 1908 with other faculty wives and community members.[116] Hope, a Chicago native, had spent time at Hull House, and the social settlement's influence was reflected in the NU's goals of "moral, social, intellectual, and religious uplift of the community and neighborhood."[117] Towards those ends the NU sponsored neighborhood activities and events such as festivals and lectures; created playgrounds and social services for children; and strove to abolish houses of prostitution, dance halls, taverns, and other examples of "vice."[118] Several Spelman graduates joined the NU, and one, Hattie Rutherford Watson, a founding member, served as its secretary and worked closely with Hope.[119] The NU borrowed the Spelman playground for the use of neighborhood children, and Lucy Tapley visited meetings along with other faculty, stating that the seminary would support the organization however it could.[120] In 1915 the organization had raised enough funds to open a settlement house staffed largely by students and faculty from Spelman and Morehouse, and later directed by Carrie Dukes, a graduate of Spelman and Columbia University.[121]

The Neighborhood Union combined many aspects of early twentieth-century black women's organizing: an interest in social welfare, especially of women and children; a cross-class organization; and concern with uplift and moral reform. Its Neighborhood House offered classes in art and music, cooking, sewing, and other domestic skills and also provided protected, supervised areas for children's play. Dividing Atlanta into neighborhood zones, the NU created local leadership, often a combination of working- and middle-class women. Historian David Godshalk, while largely critical of black male elite leadership in the city, views the NU as successful in eroding class snobbery within Atlanta's black community through its ethic of mutuality and inclusivity, perhaps ideals more acceptable in a women's club.[122] The organization did attract a broad range of women; several of the founding members worked as domestics. Unlike white reformers, members of the NU encountered crime and poverty within their own neighborhoods, and they acted aggressively to rid areas of social disorder. Although a cross-class, community-based attempt to solve real social problems and provide public safety, the NU also targeted people engaged in vice or crime, and tried to push wayward individuals or undesirable businesses out of the neighborhood. Most often, the gambling hall or tavern they closed down simply would reopen later several blocks away.[123]

The organization's attacks on working-class pleasures may suggest a narrow focus on individual moral reform, but the NU viewed the creation of respectable, and safe, neighborhoods as part of a wide-reaching political agenda. Founded the same year that amendments to Georgia's constitution disenfranchised most of the state's African Americans, the NU represents Atlanta's most significant example of a women's social welfare agency that achieved political influence just as black men lost their vote.[124] Using extensive social surveys done by its members, the NU successfully pressured city government to consider the needs of black citizens. In 1913, for example, the NU presented the board of education and the mayor a letter detailing the inadequacies of Atlanta's black elementary schools.[125] In response to this and other such petitions, the city built additional schools, improved street lighting and sanitation, and built a wall around the Neighborhood House in order to create a playground, among other actions.[126] The NU had its best luck during the mayoralty of James L. Key, who courted black support, but it also asked for and received city improvements from Mayor Walter Sims, a known member of the Ku Klux Klan.[127]

For the most part, alumnae who lived in the South did not directly take on institutionalized white supremacy, instead emphasizing social welfare and uplift. Further, Spelman's leadership did not speak out about racial violence, segregation, or disenfranchisement, and campus publications were wary about taking on such topics. The school's landmark building, however, Sisters Chapel, completed in 1927, was from its founding integrated.[128] By the 1920s, with the growth of the interracial movement and the presence of the Council for Interracial Cooperation (CIC) in Atlanta, the *Messenger* occasionally would print a speech condemning "lawlessness" (a code for lynching) and promoting the work of the CIC in creating "racial good will."[129] Some alumnae took part in the work of the CIC, which sought to improve race relations and opportunities for southern blacks without disrupting segregation. Similarly, the NU asked for more schools, not desegregated schools. Especially for alumnae in Atlanta, uplift, self-improvement, and social welfare seemed more attainable goals than the full destruction of racial segregation, and the institution itself, dependent on conservative northern funding, found the lynching issue too controversial to address.

Alumnae, however, especially those who resided outside of the South, did occasionally take a stronger stand. Ella Barksdale Brown, born in 1871 and a member of Spelman's first high school graduating class in 1887, lived after 1901 in New Jersey. Brown had a career as a teacher, journalist, and club-woman, and was a member of the NACW and NAACP. Active on behalf of civil rights generally, she was most associated with her anti-lynching efforts as well as her work expanding the teaching of black history in the public schools.[130] Her residence in New Jersey would have allowed her to be more outspoken against lynching than alumnae remaining in Georgia and other Deep South states. Yet in an undated handwritten essay (probably a speech intended for a church congregation), she both calls for full citizenship of black Americans, and also echoes language that would resonate with her education, calling for "honest, ambitious, upright, Christian manhood" to shoulder the burden of negative "public sentiment." "The only permanent safeguards" against discrimination "will be those built by our own minds," she wrote.[131] Like other prominent alumnae, Brown seemed to have viewed her education positively. She maintained a correspondence with Spelman's leadership at least through the 1950s, writing in 1951 about her accomplishments to then-president Read, and declaring, "my thoughts often turn to Spelman and the days I spent there as a young girl."[132]

Although committed to racial justice, Barksdale Brown viewed individual self-improvement part of the legacy of her education. Her example and that of the NU demonstrates the link between black women's social welfare organizations and the struggle for social justice. Women who attended Spelman felt a duty to be "leaders of their own race," and for many, the duty included moral improvement of those who, in their eyes, failed to display the respectable behavior that they themselves valued. Many Spelman graduates, active in their local churches, or YWCAs, or the NU, perceived their work, including moral uplift, as part of a larger effort to bring both better standards of living and improved political and civil rights to African Americans. In a complicated way, alumnae viewed moral, intellectual, social, and political reform as part of an interrelated agenda for racial progress and their duty as educated women.

The lives of three graduates who completed their degrees over a forty-year period demonstrate how Spelman women interpreted and implemented the values they encountered at the seminary. Although all three of these women were particularly accomplished and in many ways exceptional, they also represented the Spelman ideal championed by both students and faculty. Each of these women took her own education seriously and taught for at least part of her career. Each married an accomplished man and had at least one child, and took pride in her role as wife and mother. All three also worked in voluntary social service organizations and in local and national civil rights organizations. Although differences in age, class, and personal circumstances shaped their lives, they shared the vision of educated, respectable Christian womanhood that guided Spelman graduates over the school's first forty years.

In 1888, Selena Sloan of Thomasville, Georgia, received an academic (high school) degree from Spelman, part of the second class to graduate from the seminary. From modest circumstances, the illegitimate daughter of a white man and an African American and Native American woman who raised her alone and died while Selena was still young, she nonetheless had an exceptionally accomplished career. After graduating at the age of sixteen she enrolled in post-graduate classes, while also teaching in Atlanta grade schools. The Athens *Clipper* praised her as "a living example of the excellence of Georgia teachers." She became active in women's clubs, including the Women's Christian Temperance Union (WCTU), and in 1891 received an appointment as vice president of the organization's African American division in Georgia. Sloan also spent two years studying at Boston's Emerson School of Music. In 1893 she married Henry Rutherford Butler, one of Atlanta's first black doctors and an outspoken advocate for civil rights, and had a son, her only child, in 1900.[133] She remained in close contact with Spelman's leaders and other alumnae.[134]

Upon marriage, Sloan Butler stopped teaching, convinced that "woman's highest calling" was homemaking.[135] But she did not drop out of the public sphere, continuing her work for the WCTU and the YWCA, as well as founding the first local parent-teacher organization for African Americans. Later she became president of the National Congress of Colored Parents and Teachers. Sloan Butler also created and edited "The Woman's Advocate," a newsletter targeted to African American women. By the 1920s she had become a national figure in the YWCA and in child welfare work, attending conferences at the White House including a 1934 meeting on black education.[136] Beginning in the fall of 1937, she spent a year in London studying nursery schools and welfare work. During the war years, her son, a Harvard medical school graduate, served at Fort Huachuca in Arizona, and Sloan Butler headed a group of "Gray Ladies" sponsored by the Red Cross that nursed ill or injured troops. She also joined the local YWCA and participated locally in "interracial work," as she reported to then-president of Spelman, Florence Read.[137] After the war she returned to Atlanta, remaining active in social welfare organizations. In her last years she lived with her son and his family in Los Angeles, frequently corresponding with Spelman leaders until her death in 1964.[138] Despite this impressive career, even after the death of her husband, Sloan Butler identified her occupation as "housewife."[139]

Figure 14. Selena Sloan Butler, c. 1926. (Courtesy of Selena Sloan Butler Papers, Archives Division, Auburn Avenue Research Library on African American Culture and History, Atlanta-Fulton Public Library System)

In 1890, two years after Selena Sloan completed her degree, Claudia Thomas White entered the seminary at the age of fourteen. Unlike Sloan, White was born into the emerging black elite. She was the daughter of William Jefferson White, the well-known and influential minister of Augusta's Harmony Baptist Church and editor and publisher of the *Atlanta Baptist*. White, a strong advocate for advanced education, helped establish Georgia's first public black high school, cofounded Augusta Baptist Institute (later Morehouse), and was a charter member of Spelman. White fit the model of the "best man" as described by Glenda Gilmore—leaders who could point to their own accomplishments as a means of challenging the premise of black inferiority. During the first part of his career, White cultivated alliances with white elites and was able to count on the support of some of Augusta's white leadership. But after the turn of the century, race relations in the city, as elsewhere, worsened, and in the aftermath of the statewide sense of fear that followed the 1906 Atlanta riot, he was forced to leave the city, although he did return later that year. White remained an advocate for civil and political rights until his death in 1913.[140]

With this background, it is unsurprising that Claudia White was one of the most academically accomplished students of Spelman's early years, and later a prominent Atlanta activist. In 1894, she was one of the first students to complete the college preparatory program, and in 1897 she enrolled as one of Spelman's first two college students. She earned her B.A. in 1901, followed by a teachers' professional degree the next year. White continued her education by attending summer courses at Oberlin in German language and literature, but remained closely involved in Spelman as the cofounder and president of the alumnae association. Serving as a field worker for Spelman, White traveled throughout Georgia helping recruit students and reporting on the state of black education. Her work in the alumnae association inspired one observer to declare that "no other alumna has been so closely identified with Spelman's life and growth."[141] As both a student and alumna, White contributed frequently to the school paper the *Messenger*, including an 1897 article defending the virtue and femininity of college-educated women.[142]

After graduating, White taught at the Haines Institute in her hometown of Augusta, and then took a joint appointment at Spelman and Morehouse teaching German and ancient languages. In 1913 she married Morehouse music professor Kemper Harreld and retired from full-time teaching the following year with the birth of their daughter. White Harreld did not become idle, however, and created a second career as a clubwoman active in Atlanta's Leonard Street Orphans Home, the Colored Case Committee of the Welfare Association, the NAACP, and the Commission of Interracial Cooperation as well as both the Atlanta and the national YWCA, among other groups.[143] The Gate City Day Nursery Association received her special attention, as she spent twenty years as a board member of the organization and fifteen as its director.[144] She also taught music privately and with her husband founded the Fine Arts Study Club to support arts and music for black Atlantans, and wrote poetry.[145] One poem, "Mystic, the Detroit Hospital Maid," provides a glimpse into White Harreld's thinking. In the poem, Mystic is proud to see a wealthy black woman staying in one of the nicest rooms of the hospital, and remarks to her: "Whatever happens to one of my race/be it good or bad/It happens to me."[146] By the time of her death in 1952, Claudia White Harreld had become one of Atlanta's best-known social service and civil rights leaders.

A much younger Spelman student, Sue Elvie Bailey, credited Spelman with impressing on her a sense of duty and female accomplishment. Born in 1903 in Arkansas to a Baptist minister and an agent of the Women's American Baptist Home Mission Society, Spelman's founding organization, Bailey attended Nannie Burroughs's school in Washington, D.C., before earning a high school degree and certificate in cooking at Spelman in 1920 and in 1926 a B.A. from Oberlin College. At Oberlin Bailey began her lifelong association

Figure 15. Claudia White Harreld, who earned three degrees from Spelman: High School 1897, College 1901, Teachers' Professional 1902. (Courtesy of the Spelman College Archives)

with internationalism, particularly within the World Fellowship Committee of the YWCA. After the death of her friend, Dean of Women at Fisk University Juliette Derricotte, Bailey founded a scholarship that sent American students to study in India in her honor.[147] Bailey taught music at Hampton Institute, and worked as National Secretary for Colleges in the South for the YWCA until her marriage in 1932 to Howard Thurman, dean of the chapel of Howard University and one of the twentieth century's most influential black Baptist theologians, a direct influence on Martin Luther King Jr. The couple had two daughters.[148]

The Thurmans traveled internationally promoting their "Pilgrimage of Friendship" in 1935, meeting peace activists, including Mahatma Gandhi. In 1940 Bailey Thurman began publishing and editing the *Aframerican Woman's Journal*, the organ of the National Council of Negro Women (NCNW), and later created the organization's archives and library. She also compiled and edited the NCNW's *Historical Cookbook of the American Negro*, a collection of recipes, many of them linked to important figures or events in black history.[149] In 1944 she and her husband founded an interfaith church in San Francisco, leaving the city in 1952 after Howard Thurman accepted a position at the chapel of Boston University. In Boston Sue Thurman continued to be active in community groups as well as international organizations including the

YWCA's World Fellowship Committee.[150] She also remained involved in arts and historical organizations, including creating Boston's Black Heritage trail and founding the Museum of Afro-American History. The couple returned to San Francisco after Howard Thurman's retirement, where Sue Thurman directed the African American Historical and Cultural Society and managed the Howard Thurman Educational Trust designed to aid southern black colleges. She died in 1996. When interviewed in the 1980s, Bailey Thurman declared the sense of purpose and lack of racial animosity at Spelman deeply affected her. The friendships between black and white faculty members, and the accomplishments of women especially impressed her, and "I began to see myself as part of a noble unit that was in the process of becoming during the twenties and thirties."[151]

Women like Butler, Herrald, and Thurman exemplified the ideal Spelman alumnae, women successful as wives and mothers, professionals, and social and civil rights activists. All pointed to their time at Spelman as a major influence on their lives. Although the seminary's stress on Christian morality and social respectability might seem stifling, its students and alumnae, like these three, often considered it a means to increase their public influence. The expectations placed on Spelman graduates by their parents, teachers, and communities appear extraordinarily high. Without family support, the tension between the ideals of domesticity and that of socially responsible activist, as well as the need to contribute to family income and provide an ideal home, could become overwhelming. Several scholars have emphasized the extreme stress and emotional exhaustion that respectability placed on black women.[152] Yet most graduates accepted it as their duty as educated black women to use their influence for community and racial uplift. Their work as teachers, church members, nurses, and mothers laid the groundwork for the generation of organized women active in the broad movement for civil rights of the postwar era. Many Spelman students and alumnae joined the rank-and-file, and the son of a 1922 graduate, Alberta Williams King, became its most influential leader.[153] The commitment and determination of these women belie the view that training for respectability meant training for docility and obedience. Most Spelman alumnae embraced the challenge of becoming race leaders, a female talented tenth.

Conclusion

Race, Respectability, and Sexuality in Women's Education

The Lucy Cobb Institute and Spelman Seminary represent two attempts to prepare southern women and girls for a new century. Founders and faculty of both schools strove to mold young women who would demonstrate the modernity and progressiveness of the South, as the schools themselves defined them. Race, class, and ideology shaped both the definition and form of secondary education offered at both schools, creating some profound differences. Perhaps more surprising, the schools shared some remarkable similarities.

Both Lucy Cobb and Spelman demonstrated a deep concern with morality and respectability. The two schools wanted to create women whose impeccable behavior would shield their public activism from reproach. Cities and towns gave the granddaughters of slaves and granddaughters of slaveholders new opportunities, yet both groups of women could be vulnerable in the New South's fast growing towns and cities. Teachers of elite white and aspiring African American young women viewed female economic and political participation as intimately tied with sexual purity. Sexual modesty and respectability, teachers believed, would provide protection against accusations of immorality for young women venturing into the public sphere.

For white southern women, sexual purity had long been central to "true womanhood" and a buttress of white supremacy. In the antebellum era, a white woman's chastity guaranteed her family's racial purity, and any hint of impropriety could destroy her own and her family's reputation.[1] In the urbanizing New South, sexual reputation remained closely tied to elite white feminine identity. Proper dress, manners, and decorum indicated family status as a young woman encountered people of all social backgrounds and classes. Additionally, white supremacy was dependent upon white female sexual propriety. If women acted, in Mildred Rutherford's own words, "so as to not deserve any better," they would destroy the keystone of the southern racial hierarchy.[2] Segregation and disenfranchisement, justified as means of protecting white women, required their conformity to a respectable and chaste femininity.

With the aid of the respectability earned through their Lucy Cobb education, young women could take advantage of new opportunities in the South's towns and cities. As a private, elite secondary school, Lucy Cobb offered an education in manners, but at the same time did not view its education as limited to training in gentility. The strict rules Rutherford imposed on her students allowed Lucies to engage freely in intellectual and social pursuits in the sheltered world of the campus that trained them for later public activism. While Rutherford attempted to produce women whose manners and behavior conformed to an elite model of antebellum femininity, Lucy Cobb also offered an education that prepared its graduates for the changed circumstances of the postwar South. Protected by the cloak of antebellum tradition, Lucies would shape New South society in overtly public roles as clubwomen and teachers or other professionals.

Lucy Cobb graduates, their instructors hoped, would take advantage of new, more public roles for white women to defend their racial and class interests, as faculty defined them. For Rutherford, this meant following her example in rejecting woman suffrage, defending states' rights, and supporting industrial progress. Despite the nostalgic tone of her speeches and publications glorifying the Confederacy and the antebellum era, Rutherford was an active participant in the New South, striving to create a modern society that would fully rejoin the Union but on its own terms. These terms included "self-rule" and open defiance of the fourteenth and fifteenth amendments to the Constitution. "Lucies," she anticipated, would join her in promoting economic development, social conservatism, and elite political hegemony. Yet as many examples demonstrate, Rutherford could not fully control how students interpreted and used their education. Younger Lucies had their own understanding of how they might use their education to improve southern society.

As at Lucy Cobb, Spelman's faculty also linked increased public opportunities for its students with sexual modesty. The African American women who attended the Atlanta seminary faced a much more difficult challenge in proving their respectability than did their counterparts at Lucy Cobb. For black women, the stereotype of the "black Jezebel" dated back to slavery and served as a way to excuse sexual mistreatment by white male slaveholders.[3]

After emancipation, whites continued to use black women's supposed las-civiousness to attempt to discredit their work towards racial and personal betterment. As one white woman wrote, "I cannot imagine such a thing as a respectable black woman."[4] As they sought public authority on behalf of their communities, African American women viewed respectability as armor against such insults. Spelman viewed its mission as creating modest, respectable women whose self-discipline would defy the stereotype of the sexually aggressive black woman and give them the opportunity to use their education on behalf of racial uplift.

The seminary's means of ensuring respectability was industrial educa-tion. Because Spelman College is now considered one of the academically top-ranking small liberal arts colleges in the nation, the focus on industrial training during its early years is at first surprising. Historians continue to associate industrial instruction with racial accommodationism, viewing it as second-class education for second-class citizenship. But at least at Spelman, industrial education served as moral instruction meant to prepare African American women to become race leaders. The white northern missionaries who founded Spelman believed that by instilling their students with middle-class values of thrift, sobriety, discipline, self-reliance, and industry, as well as sexual purity, they would allow black women to work towards racial uplift as mothers, nurses, teachers, and community leaders. Rather than "schooling for the new slavery," Spelman's faculty viewed industrial education as the part of its effort to achieve African American economic, social, and even political progress.[5]

Many among the African American elite as well as Spelman students and alumnae viewed industrial and moral education as part of an overall program of race uplift. Believing in the political utility of respectability, they had faith that modest appearance, dedication to Christianity, and personal morality would overturn stereotypes of blacks as lazy, loud, dirty, and promiscuous, and thereby demonstrate readiness for full citizenship. As nurses, mothers, social workers, and especially teachers, Spelman alumnae employed an image of respectable black womanhood to labor more effectively for racial progress and social justice—in effect, to create a female "talented tenth." Notably, striving for respectability did not preclude questioning white supremacy. Some alumnae created community organizations to make up for paltry funding given to public social welfare services and schools. Others joined clubs or other organizations that fought for increased civil rights and resisted continued defiance of the Reconstruction amendments by southern states. To Spelman alumnae, a truly new South would be a racially equal South. Yet of course alumnae worked within racial restraints, even within their own institution. It is worth noting that Spelman students were not able to have the effect on their alma mater that Lucy Cobb graduates did. Although several Spelman graduates did teach at the school, the seminary remained directed and controlled by white women until 1953 (when Spelman's first black, and first male, president took office).

By 1930, both schools had undergone dramatic changes. Despite Mildred Rutherford's determined efforts to create an endowment in 1925, the Lucy Cobb Institute never gained financial stability. Although the school's close association with the Cobb family had been part of its appeal, it may also have limited the development of leadership outside of the family. Rutherford proved truly irreplaceable. After her death in 1928, two male principals—the first nonalumnae to lead the school since 1880—struggled to keep the school open. In 1931 the Lucy Cobb Institute closed its doors; the affiliated elementary school would stay open another ten years. By the 1930s the seminary model had largely become obsolete. White women had broader academic opportunities, and strict rules of conduct associated with seminaries seemed old-fashioned. The women who would have attended the Lucy Cobb could instead enroll in local public high schools and go on to southern women's colleges such as Agnes Scott or to the State Normal in Athens. As juniors they could transfer to the University of Georgia. As an Athens journalist noted in reporting the school's closure: "the day is past when girls are satisfied with merely being 'polished up.'"[6] With more educational and social opportunities elsewhere, young women turned away from the seminary's cloistered campus.

Spelman, too, went through significant changes by 1930. Unlike Lucy Cobb, however, the Atlanta school made the transition from seminary to college successfully. In 1923, Spelman obtained a grant from the General Education Board (GEB) to build a science building, allowing the school to offer a complete college course independent of Morehouse. The following year the school became formally incorporated as Spelman College, and by 1927 received recognition from the Georgia Department of Education as a top-grade college. That year, Lucy Tapley stepped down from her leadership role. The top choice for her successor, Florence Read, a Mount Holyoke graduate who had worked at the Rockefeller Foundation and at Reed College in Oregon, refused to take the position unless the board secured an endowment. Although unsuccessful in the past, this time the board, led by University of Chicago vice-president Trevor Arnett, convinced the GEB to donate one-and-a-half million dollars towards an endowment. Additional funding came from the Laura Spelman Rockefeller Memorial Fund, the Julius Rosenwald Fund, and the WABHMS. Read immediately worked to transform Spelman into a true liberal arts college. Within two years she closed the elementary school, the high school, and the nurse-training department, and expanded the library. During her long tenure as president, lasting until 1953, Florence Reed worked to complete the school's evolution from seminary to college. Since the 1950s the college has continued to grow, and has been recognized as one of the leading small liberal arts colleges in the nation.[7]

What accounts for Spelman's success? A key difference is that, because of its long relationship with the Rockefeller family and the GEB, it achieved securing an endowment, whereas Lucy Cobb did not. Additionally, and somewhat ironically, the college succeeded because it targeted women excluded from most of the South's higher educational institutions. Whereas women who might have become Lucies enjoyed greater opportunities at both private and public colleges and universities, black women in the 1920s and 1930s had few options. Spelman moved away from the strict rules and work requirements associated with its history as a seminary, and unlike Lucy Cobb, was able to reinvent itself as a vital institution meeting the needs of its students.

A comparison between these two schools points to some significant and surprising similarities. Both schools were compelled to reckon with major economic, social, and political changes as the South sought to modernize its economy and cement sectional reunification while maintaining local control over race relations. Lucy Cobb and Spelman offered serious academic and vocational curricula intended to prepare women to take an active part in this economic and social transformation, and both viewed control of female sexuality as central to increased freedom for women. And, in each, alumnae used their education to further their own goals, relying on the skills and knowledge their education provided to determine the needs of their societies and their roles within them.

Notes

Introduction

1. [Henry Morehouse], "The Worth of Spelman Seminary to the World," *Spelman Messenger*, June 1896, 1–8 (quotations page 3).

2. "Lucy Cobb Institute A Giant Factor in the Education of Young Women," Dec. 10, 1897, Lucy Cobb Scrapbook, 1858–1908, box 4, Mildred Lewis Rutherford Scrapbooks, Hargrett Library, University of Georgia, Athens, Georgia (hereafter Hargrett Library).

3. "Catalogue of the Lucy Cobb Institute," 1903, 12, Special Collections Hargrett Rare Books, Hargrett Library.

4. David Tyack, *The One Best System: A History of American Urban Education* (Cambridge, Mass.: Harvard University Press, 1974); Michael B. Katz, *The Irony of Early School Reform: Educational Innovation in Mid-Nineteenth Century Massachusetts* (Cambridge, Mass.: Harvard University Press, 1968); Michael B. Katz, *Class, Bureaucracy, and Schools: The Illusion of Educational Change in America* (New York: Praeger, 1971); Clarence J. Karier, Paul Voilas, and Joel Spring, *Roots of Crisis: American Education in the Twentieth Century* (New York: Rand McNally, 1973).

5. James Anderson, *The Education of Blacks in the South, 1860–1935* (Chapel Hill: University of North Carolina Press, 1988); Adam Fairclough, *A Class of Their Own: Black Teachers in the Segregated South* (Cambridge, Mass.: Harvard University Press, 2007); Heather Andrea Williams, *African American Education in Slavery and Freedom* (Chapel Hill: University of North Carolina Press, 2005); Ron E. Butchart, *Schooling the Freedpeople: Teaching, Learning, and the Struggle for Black Freedom, 1861–1876* (Chapel Hill: University of North Carolina Press, 2010).

6. Walter J. Fraser Jr., R. Frank Saunders Jr., and Jon L. Wakelyn, eds., *The Web of Southern Social Relations: Women, Family, and Education* (Athens: University of Georgia Press, 1985), 4–7, 16–19; William A. Link, *A Hard Country and a Lonely Place:*

Schooling, Society, and Reform in Rural Virginia (Chapel Hill: University of North Carolina Press, 1986), 85–91; James L. Leloudis, *Schooling the New South: Pedagogy, Self, and Society in North Carolina, 1880–1920* (Chapel Hill: University of North Carolina Press, 1996), 29–34, 70–71, 113, 140–41, 145–46; Wayne J. Urban, ed., *Essays in Twentieth-Century Southern Education: Exceptionalism and Its Limits* (New York: Garland Publishing, 1999); Dan R. Frost, *Thinking Confederates: Academia and the Idea of Progress in the New South* (Knoxville: University of Tennessee Press, 2000); Rebecca S. Montgomery, *The Politics of Education in The New South: Women and Reform in Georgia* (Baton Rouge: Louisiana State University Press, 2006); Ann Short Chirhart, *Torches of Light: Georgia Teachers and the Coming of the Modern South* (Athens: University of Georgia Press, 2005).

7. Ronald K. Goodenow and Arthur O. White, *Education and the Rise of the New South* (Boston: G. K. Hall & Co., 1981); Fraser, Saunders, and Wakelyn, eds., *Web of Southern Social Relations*; Anderson, *Education of Blacks in the South*; Link, *A Hard Country and Lonely Place*; Leloudis, *Schooling the New South*; Urban, ed., *Essays in Twentieth-Century Southern Education*.

8. Linda Kerber, "'Why Should Girls be Learn'd and Wise?': Two Centuries of Higher Education for Women as Seen through the Unfinished Work of Alice Mary Baldwin," in *Women and Higher Education in American History*, ed. John Mack Faragher and Florence Howe (New York: Norton, 1988), 25–26; Christie Anne Farnham, *The Education of the Southern Belle: Higher Education and Student Socialization in the Antebellum South* (New York: New York University Press, 1994), 37, 199–20 (fnt 13).

9. Farnham, *Education of the Southern Belle*; Catherine Clinton, *The Plantation Mistress: Woman's World in the Old South* (New York: Pantheon Books, 1982); Jean E. Friedman, *The Enclosed Garden: Women and Community in the Evangelical South, 1830–1900* (Chapel Hill: University of North Carolina Press, 1985); Elizabeth Fox-Genovese, *Within the Plantation Household: Black and White Women of the Old South* (Chapel Hill: University of North Carolina Press, 1988); Stephanie McCurry, *Masters of Small Worlds: Yeoman Households, Gender Relations, and the Political Culture of the Antebellum South Carolina Low Country* (New York: Oxford University Press, 1995).

10. Farnham, *The Education of the Southern Belle*, 14–18, 28–29.

11. Amy Friedlander, "A More Perfect Christian Womanhood: Higher Learning for a New South," in Goodenow and White, *Education and the Rise of the New South*, 72–91; Barbara Miller Solomon, *In the Company of Educated Women: A History of Women and Higher Education in America* (New Haven: Yale University Press, 1985); Faragher and Howe, eds., *Women and Higher Education in American History*; Helen Lefkowitz Horowitz, *Alma Mater: Design and Experience in the Women's Colleges from Their Nineteenth Century Beginnings to the 1930s* (Amherst: University of Massachusetts Press, 1993 [second edition]); Lynn D. Gordon, *Gender and Higher Education in the Progressive Era* (New Haven: Yale University Press, 1990); Amy McCandless, *The Past in the Present: Women's Higher Education in the Twentieth-Century South* (Tuscaloosa: University of Alabama Press, 1999); Leloudis, *Schooling the New South*;

Ann Mari May, ed., *The "Woman Question" and Higher Education: Perspectives on Gender and Knowledge Production in America* (Cheltenham, UK: Edward Elgar, 2008). The Morrill Act gave federal land to states to found universities, most of which admitted female state residents.

12. Linda Kerber, *Women of the Republic: Intellect and Ideology in Revolutionary America* (Chapel Hill: University of North Carolina Press, 1980); Mary Beth Norton, *Liberty's Daughters: The Revolutionary Experience of American Women, 1750–1800* (Boston: Little, Brown, 1980); Jan Lewis, "The Republican Wife: Virtue and Seduction in the Early Republic," *The William and Mary Quarterly* 44, no. 4 (Oct. 1987): 689–721; Ruth Bloch, "The Gendered Meaning of Virtue in Revolutionary America," *Signs* 13 (1987): 37–58; Rosemarie Zagarri, "Morals, Manners, and the Republican Mother," *American Quarterly* 44, no. 2 (June 1992): 192–215; Jan Lewis, "Of Every Age, Sex and Condition: The Representation of Women in the Constitution," *Journal of the Early Republic* 15, no. 3 (Autumn 1995): 359–89; Carol Berkin, *Revolutionary Mothers: Women in the Struggle for America's Independence* (New York: Knopf, 2005); Mary Kelley, *Learning to Stand and Speak: Women, Education, and Public Life in America's Republic* (Chapel Hill: University of North Carolina Press, 2006).

13. Kelley, *Learning to Stand and Speak*, 9–10, 53; Margaret A. Nash, *Women's Education in the United States, 1780–1840* (New York: Palgrave Macmillan, 2005), 54, 57–61.

14. Daniel Scott Smith and Michael S. Hindus, "Premarital Pregnancy in America 1640–1971: An Overview and Interpretation," *Journal of Interdisciplinary History* 5, no. 4 (Spring 1975): 537–570; Cornelia Hughes Dayton, "Taking the Trade: Abortion and Gender Relations in an Eighteenth-Century New England Village," *The William and Mary Quarterly Third Series* 48, no. 1 (January 1991): 19–49; Laurel Thather Ulrich, *A Midwife's Tale: The Life of Martha Ballard, Based on Her Diary, 1785–1812* (New York: Knopf, 1990).

15. Susanna Rowson, *Charlotte Temple*, ed. Cathy Davidson (New York: Oxford University Press, 1986); Smith and Hindus, "Premarital Pregnancy in America 1640–1971," 549–52; Nancy Cott, "Passionlessness: An Interpretation of Victorian Sexual Ideology, 1790–1850," *Signs* 4 (Winter 1978): 219–36; Patricia Cline Cohen, *The Murder of Helen Jewett: The Life and Death of a Prostitute in Nineteenth-Century New York* (New York: Knopf, 1998); Cathy Davidson, *Revolution and the Word: The Rise of the Novel in America*, expanded edition (Oxford: Oxford University Press, 2004); Karen J. Renner, "Seduction, Prostitution, and the Control of Female Desire in Popular Antebellum Fiction," *Nineteenth-Century Literature* 65, no. 2 (September 2010): 166–91; Bonnie Laughlin Schultz, "Introduction" to *How Did Susanna Rowson and Other Reformers Promote Higher Education as an Antidote to Women's Sexual Vulnerability, 1780–1820?*, ed. Schultz, in Kathryn Kish Sklar and Thomas Dublin, eds., *Women and Social Movements in the United States, 1600–2000* (Alexander Street Press, online resource).

16. Susan E. Klepp, *Revolutionary Conceptions: Women, Fertility, and Family Limitation in America, 1760–1820* (Chapel Hill: University of North Carolina Press, 2009). See also Cott, "Passionlessness," and Nash, *Women's Education in the United States.*

17. Helen Lefkowitz Horowitz, "The Body in the Library," in May, ed., *The Woman Question and Higher Education,* 11–31.

18. Horowitz, *Alma Mater,* 4–5.

19. Deborah Grey White, *Ar'n't I a Woman? Female Slaves in the Plantation South,* rev. ed. (New York: W. W. Norton, 1999).

20. April Haynes, "The Trials of Frederick Hollick: Obscenity, Sex Education, and Medical Democracy in the Antebellum United States," *Journal of the History of Sexuality* 12, no. 4 (October 2003): 543–74.

21. A major theme of Harriet Jacobs's narrative, for example, is the vulnerability of slave women to sexual abuse and their own attempts to protect themselves from violence and exploitation. Harriet Jacobs, *Incidents in the Life of a Slave Girl Written by Herself,* ed. Jean Fagan Yellin (Cambridge, Mass.: Harvard University Press, 2000).

22. Darlene Clark Hine, "Rape and the Inner Lives of Black Women in the Middle West," *Signs* 14, no. 4 (Summer 1989): 912–20; Martha Hodes, "The Sexualization of Reconstruction Politics: White Women and Black Men in the South after the Civil War," *Journal of the History of Sexuality* 3, no. 3 (January 1993): 402–17; Glenda Gilmore, *Gender and Jim Crow: Women and the Politics of White Supremacy in North Carolina, 1896–1920* (Chapel Hill: University of North Carolina Press, 1996), 104, 140–41.

23. C. Vann Woodward, *Origins of the New South, 1877–1913* (Baton Rouge: Louisiana State University Press, 1951); Dewey W. Grantham, *Southern Progressivism: The Reconciliation of Progress and Tradition* (Knoxville: University of Tennessee Press, 1983); Numan V. Bartley, *The Creation of Modern Georgia* (Athens: University of Georgia Press, 1983); Pete Daniels, *Breaking the Land: The Transformation of Cotton, Tobacco, and Rice Cultures Since 1880* (Urbana: University of Illinois Press, 1985); Edward L. Ayers, *The Promise of the New South: Life After Reconstruction* (New York: Oxford University Press, 1995); George Fredrickson, *The Black Image in the White Mind: The Debate on Afro-American Character and Destiny, 1817–1914* (New York: Harper & Row, 1971); Joel Williamson, *A Rage for Order: Black-White Relations in the American South Since Emancipation* (New York: Oxford University Press, 1986); Gavin Wright, *Old South, New South: Revolutions in the Southern Economy Since the Civil War* (New York: Basic Books, 1986); James C. Cobb, "Beyond Planters and Industrialists: A New Perspective on the New South," *Journal of Southern History* 54 (February 1988): 45–68; James C. Cobb, *The Selling of the South: The Southern Crusade for Industrial Development, 1936–1990* (Urbana: University of Illinois Press, 1993); Paul Cimbala and Barton C. Shaw, *Making a New South: Race, Leadership, and Community after the Civil War* (Gainesville: University Press of Florida, 2007).

24. Charles E. Wynes, "Part IV: 1865–1890" in Kenneth Coleman, general editor, *A History of Georgia* (Athens: University of Georgia Press, 1977, 1991), 207, 225–237, 252–53.

25. Woodward, *Origins of the New South;* Fredrickson, *Black Image in the White Mind;* Williamson, *Rage for Order;* Ayers, *Promise of the New South;* Gilmore, *Gender and Jim Crow.*

26. Harold H. Martin, *Georgia: A Bicentennial History* (New York: Norton and American Association for State and Local History, 1977), 125–28; Wynes, "Part IV:

1865–1890," 225–229, 247–49; Charles L. Flynn, Jr., *White Land, Black Labor: Caste and Class in Late Nineteenth Century Georgia* (Baton Rouge: Louisiana State University Press, 1983); Tera W. Hunter, *To 'Joy My Freedom: Southern Black Women's Lives and Labors after the Civil War* (Cambridge, Mass.: Harvard University Press, 1997), 21–25; Ronald H. Bayor, *Race and the Shaping of Twentieth-Century Atlanta* (Chapel Hill: University of North Carolina Press, 1996), 3–12.

27. Stephanie J. Shaw, *What a Woman Ought to Be and Do: Black Professional Women Workers During the Jim Crow Era* (Chicago: University of Chicago Press, 1996); Gilmore, *Gender and Jim Crow*; Hunter, *To 'Joy My Freedom*.

28. Caroline Janney, *Burying the Dead but Not the Past: Ladies' Memorial Associations and the Lost Cause* (Chapel Hill: University of North Carolina Press, 2007).

29. Jane Turner Censer, *The Reconstruction of White Southern Womanhood, 1865–1895* (Baton Rouge: Louisiana State University Press, 2003), especially chapter 5.

30. Elizabeth Lasch-Quinn, *Black Neighbors: Race and the Limits of Reform in the American Settlement House Movement, 1890–1945* (Chapel Hill: University of North Carolina Press, 1993); Sarah Wilkerson-Freeman, "The Feminization of the American State: The Odyssey of a Southern Vanguard, 1898–1940" (Ph.D. dissertation, University of North Carolina, Chapel Hill, 1995); Gilmore, *Gender and Jim Crow*; Shaw, *What a Woman Ought to Be and Do*; Anastasia Sims, *The Power of Femininity in the New South: Women's Organizations and Politics in North Carolina, 1880–1930* (Columbia: University of South Carolina Press, 1997); Elna Green, *Southern Strategies: Southern Women and the Woman Suffrage Question* (Chapel Hill: University of North Carolina Press, 1997); Elizabeth Hayes-Turner, *Women, Culture, and Community: Religion and Reform in Galveston, 1880–1920* (New York: Oxford University Press, 1997); Ann D. Gordon with Bettye Collier-Thomas, John H. Bracey, Arlene Voski Avakian, and Joyce Avrech Berkman, eds., *African American Women and the Vote, 1837–1965* (Amherst: University of Massachusetts Press, 1997); Elna Green, ed., *Before the New Deal: Social Welfare in the South, 1830–1930* (Athens: University of Georgia Press, 1999); Patricia Schechter, *Ida B. Wells-Barnett and American Reform, 1880–1930* (Chapel Hill: University of North Carolina Press, 2001); Censer, *The Reconstruction of White Southern Womanhood*; Bruce L. Clayton and John A. Salmond, eds., *"Lives Full of Struggle and Triumph": Southern Women, Their Institutions, and Their Communities* (Gainesville: University Press of Florida, 2003); Joan Marie Johnson, *Southern Ladies, New Women: Race, Region, and Clubwomen in South Carolina, 1890–1930* (University Press of Florida, 2004).

31. Wynes, "Part IV: 1865–1890," 207–208, 214–16, 219, 223–24, 238–41; William F. Holmes, "Part Five: 1890–1940," in Coleman, ed., *A History of Georgia*, 279; Martin, *Georgia: A Bicentennial History*, 118–20, 131; Chirhart, *Torches of Light*, 24; Georgia Constitution of 1877 (http://georgiainfo.galileo.usg.edu/con1877c.htm).

32. Anderson, *Education of Blacks in the New South*; Chirhart, *Torches of Light*, 24–25, 93, 96; Bayor, *Race and the Shaping of Twentieth Century Atlanta*, 7, 10–11, 197–205.

33. "Lucy Cobb Institute A Giant Factor in the Education of Young Women."

34. Wayne J. Urban, "Educational Reform in a New South City: Atlanta, 1890–1925," in Goodenow and White, eds., *Education and the Rise of the New South*, 114–30.

35. Robyn Muncy, *Creating a Female Dominion in American Reform, 1890–1935* (New York: Oxford University Press, 1991); Theda Skocpol, *Protecting Soldiers and Mothers: The Political Origins of Social Policy in the United States* (Cambridge, Mass.: Belknap Press of Harvard University Press, 1992); Kathryn Kish Sklar, "The Historical Foundations of a Women's Power in the Creation of the American Welfare State, 1830–1930," in Seth Koven and Sonya Michel, eds., *Mothers of a New World: Maternalist Politics and the Origins of Welfare States* (New York: Routledge, 1993), 43–93; Molly Ladd-Taylor, *Mother-work: Women, Child Welfare, and the State, 1890–1930* (Urbana: University of Illinois Press, 1994); Linda Gordon, *Pitied But Not Entitled: Single Mothers and the History of Welfare, 1890–1935* (Cambridge, Mass.: Harvard University Press, 1994); Gwendolyn Mink, *Wages of Motherhood: Inequality in the Welfare State, 1917–1942* (Ithaca: Cornell University Press, 1995).

36. Evelyn Brooks Higginbotham, "African American Women's History and the Metalanguage of Race," *Signs* 17 (Winter 1992): 251–74; Nancy Hewitt, "Compounding Differences," *Feminist Studies* 18 (Summer 1992): 313–26; Nell Irvin Painter, *Southern History Across the Color Line* (Chapel Hill: University of North Carolina Press, 2002).

Chapter 1. The "Perfection of Sacred Womanhood"

1. Margaret Anne Womack, "Mildred Lewis Rutherford: Exponent of Southern Culture" (MA thesis, University of Georgia, 1947), 11–12.

2. Laura gave birth to six daughters and two sons; one daughter and one son died as toddlers. Her daughter Marion was born in 1857 and died in 1859; another daughter, Laura, was born in 1859. Merrow Egerton Sorley, *Lewis of Warner Hall: The History of a Family* (1935; reprint Baltimore: Geneological Publishing, 2000), 463–63.

3. "Female Education in Athens," typewritten copy, Lucy Cobb Institute File, Athens-Clarke County Heritage Foundation, Athens, Georgia (hereafter cited as Athens Heritage Foundation); Womack, "Mildred Lewis Rutherford," 12–13; Phyllis Jenkins Barrow, "History of Lucy Cobb Institute, 1858–1950" (MA thesis, University of Georgia, 1951); reprinted in Phinizy Spalding, comp. and ed., *Higher Education for Women in the South: A History of Lucy Cobb Institute, 1858–1994* (Athens, Ga.: Georgia Southern Press, 1994), 11–12; William B. McCash, *Thomas R. R. Cobb: The Making of a Southern Nationalist* (Macon, Ga.: Mercer University Press, 2004), 76, 100–9; T. R. R. Cobb to H. R. J. Long, 28 March 1858, Lucy Cobb Institute File, Athens Heritage Foundation; "An Act to Incorporate the 'Lucy Cobb Institute' for the education of young ladies, in the town of Athens," Georgia Laws, 1859, Lucy Cobb Institute Stock Books and Minutes (hereafter Lucy Cobb Institute Stock Books), Hargrett Library, University of Georgia, Athens (hereafter Hargrett Library).

4. Marjorie Spruill Wheeler, *New Women of the New South: The Leaders of the Woman Suffrage Movement in the Southern States* (New York: Oxford University Press, 1993); Glenda Gilmore, *Gender and Jim Crow: Women and the Politics of White Supremacy in North Carolina, 1896–1920* (Chapel Hill: University of North Carolina Press, 1996); Anastatia Sims, *The Power of Femininity in the New South: Women's*

Organizations and Politics in North Carolina, 1880–1930 (Columbia: University of South Carolina Press, 1997); Elna Green, *Southern Strategies: Southern Women and the Woman Suffrage Question* (Chapel Hill: University of North Carolina Press, 1997); Jane Turner Censer, *The Reconstruction of White Southern Womanhood, 1865–1895* (Baton Rouge: Louisiana State University Press, 2003); Joan Marie Johnson, *Southern Ladies, New Women: Race, Region and Clubwomen in South Carolina, 1890–1930* (Gainesville: University Press of Florida, 2004).

5. Amy McCandless, *The Past in the Present: Women's Higher Education in the Twentieth-Century South* (Tuscaloosa: University of Alabama Press, 1999), 18.

6. Johnson, *Southern Ladies, New Women*, 2–3, 27, 204–5.

7. Ernest C. Hynds, *Antebellum Athens and Clarke County, Georgia* (Athens: University of Georgia Press, 1974), 2–5, 7–8, 22; Frances Taliaferro Thomas, *A Portrait of Historic Athens & Clarke County* (Athens: University of Georgia Press, 1992), 39–40. Two institutions claim the title of the nation's "first public university": the University of Georgia received its charter in 1785, but did not accept students until 1801. The University of North Carolina, chartered in 1789, enrolled its first students in 1795.

8. Thomas, *Portrait of Athens*, 64; Barrow, "History of Lucy Cobb," 12; Photograph, c. 1893, folder 2, box 4, Mildred Lewis Rutherford Papers, Hargrett Library (hereafter Rutherford Papers).

9. Hynds, *Antebellum Athens*, 25, 29, 33. Hynds reports that $200,000 of the $284,841 invested in the country was invested in the factories. Together, the factories had 5,630 spindles and two dyeing and printing centers; p. 25.

10. Hynds, *Antebellum Athens*, 27, 30, 32, 174; Thomas, *Portrait of Athens*, 46.

11. "Substance of Remarks Made By Thomas R. R. Cobb, Esq., Before the General Assembly of Georgia, November 12th, 1860"; "Journal of the Public and Secret Proceedings of the Convention of the People of Georgia"; and "Appendix 2: Georgia in the Confederacy"; all from *The Confederate Records of the State of Georgia*, compiled and published under Authority of The Legislature by Allen D. Candler, A. M., L.L.D. Vol. 1 (Atlanta: Chas. P. Byrd, State Printer, 1909), 157–182, 214, 292–93, 748. "Genealogy," no folder, box 2, Lipscomb Family Papers, Hargrett Library; unidentified newspaper clipping on Howell Cobb, folder 15, box 30, E. M. Coulter Manuscripts, Hargrett Library (hereafter Coulter Manuscripts); Hynds, *Antebellum Athens*, 63–67; Thomas, *Portrait of Athens*, 71–78; Numan V. Bartley, *The Creation of Modern Georgia* (Athens: University of Georgia Press, 1983), 29, 45; Lewis Nicholas Wynne, *The Continuity of Cotton: Planter Politics in Georgia, 1865–1892* (Macon, Ga.: Mercer University Press, 1986), 56, 64, 102; Tom Watson Brown, "The Military Career of T.R.R. Cobb," *Georgia Historical Quarterly* 45, no. 4 (December 1961): 345–62; McCash, *Thomas R. R. Cobb*.

12. The university held its vacation in the late fall because of the high incidence of malaria in southern Georgia, the home of most students, in the summer months. Virginia Pettigrew Clare, *Thunder and Stars* (Oglethorpe, Ga.: Oglethorpe University Press, 1941), 11.

13. Clare, *Thunder and Stars*, 22, 52, 82; Womack, "Mildred Lewis Rutherford," 4; Thomas Dyer, *The University of Georgia: A Bicentennial History, 1785–1985* (Athens: University of Georgia Press, 1985), 96.

14. Clare, *Thunder and Stars*, 73–74, 89; Womack, "Mildred Lewis Rutherford," 6–7; Gaines Foster, *Ghosts of the Confederacy: Defeat, the Lost Cause, the Emergence of the New South* (New York: Oxford University Press, 1987), 38–40; LeeAnn Whites, "'Stand by Your Man': The Ladies Memorial Association and the Reconstruction of Southern White Manhood," in *Women of the American South: A Multicultural Reader*, ed. Christie Anne Farnham (New York: New York University Press, 1997), 133–49; Censer, *Reconstruction of White Southern Womanhood*, 191–203; Caroline Janney, *Burying the Dead but Not the Past: Ladies' Memorial Associations and the Lost Cause* (Chapel Hill: University of North Carolina Press, 2007).

15. Womack, "Mildred Lewis Rutherford," 14–15; Clare, *Thunder and Stars*, 99, 107–8; Thomas, *Portrait of Athens*, 101; Kenneth Coleman, *Confederate Athens* (Athens: University of Georgia Press, 1967); Joseph T. Glatthaar, *The March to the Sea and Beyond: Sherman's Troops in the Savannah and Carolinas Campaigns* (New York: New York University Press, 1985), 9. Her sense of loss comes through especially clearly in a 1926 sketch, "Memories of Christmas on a Southern Plantation," in which she described an idyllic childhood Christmas spent playing with her personal slave and indulging in rich foods. Reprinted in Spalding, *Higher Education for Women in the South*, 211–16.

16. Christie Anne Farnham, *The Education of the Southern Belle: Higher Education and Student Socialization in the Antebellum South* (New York: New York University Press, 1994), 14–17; McCandless, *The Past in the Present*.

17. Farnham, *Education of the Southern Belle*, 2–3, 17–18, 28–32.

18. Ann Short Chirhart, *Torches of Light: Georgia Teachers and the Coming of the Modern South* (Athens: University of Georgia Press, 2005), 25–27; William A. Link, *The Paradox of Southern Progressivism, 1880–1930* (Chapel Hill: University of North Carolina Press, 1992), 269–283; James L. Leloudis, *Schooling the New South: Pedagogy, Self, and Society in North Carolina, 1880–1920* (Chapel Hill: University of North Carolina Press, 1996), 23–24, 32–35, and chapter 4, especially 127–29.

19. McCash, *Thomas R. R. Cobb*, 104–5.

20. It also lost the support of Thomas Cobb, who, in 1861, after one of his daughters had a dispute with an instructor, withdrew both of his children from the school and resigned his trusteeship. McCash, *Thomas R. R. Cobb*, 108–9.

21. "Announcement of opening of Lucy Cobb Institute, 1859," folder 15, box 30, Coulter Manuscripts; Mildred Lewis Rutherford, "The Early History of the Lucy Cobb," *The Lightning Bug* (March/April 1926), 9; Barrow, "History of Lucy Cobb Institute," 13, 18; Coleman, *Confederate Athens*, 126–31. Farnham notes that these subjects were not unusual in antebellum women's education. Female academies modeled their curricula on male colleges, which emphasized the classics, and it was not considered improper for southern girls to learn Greek and Latin. *Education of the Southern Belle*, 72–73, 86 (on wax flowers).

22. Rutherford, "Early History of the Lucy Cobb," 10; Barrow, "History of Lucy Cobb Institute," 21–22; Farnham, *Education of the Southern Belle*, 65, 182.

23. "Amendment to Incorporation," Georgia Laws, 1872, Lucy Cobb Institute Stock Books. Lack of standardization meant that many more schools claimed to offer a college-level education than did so in actuality. McCandless, *The Past in the Present*, 37. See the many articles on commencement and other events collected in Lucy Cobb Scrapbook, 1858–1908, and Lucy Cobb Scrapbook, 1896–1901, box 4, Mildred Lewis Rutherford Scrapbooks, Hargrett Library (hereafter Rutherford Scrapbooks). As Jane Censer notes, after the Civil War southern newspapers routinely reported on dances, performances, and school events for young women, suggesting that postwar women accepted and even sought out public notice in ways that would have been impermissible in the antebellum era. Censer, *Reconstruction of White Southern Womanhood*, 23–24.

24. Censer, *Reconstruction of White Southern Womanhood*, 165.

25. Mary Morris Miller, "Madame Sophie Sosnowski," *Georgia Historical Quarterly* 38, no. 3 (September 1954): 249–52; Mary Harriet White, "Madame Sophie Sosnowski, Educator of Young Ladies," *Georgia Historical Quarterly* 50, no. 3 (September 1966): 283–87.

26. Two daughters died in childhood, as did a son. The eldest child, John Cobb Rutherford, became a lawyer. "Genealogy" in Lipscomb Family Papers; Mildred Lewis Rutherford, handwritten genealogy, folder 1, box 1, Rutherford Papers.

27. Rutherford, "Early History of the Lucy Cobb," 9–28; Womack, "Mildred Lewis Rutherford," 16–17; Barrow, "History of Lucy Cobb Institute," 25; Margaret Anne Moss, "Miss Millie Rutherford, Southerner," *The Georgia Review* 7, no. 1 (Spring 1953): 56–66.

28. Hazelle Beard Tuthill, "Mildred Lewis Rutherford" (MA thesis, University of South Carolina, 1929), 27 (quotation), 30; Katherine Trussell Wilson, LaGrange Trussell DuPree, and Phyllis Jenkins Barrow, comps., "Interview with Bessie Mell Lane," in Spalding, *Higher Education for Women in the South*, 266; interview with Phyllis Jenkins Barrow by author, Athens, Georgia, September 1999.

29. Rutherford, "Early History of the Lucy Cobb," 12; Tuthill, "Mildred Lewis Rutherford," 32; Womack, "Mildred Lewis Rutherford," 16–18; Clare, *Thunder and Stars*, 130–35.

30. Censer, *Reconstruction of White Southern Womanhood*, 30–41, 173–175, 180. Censer notes that many teachers barely mentioned their experience within the classroom in their correspondence; rather, they focused on their self-sufficiency, earning power, and "influence" over the next generation. This proved to be true for Rutherford as well.

31. Womack, "Mildred Lewis Rutherford," 97–99, 102.

32. Susan Marshall, *Splintered Sisterhood: Gender and Class in the Campaign against Woman Suffrage* (Madison: University of Wisconsin Press, 1997), 120–22, "barbarism" quote p. 122; Green, *Southern Strategies*, 80–91; Elizabeth Gillespie McRae, "Caretakers of Southern Civilization: Georgia Women and the Anti-Suffrage Campaign,

1914–1920," *Georgia Historical Quarterly* 82, no. 4 (Winter 1991), 801–28. Gail Bederman, *Manliness and Civilization: A Cultural History of Gender and Race in the United States, 1880–1917* (Chicago: University of Chicago Press, 1995), 23–25, discusses the link Americans made between racial hierarchy, civilization, and gender difference.

33. Farnham, *Education of the Southern Belle*, 181–82.

34. Farnham, *Education of the Southern Belle*, 127–28; 172–74.

35. Tuthill, "Mildred Lewis Rutherford," 30, 44, 49–55; Womack, "Mildred Lewis Rutherford," 26, chapter 4; Clare, *Thunder and Stars*, 172–73, 211–12; Wilson, DuPree, and Barrow, "Interview with Bessie Mell Lane," 264 (quotation). Folders 15–26, box 2 of the Mell-Rutherford Family Papers, Hargrett Library, University of Georgia, contain several letters written by Rutherford's niece Mildred Mell during a visit of Lucy Cobb students to Europe in 1910.

36. Joan Marie Johnson, *Southern Women at the Seven Sister Colleges: Feminist Values and Social Activism, 1875–1915* (Athens: University of Georgia Press, 2008), 17–20, notes the preoccupation with femininity in southern seminaries and women's colleges.

37. "Catalogue of the Lucy Cobb Institute," 1883, 12, Rare Books Collection, Hargrett Library; Rutherford, "Early History of the Lucy Cobb," 13; Mildred Lewis Rutherford, "Sketch of Lucy Cobb Institute," in H. J. Rowe, ed., *History of Athens and Clarke County* (Athens: H. L. Rowe, 1923), 75; Florida Orr, "The Lucy Cobb: Reminiscence by an 'Old Pupil,'" *Athens Banner-Watchman*, June 1887, in Lucy Cobb Institute Scrapbook, 1858–1908, box 4, Mildred Rutherford Scrapbooks.

38. Lynn Gordon, *Gender and Higher Education in the Progressive Era* (New Haven: Yale University Press, 1990), 171.

39. Clare, *Thunder and Stars*, 147, 149; Barrow, "History of Lucy Cobb Institute," 30 (quotation).

40. The 1883 catalogue shows that 36 students took instrumental music, 14 vocal music, 52 French (included in tuition for primary grades only), 9 art, and 39 elocution. Cooking, dressmaking, and portrait, oil, and china painting were also offered that year, but the catalogue does not note how many students chose to enroll in these optional (with fees) classes. "Catalogue of the Lucy Cobb Institute," 1883, 3, 7–9, 14–15; McCandless, *Past in the Present*, 30–31; Farnham, *Education of the Southern Belle*, 86–88; Censer, *Reconstruction of White Southern Womanhood*, 17–18, 64, 80–82.

41. "Catalogue of the Lucy Cobb Institute," 1883, 10–11, 15–16; "Announcement of Lucy Cobb Institute, Athens, Georgia," 1890, Lucy Cobb Institute Scrapbook, 1858–1908, box 4, Rutherford Scrapbooks.

42. Farnham, *Education of the Southern Belle*, 23, 69–73; Johnson, *Southern Women at the Seven Sisters*, 25–26. Columbia Female College, Catalogue, 1887–89, 14–23; Columbia Female College, Catalogue, 1900–1901, 54–46; Columbia Female College, Catalogue, 1910–11, 3–6, 30–39, South Caroliniana Library, University of South Carolina, Columbia; Maude Moore, "History of the College for Women, Columbia, SC," (MA thesis, University of South Carolina, 1932).

43. "Catalogue of the Lucy Cobb Institute," 1883, 10–11.

44. "Announcement of Lucy Cobb Institute," 1890.

45. Charles Morton Strahan, "The Lucy Cobb Institute" in *Clark County, Ga. and the City of Athens* (Athens, Ga.: Copyrighted by author, no publisher, 1893), 64–66 (quotation p. 65).

46. "Catalogue of the Lucy Cobb Institute," 1883, 3, 15–16; "Announcement of Lucy Cobb Institute," 1890; Rutherford, "Early Years of Lucy Cobb," 14.

47. Orr, "Reminiscence by an 'Old Pupil.'"

48. Notice for laying of cornerstone of Seney-Stovall Chapel, 12 May 1882, and "Free Concert, Seney-Stovall Chapel," 1883, file 10, box 2, Rutherford Papers; notice for concert in new chapel, 1883, folder 15, box 30, Coulter Manuscripts; untitled manuscript describing the Friends of Lucy Cobb, Lucy Cobb Institute File, Athens Heritage Foundation; Rutherford, "History of Lucy Cobb Institute," 13–14; Barrow, "History of Lucy Cobb Institute," 27–28.

49. "Catalogue of the Lucy Cobb Institute," 1883, 14; "Announcement of Lucy Cobb Institute," 1890.

50. McCandless, *The Past in the Present*, 56. The College for Women in Columbia, S.C., similarly allowed male visitors only with parental permission and during restricted hours. Moore, "History of the College for Women," 48.

51. "Announcement of Lucy Cobb Institute," 1890 (quotations); Barrow, "History of Lucy Cobb Institute," 35.

52. Shira Birnbaum, "Making Southern Belles in Progressive Era Florida: Gender in the Formal and Hidden Curriculum of the Florida Female College," *Frontiers* 16, no. 2/3 (1996): 218–46, especially 235–36.

53. Farnham, *Education of the Southern Belle*, 138.

54. Dyer, *History of the University of Georgia*, 177–78 (quotation p. 178).

55. Barrow, "History of Lucy Cobb," 31.

56. Johnson, *Southern Women at the Seven Sisters*, 18–21, 29, 34–36.

57. McCandless, *The Past in the Present*, 33–34; Birnbaum, "Making Southern Belles in Progressive Era Florida."

58. Victoria Bynum, *Unruly Women: The Politics of Social and Sexual Control in the Old South* (Chapel Hill: University of North Carolina Press, 1992), 9–10.

59. Wynne, *Continuity of Cotton*, 179–184; Bartley, *Creation of Modern Georgia*, 103–6; Thomas, *Portrait of Athens*, 103–4. This is not to say that planters and "new men" did not share political, economic, and even familial ties. See James C. Cobb, "Beyond Planters and Industrialists: A New Perspective on the New South," *Journal of Southern History* 54 (February 1988): 45–68.

60. Birnbaum, "Making Southern Belles in Progressive Era Florida," 219, 231; Pamela Dean, "Learning to Be New Women: Campus Culture at the North Carolina Normal and Industrial College," *The North Carolina Historical Review* 68, no. 3 (July 1991): 286–306.

61. Clare, *Thunder and Stars*, 141.

62. Susan E. Klepp, *Revolutionary Conceptions: Women, Fertility, and Family Limitation in America, 1760–1820* (Chapel Hill: University of North Carolina Press, 2009);

Margaret A. Nash, *Women's Education in the United States, 1780–1840* (New York: Palgrave Macmillan, 2005); Bonnie Laughlin Schultz, "Introduction" to *How Did Susanna Rowson and Other Reformers Promote Higher Education as an Antidote to Women's Sexual Vulnerability, 1780–1820?*, ed. Schultz, in Kathryn Kish Sklar and Thomas Dublin, eds., *Women and Social Movements in the United States, 1600–2000*.

63. Helen Lefkowitz Horowitz, *Alma Mater: Design and Experience in the Women's Colleges from Their Nineteenth Century Beginnings to the 1930s* (Amherst: University of Massachusetts Press, 1993 [second edition]); 65–66, 166–67.

64. Mildred Rutherford Mell to Rosa Smith, May 31, 1910, and June 10, 1910, folder 17, box 2, Mell-Rutherford family papers; diary, (Mary) Edna Pope, March 11, 1893, file 1, box 1, Friends of Lucy Cobb and Seney-Stovall Collection, Hargrett Library.

65. Rufus B. Spain, *At Ease in Zion: A Social History of Southern Baptists, 1865–1900* (Tuscaloosa: The University of Alabama Press, 2003 [Vanderbilt University Press, 1967]), 198–208; Paul Harvey, *Redeeming the South: Religious Cultures and Racial Identities among Southern Baptists, 1865–1925* (Chapel Hill: University of North Carolina Press, 1997), 86–88.

66. "Lucy Cobb Institute Annual Announcement, 1902–1903," 17, 44–45, Rare Books Collection, Hargrett Library; Mildred Lewis Rutherford, *Bible Questions With Reference in the Old Testament* (Athens, Ga.: MacGregor Co. [?], 1890); Tuthill, "Mildred Lewis Rutherford," 44; Clare, *Thunder and Stars*, 141, 143; Barrow, "History of Lucy Cobb Institute," 27.

67. Rutherford, *Bible Questions*; Mildred Lewis Rutherford, *English Authors: A Handbook of English Literature from Chaucer to Living Writers* (Atlanta: Constitutional Book Company, 1890); Mildred Lewis Rutherford, *American Authors* (Atlanta: Franklin Printing and Publishing Co., 1894); Mildred Lewis Rutherford, *French Authors* (Atlanta: Franklin Printing and Publishing Co., 1906); Mildred Lewis Rutherford, *The South in History and Literature: A Hand-book of Southern Authors from the Settlement of Jamestown, 1607, to Living Writers* (Atlanta: Franklin Printing and Publishing Co., 1906).

68. Farnham, *Education of the Southern Belle*, 45–46.

69. Rutherford, *English Authors*, 36–37 (third quotation p. 36), 149 (first quotation), 411 (second quotation); Womack, "Mildred Lewis Rutherford," 31–35.

70. Rutherford, *American Authors*, 14–15, 79–85, 108–18.

71. Womack, "Mildred Lewis Rutherford," 42–44.

72. "Report of State Historian, Mildred Rutherford, Athens, Ga.," n.d.; Mildred Rutherford, State Historian, and Lillian Martin, Assistant State Historian, "Letter to All Chapter Historians, Georgia Division, U.D.C."; all in folder 4, box 4, Mildred Lewis Rutherford Papers; Rutherford, "Life Sketch of Miss Mildred Rutherford," 105–6; Womack, "Mildred Lewis Rutherford," 7, 73–74.

73. Mary B. Poppenheim, et al., *The History of the United Daughters of the Confederacy* (3 volumes in 2; Raleigh, N.C.: Edwards and Broughton Co., 1956), I, 1–12; Foster, *Ghosts of the Confederacy*, 172–74; Angie Parrott, "'Love Makes Memory Eternal': The United Daughters of the Confederacy in Richmond, Virginia 1897–1920," in Edward

L. Ayers and John C. Willis, eds., *The Edge of the South: Life in Nineteenth Century Virginia* (Charlottesville: University of Virginia Press, 1991), 219–238; Karen L. Cox, *Dixie's Daughters: The United Daughters of the Confederacy and the Preservation of Southern Culture* (Gainesville: University Press of Florida, 2003); Sarah E. Gardner, *Blood and Irony: Southern White Women's Narratives of the Civil War, 1861–1937* (Chapel Hill: University of North Carolina Press, 2004); Francesca Morgan, *Women and Patriotism in Jim Crow America* (Chapel Hill: University of North Carolina Press, 2005).

74. Gardner, *Blood and Irony*, 4, 157–58; Johnson, *Southern Ladies, New Women*, 32–38.

75. Cox, *Dixie's Daughters*.

76. Jennie Smith, "Lucy Cobb Institute," folder 1, box 1, Lucy Cobb Institute Collection, Hargrett Library; Mildred Lewis Rutherford, *What the South May Claim* (Athens, Ga.: McGregor Co., 1916 [?]), 37, 42; Womack, "Mildred Lewis Rutherford," 85, 93, 104; Fred Arthur Bailey, "Mildred Lewis Rutherford and the Patrician Cult of the Old South," *Georgia Historical Quarterly* 77 (Fall 1994): 509–35; Gardner, *Blood and Irony*, 125–26, 162–64.

77. Mildred Lewis Rutherford, "The South in the Building of the Nation" (1912), "Thirteen Periods of United States History" (1912), "Wrongs of History Righted" (1914), and "Historical Sins of Omission and Commission" (1915), in Mildred Lewis Rutherford, *Four Addresses by Mildred Lewis Rutherford* (Birmingham, Ala.: Mildred Lewis Rutherford Historical Circle Printers, 1922); Mildred Lewis Rutherford, *The Civilization of the Old South: What Made It; What Destroyed It; What Has Replaced It* (Athens, Ga.: McGregor Co., 1917); Mildred Lewis Rutherford, *Truths of History: A Fair, Unbiased, Impartial, Unprejudiced, and Conscientious Study of History* (Athens, Ga.: McGregor Co., n.d.); Mildred Lewis Rutherford, *The South Must Have Her Rightful Place in History* (Athens, Ga.: McGregor Co., 1923).

78. Rutherford, "The South in the Building of the Nation," 7–9; Rutherford, "Wrongs of History Righted," 49–51; Rutherford, *Civilization of the Old South*, especially 6–17; Mildred Lewis Rutherford, "Memories of Christmas on a Southern Plantation"; Spalding, *Higher Education in the South*, 211–16. The interest of the UDC in southern soldiers' heroism during its first decade is documented in Poppenheim, et al., *History of the United Daughters*, I, 26, 30; Rowland, "Work of Southern Women," 169; Johnson, *Southern Ladies*, 38–42.

79. Rutherford, "Historical Sins," 113 (quotation); Rutherford, "Wrongs of History Righted," especially 49–50; Rutherford, *Truths of History*, 1–7.

80. Rutherford, *Civilization of the Old South*, 6–7, 30–31, 33; Rutherford, *The South Must Have Her Rightful Place in History*, 18–19; Rutherford, "Memories of Christmas," 213, 216.

81. Rutherford, *What the South May Claim*, 17; Rutherford, "Historical Sins," 108–111; Rutherford, *Truths of History*, 19–21.

82. Rutherford, *Civilization of the Old South*, 7 (first quotation), 15, 40–42 (second quotation on p. 40). This kind of sentimental style characterized UDC histories

in general, and members resisted the new idea of scientific objectivity in history. Gardner, *Blood and Irony*, 120–23.

83. Rutherford, "Thirteen Periods," 40; Rutherford, *Civilization of the Old South*, 42.

84. Bederman, *Manliness and Civilization*, 159–61.

85. Rutherford, *Civilization of the Old South*, 39–40. UDC members across the South expressed views similar to Rutherford's in the 1915 essay contest, "Women of the Confederacy." Some of the essays are collected in the Mildred Rutherford Notebooks, Vol. XL: "Women of the Confederacy," United Daughters of the Confederacy Collection, American Civil War Museum, Richmond, VA.

86. "Lecture Talks by Miss Rutherford"; Womack, "Mildred Lewis Rutherford," 85–86, 91, 97, 102; Bailey, "Mildred Lewis Rutherford"; Marshall, *Splintered Sisterhood*, 109–23; Green, *Southern Strategies*, 40, 83–85.

87. Green, *Southern Strategies*, 63.

88. Grace Elizabeth Hale, "'Some Women Have Never Been Reconstructed': Mildred L. Rutherford, Lucy M. Stanton, and the Racial Politics of White Southern Womanhood, 1900–1930," in *Georgia in Black and White*, ed. John Inscoe (Athens: University of Georgia Press, 1994), 173–201, especially 179. Rutherford's views of African Americans' and women's social places are part of a hierarchical worldview; Elna Green labeled this interconnectedness as a "triangular structure" of society in which hierarchies of race, class, and gender reinforced and were dependent on each other. Green, *Southern Strategies*, 90.

89. Green, *Southern Strategies*; McRae, "Caretakers of Southern Civilization," 803–4.

90. McRae, "Caretakers of Southern Civilization," quotation p. 806; LeeAnn Whites, "Rebecca Latimer Felton: The Problem of Protection in the New South," in *Visible Women: New Essays on American Activism*, eds. Nancy A. Hewitt and Suzanne Lebsock (Urbana: University of Illinois Press, 1993), 41–61.

91. Accusing suffragists of sexual immodesty and abandonment of womanly virtue was a standard weapon used against woman suffrage. Camhi, *Women Against Women*, 64–65; Andrea Moore Keer, "White Women's Rights, Black Men's Wrongs, Free Love, Blackmail, and the Formation of the American Woman Suffrage Association," in Marjorie Spruill Wheeler, ed., *One Woman, One Vote: Rediscovering the Woman Suffrage Movement* (Troutdale, Ore.: NewSage Press, 1995), 61–79, especially 73–74; Susan Marshall, *Splintered Sisterhood: Gender and Class in the Campaign against Woman Suffrage* (Madison: University of Wisconsin Press, 1997), 121, 191.

92. Green, *Southern Strategies*, 87–91; Williamson, *Rage for Order*, 186–191 (quotation on p. 188); Glenda Gilmore, *Gender and Jim Crow: Women and the Politics of White Supremacy in North Carolina, 1896–1920* (Chapel Hill: University of North Carolina Press, 1996), 95–99.

93. Harold H. Martin, *Georgia: A Bicentennial History* (Nashville, Tenn.: American Association for State and Local History, 1977) 144–46; Numan V. Bartley, *The Creation of Modern Georgia* (Athens: University of Georgia Press, 1983), 151–53; Williamson,

Rage for Order, 141–151, especially 150; Gregory Mixon, *The Atlanta Riot: Race, Class, and Violence in a New South City* (Gainesville: University Press of Florida, 2005). In research done for his walking tour of the Atlanta Race Riot, Clifford Kuhn found evidence that the death toll has been underestimated and was at least three dozen and probably much higher. 1906 Race Riot Tour, Atlanta, Georgia (author took the tour in 2014).

94. Smith married "Birdie" Cobb, Lucy Cobb's sister. He helped raise money for the Lucy Cobb Institute during its endowment campaign in 1925 and became a board member in 1926. Lamar Rutherford Lipscomb to Hoke Smith, 23 March 1925; Hoke Smith to Mildred Rutherford, 25 March 1925; Mildred Rutherford to Hoke Smith, 20 April 1925; Billups Phinizy to Hoke Smith, 15 April 1926; all in folder 15, box 30, Coulter Manuscripts, Hargrett Library; Dewey W. Grantham, *Hoke Smith and the Politics of the New South* (Baton Rouge: Louisiana State University Press, 1956).

95. Grace Elizabeth Hale, *Making Whiteness: The Culture of Segregation in the South, 1890–1940* (New York: Random House, 1998); Johnson, *Southern Ladies, New Women*, 205.

96. Sarah H. Case, "Confederate Historian's New South Creed," *Journal of Southern History* (August 2002), 599–628.

97. John E. Drewry, "Some of Our Lucy Cobb Girls," *The Lightning Bug* (November 1925), 44–45; John E. Drewry, "Some of Our Lucy Cobb Girls" and "The Old Fashioned Women, Atlanta, Ga.," *The Lightning Bug* (January 1926), 36–37; scrapbook of clippings (including marriage announcements), Lucy Cobb Alumnae Association, box 4, Lucy Cobb Institute Collection, Hargrett Library; *Women of Georgia: A Ready and Accurate Reference Book for Newspapers and Librarian[s]* (Atlanta: Georgia Press Reference Association, 1927), 39, 67, 124, 137, 150–51, 155, 156, 127.

98. Clare, *Thunder and Stars*, 11, 21; Thomas, *Portrait of Athens*, 46; Rutherford, handwritten note tracing her genealogy; Rutherford, "Early History of the Lucy Cobb," 16; Bessie Mell Lane, "Mildred Rutherford Mell (1889–1982)," in Spalding, *Higher Education for Women in the South*, 257.

99. Barrow, "History of Lucy Cobb," 31, quotation; Lamar Rutherford Lipscomb, "Pranks of Miss Millie," in *Essays Wise and Otherwise* ([Atlanta?]: Mildred Seydel Publishing, 1957), 68–74; Clare, *Thunder and Stars*.

100. Anne Bates Windship, memorial letter, 1928, folder 1, box 1, Rutherford Papers; "Letters from H + H," folder 1, box 1, Rutherford Papers; "Miss Mildred Rutherford Paid Tributes By Former Lucy Cobb Girls," unidentified newspaper clipping, 1928, folder 3, box 4, Rutherford Papers; "Athens Remembers," *Athens Banner-Herald*, n.d., folder 3, box 1, Rutherford Scrapbooks; Wilson, DuPree, and Barrow, comps., "Interview with Bessie Mell Lane," 266.

101. "Outline of Work, 1908–1909, Mildred Rutherford Literary Society, State Normal School, Athens, Georgia"; "Bulletin of the University of Georgia, The State Normal School, 1911," 24; and "Mildred Rutherford Society, 1916–1917, State Normal School, Athens, Georgia"; all in box 1, State Normal School Records, Administrative

Subject Folder, Senior Essays and Microfilm, 1904–33, University Archives, Hargrett Library.

102. Lipscomb, "Pranks of Miss Millie," 69.

103. Mildred Rutherford to Edna Pope, Aug. 16, 1892, and diary, (Mary) Edna Pope. Quote from March 11 entry.

104. Diary, (Mary) Edna Pope, March 11, April 25, April 30 (quotation), "Saturday" [in May], June 28, July 11.

105. The fact that several of these survive as part of family collections at the University of Georgia attests to their significance to the alumnae.

106. Irene Felker Scrapbook, Hargrett Library.

107. Sarah A. McElmurray Scrapbook, Hargrett Library.

108. "Lizzie Carither's Diary, 1892," box 3, Harden-Jackson-Carithers Collection, Hargrett Library. See for example entries for January 12, June 15, September 11, October 20, and November 7.

109. "Miss Rutherford's Scrap book," box 3, Harden-Jackson-Carithers Collection, Hargrett Library.

110. Orr, "Reminiscences by an 'Old Pupil'"; Evangeline Bower to Papa [1894], folder 7, box 1, Bower Family Papers, Hargrett Library.

111. Clare, *Thunder and Stars*, 222–23. Clare also gave the example that rather than ordering her students to wipe off their shoes before entering the school, Rutherford scrubbed the floor on her hands and knees, thus embarrassing the girls and ensuring that they cleaned off their shoes. Clare, *Thunder and Stars*, 143.

112. "Death of Professor Frank A. Lipscomb" [March 1874], unidentified newspaper clipping, Frank A. Lipscomb file, box 69, Georgiana Vertical Files: Biographical, Hargrett Library; Tuthill, "Mildred Lewis Rutherford," 18; Rutherford, "Early History of Lucy Cobb," 16; Barrow, "History of the Lucy Cobb Institute," 33; Dyer, *History of the University of Georgia*, 99–100.

113. "Athens Woman's Club," folder 1; Mrs. P. B. Parker to M. A. Lipscomb, February 27, 1913, folder 5; Parker to Lipscomb, March 14, 1913, folder 5; all in box 1, Lipscomb Family Papers, Hargrett Library; "Local Notes," *Lucy Cobb Magazine* (1) January 1907, (1): 28; Georgia Federation of Women's Clubs Yearbook 1906–07, 4–15, Georgia Federation of Women's Clubs Collection, Georgia State Archives, Atlanta, Georgia; "Women's Club News in Georgia," *The Atlanta Constitution*, April 7, 1907, "Georgia Women Fighting the Convict Lease," *New York Times*, September 6, 1908; Mrs. M.A. Lipscomb, "A Greeting to the Georgia Federation," *Atlanta Constitution* January 12, 1908, all in Scrapbook, Georgia Federation of Women's Clubs Collection, Georgia State Archives.

114. Carol Stevens Hancock, *The Light in the Mountains: A History of Tallulah Falls School* (Toccoa, Ga.: Commercial Printing Company), 1975; "Tallulah Falls Industrial School Formally Dedicated on Wednesday," *Atlanta Constitution*, July 4, 1909, Scrapbook, Georgia Federation of Women's Clubs Collection, Georgia State Archives.

115. Robyn Muncy, *Creating a Female Dominion in American Reform, 1890–1935* (New York: Oxford University Press, 1991); Theda Skocpol, *Protecting Soldiers and Mothers: The Political Origins of Social Policy in the United States* (Cambridge, Mass.:

Belknap Press of Harvard University Press, 1992); Kathryn Kish Sklar, "The Historical Foundations of a Women's Power in the Creation of the American Welfare State, 1830–1930," in Seth Koven and Sonya Michel, eds., *Mothers of a New World: Maternalist Politics and the Origins of Welfare States* (New York: Routledge, 1993), 43–93; Molly Ladd-Taylor, *Mother-work: Women, Child Welfare, and the State, 1890–1930* (Urbana: University of Illinois Press, 1994); Linda Gordon, *Pitied But Not Entitled: Single Mothers and the History of Welfare, 1890–1935* (Cambridge, Mass.: Harvard University Press, 1994); Gwendolyn Mink, *Wages of Motherhood: Inequality in the Welfare State, 1917–1942* (Ithaca: Cornell University Press, 1995).

116. "Address of Mrs. M. A. Lipscomb, President of the Georgia Federation of Women's Clubs, at Valdosta," Georgia Federation of Women's Clubs Annual Report 1908, 15, Georgia Federation of Women's Clubs Collection, Georgia State Archives.

117. J. Morgan Kousser, "Progressivism—For Middle-Class Whites Only: North Carolina Education, 1880–1910," *Journal of Southern History* 46, no. 2 (May 1980): 169–94; C. Vann Woodward, *Origins of the New South, 1877–1913* (Baton Rouge: Louisiana State University Press, 1951). Kathleen Blee analyzes the mix of support for both white supremacy and gender equality among members of the Women's KKK. Blee, *Women of the Klan: Racism and Gender in the 1920s* (Berkeley: University of California Press, 1991).

118. Birnbaum, "Making Southern Belles in Progressive Era Florida," 219.

119. "Address of Mrs. M. A. Lipscomb, President of the Georgia Federation of Women's Clubs, at Valdosta," 12.

120. Clipping, "Compensation for Freed Slaves" [*Atlanta Daily Chronicle* ??], folder 2, box 1, Lipscomb Family Papers, Hargrett Library. While president of the Athens Woman's Club Lipscomb held joint meetings between the local UDC and the AWC to discuss the creation of the Winnie Davis (daughter of Confederate president Jefferson Davis) memorial and other activities. Athens Woman's Club minutes, 1899–1911, p. 8, 35, 53, 72, insert 13, Heritage Room, Athens-Clarke County Library, Athens, Georgia (http://dlg.galileo.usg.edu/athenswomansclub/awc001.php).

121. "Address of Mrs. M. A. Lipscomb, President of the Georgia Federation of Women's Clubs, at Valdosta," 13.

122. Both a disenfranchisement bill and abolition of convict lease occurred during his governorship and with his support. Dewey W. Grantham Jr., *Hoke Smith and the Politics of the New South* (Baton Rouge: Louisiana University Press, 1967 [1958]), 23, 158–62, 173–74; Holmes, "Part Five: 1890–1940" in Coleman, ed., *A History of Georgia*, 286. On the centrality of the convict lease system to the South's postwar economy, see Matthew J. Mancini, *One Dies, Get Another: Convict Leasing in the American South, 1866–1928* (Columbia: University of South Carolina Press, 1996); David M. Oshinsky, *Worse than Slavery: Parchment Farm and the Ordeal of Jim Crow Justice* (New York: Free Press, 1996).

123. Laurel Thatcher Ulrich, "'A Quilt unlike Any Other': Rediscovering the Work of Harriet Powers," in *Writing Women's History: A Tribute to Anne Firor Scott*, ed. Elizabeth Anne Payne (Jackson: University Press of Mississippi, 2011), 99.

124. Although accounts suggest that Dot stayed with Rutherford until her death in 1910, a letter from 1905 suggests that she had left Athens to live with her daughter in Malden, Massachusetts. The letter questions the myth of "Aunt Dot" in several ways—it is well written, indicating fluent literacy; it is affectionate, but not fawning; and it contradicts the story that Dot never left the Rutherford family. Dot to "My dear 'Miss Mary Ann,'" October 23, 1905, Friends of Lucy Cobb and Seney-Stovall Collection, folder 4, box 1. Rutherford's biographer suggests that Dot went to Massachusetts to visit her children but unexpectedly died on the trip—however, the five-year lag between the letter and her death suggests otherwise (unless she made several trips to the Boston area). Clare, *Thunder and Stars*, 210.

125. Orr, "Reminiscences by an 'Old Pupil'" (first quotation); "A Word to the Alumnae of Lucy Cobb and to the Citizens of Athens," 2, folder 9, box 2, Rutherford Papers (second quotation); D. G. Bickers, "The Spirit of Lucy Cobb" [reprinted from "Introduction to Lucy Cobb," *Athens Banner-Herald*, September 19, 1917], in "Lucy Cobb Institute Sixty-Sixth Annual Announcement, 1858–1923," 1923, 10–12, Rare Books Collection, Hargrett Library; Barrow, "Higher Education," 29; Clare, *Thunder and Stars*, 107, 205.

126. Hale, *Making Whiteness*.

127. June O. Patton, "Moonlight and Magnolias in Southern Education: The Black Mammy Memorial Institute," *Journal of Negro History* 65, no. 2 (Spring 1980): 149–55.

128. Patton, "Moonlight and Magnolias," 153–54.

129. M. A. Lipscomb, "Duty of Anglo-American Women in Times of Threatened Hostility," *Lucy Cobb Magazine* (June 1906): 161–70 (quotation 165).

130. Henry Shapiro, *Appalachia on Our Mind: The Southern Mountains and Mountaineers in the American Consciousness, 1870–1920* (Chapel Hill: University of North Carolina Press, 1978); T. J. Jackson Lears, *No Place of Grace: Antimodernism and the Transformation of American Culture, 1880–1920* (New York: Pantheon Books, 1981); David E. Whisnant, *All That Is Native and Fine: The Politics of Culture in an American Region* (Chapel Hill: University of North Carolina Press, 1983); Allan Batteau, *The Invention of Appalachia* (Tucson: University of Arizona Press, 1990); Deborah L. Blackwell, "The Ability to "Do Much Larger Work': Gender and Reform in Appalachia" (PhD dissertation, University of Kentucky, 1998); Jane S. Becker, *Selling Tradition: Appalachia and the Construction of an American Folk, 1930–1940* (Chapel Hill: University of North Carolina Press, 1998); Sarah Case, "Katherine Pettit and May Stone: The Cultural Politics of Mountain Reform," in *Kentucky Women: Their Lives and Times,* ed. Melissa McEuen and Tom Appleton (Athens: University of Georgia Press, 2015).

131. Unidentified newspaper clipping [1896?], Lucy Cobb Institute Scrapbook, n.d., box 4, Rutherford Scrapbooks.

132. "Lucy Cobb Institute Opened Yesterday," *Athens Weekly-Banner*, September 15, 1905, Lucy Cobb Institute File, Athens-Clarke County Library; "Lucy Cobb Institute Annual Announcement, 1902–1903," 4.

133. "To Make Improvements. Lucy Cobb Teachers Start a Subscription," unidentified newspaper clipping [1895], Lucy Cobb Institute Scrapbook, 1858–1908, box 4,

Rutherford Scrapbooks (quotation); "Lucy Cobb Institute Annual Announcement, 1904–1905," 37–38, Rare Books Collection, Hargrett Library.

134. Rutherford, "Early History of the Lucy Cobb," 16; Barrow, "History of Lucy Cobb Institute," 33–34, 49.

135. "Lucy Cobb Institute Annual Announcement, 1902–1903," 5, 11–26; *Nods and Becks*, 1899, 13.

136. "Lucy Cobb Institute Annual Announcement, 1902–1903," 13–14 (quotation p. 13).

137. Nov. 7, 1892, entry, Lizzie Carither's Diary.

138. "They had their April Joke, and Will be Sent Home from the Lucy Cobb Institute To-Day," *New York Times*, April 2, 1897; Ralph T. Jones, "Athens Man Recalls Exciting April 1, 1897, When 18 Lucy Cobb Girls Ran Away as a Joke," unidentified newspaper clipping, Lucy Cobb Institute Scrapbook, 1858–1908, box 4, Rutherford Scrapbooks.

139. Gordon Bower to "My dear father," 11 January 1897, folder 10, box 1, Bower Family Papers, Hargrett Library. Bower's brother had been arrested in a similar incident four years earlier. Newspaper clippings, folder 6, box 1, Bower Family Papers.

140. "The Lucy Cobb from my standpoint," unidentified newspaper clipping, Lucy Cobb Institute Scrapbook 1858–1908, box 4, Rutherford Scrapbooks.

141. Farnham, *Education of the Southern Belle*, 139–40.

142. "Thirteen blondes and thirteen brunettes graduate from Lucy Cobb Institute," unidentified newspaper clipping, n.d., Lucy Cobb Institute Scrapbook, 1858–1908, Rutherford Scrapbooks.

143. D. G. Bickers, "Spirit of Lucy Cobb," 10 (first quotation), 11 (second quotation).

144. Strahan, "The Lucy Cobb Institute," 66; "Lucy Cobb to Open Its 60th Session Today" [Sept. 19, 1917], unidentified newspaper clipping, Athens-Clarke County Heritage Foundation; "Constitutionals. General Gossip and Editorial Short Stops Caught on the Run," *Atlanta Constitution*, n.d., Lucy Cobb Institute Scrapbook, 1858–1908, box 4, Rutherford Scrapbooks (quotations). See also other clippings collected in the Lucy Cobb Institute Scrapbook, 1858–1908.

Chapter 2. Clubwomen, Educators, and a Congresswoman

1. *Nods and Becks*, 1903, 37–39; *Nods and Becks*, 1905, 26–28; *Lucy Cobb Magazine*, June 1906, 184–87; Lucile Peacock, "Athens Girls Who Graduated at Lucy Cobb: With the Class Prophecy of the Class of 1911 by Its Own Historian," *Athens Banner*, June 4, 1911, folder 9, box 1, Rutherford Papers.

2. *Nods and Becks*, 1899; "Lucy Cobb Annual 'Nods and Becks,'" unidentified newspaper clipping, Lucy Cobb Institute Scrapbook, n.d., box 4, Rutherford Scrapbooks.

3. *Nods and Becks*, 1902; *Lucy Cobb Magazine*, June 1905, 203. On the significance of the YWCA, see Nancy Marie Robertson, *Christian Sisterhood, Race Relations, and the YWCA, 1906–46* (Urbana: University of Illinois Press, 2007).

4. Scrapbook of clippings, Lucy Cobb Alumnae Association, box 4, Lucy Cobb Institute Collection, Hargrett Library; *Women of Georgia: A Ready and Accurate*

Reference Book for Newspapers and Librarian[s] (Atlanta: Georgia Press Reference Association, 1927), 39, 67, 124, 137, 150–51, 155, 156, 127.

5. *Minutes of the Fourth Annual Meeting of the United Daughters of the Confederacy, Nov. 10–12, 1897* (Nashville, Tenn.: Press of Foster and Webb, 1898), 74.

6. Lucy Cobb Alumnae Association, handwritten minutes, June 2, 1924, folder 2, box 1, Lipscomb-Lucy Cobb Institute Collection, Hargrett Library.

7. Frances Taliaferro Thomas, *A Portrait of Historic Athens & Clarke County* (Athens: University of Georgia Press, 1992), 149; list of Athens Chapter, UDC (chartered 1896), folder 4, box 4, Mildred Lewis Rutherford Papers; letter to "Dear Alumnae," n.d., and sections of Minute book of the L.C.I. Alumnae Association, 1902, folder 2, box 1, Lipscomb-Lucy Cobb Institute Collection.

8. Untitled newspaper clipping [1895], folder 2, box 1, Lucy Cobb Institute Collection.

9. The daughter of Nellie and Billups Phinizy, Martha (known as Mattie Sue), graduated from Lucy Cobb in 1908 and then married LeRoy Pratt Percy in 1915 and had Walker Percy in 1916. LeRoy Percy died in 1929 of suicide, Mattie Sue two years later in an auto accident suspected of also being a suicide. Zella Armstrong, Janie Preston Collup French, *Notable Southern Families* (Chattanooga, Tenn.: Lookout Publishing Co., 1918), 170; "Walker Percy Is Dead at 74; A Novelist of the New South," *New York Times*, May 11, 1990; Patrick H. Samway, *Walker Percy, A Life* (Farrar, Straus and Giroux, 1997), accessed online, http://www.nytimes.com/books/first/s/samway-percy.html; Alumnae List (from Spalding, *Higher Education*), 129; H. M. Gelfand, "Phinizy Spalding (1930–1994)," *New Georgia Encyclopedia*, http://www.georgiaencyclopedia.org/articles/history-archaeology/phinizy-spalding-1930–1994; Harvey H. Jackson III, "Billups Phinizy Spalding: A Tribute," *Georgia Historical Quarterly* 78 (Fall 1994) [pages unnumbered].

10. Jane Turner Censer, *The Reconstruction of White Southern Womanhood, 1865–1895* (Baton Rouge: Louisiana State University Press, 2003), 170–71.

11. Shira Birnbaum, "Making Southern Belles in Progressive Era Florida: Gender in the Formal and Hidden Curriculum of the Florida Female College," *Frontiers* 16, no. 2/3 (1996): 218–46.

12. Jno. C. Whitner, "Woman: God-made. Her true culture, and her sphere of work" [commencement address], Lucy Cobb Institute, Athens, Georgia, 17 June 1885, pamphlet in Lucy Cobb Institute Scrapbook, 1858–1908, box 4, Rutherford Scrapbooks.

13. James Leloudis, *Schooling the New South: Pedagogy, Self, and Society in North Carolina, 1880–1920* (Chapel Hill: University of North Carolina Press, 1996); Ann Short Chirhart, *Torches of Light: Georgia Teachers and the Coming of the New South* (Athens: University of Georgia Press, 2005); Rebecca S. Montgomery, *The Politics of Education in the New South: Women and Reform in Georgia, 1890–1930* (Baton Rouge: Louisiana State University Press, 2006); Pamela Dean, "Learning to Be New Women: Campus Culture at the North Carolina Normal and Industrial College," *The North Carolina Historical Review* 68, no. 3 (July 1991): 286–306.

14. On Breckinridge see Joan Marie Johnson, *Southern Women at the Seven Sister Colleges: Feminist Values and Social Activism, 1875–1915* (Athens: University of Georgia Press, 2008), 109–10, 128–31; Anya Jabour, "Sophonisba Preston Breckinridge: Homegrown Heroine," in *Kentucky Women: Their Lives and Times*, ed. Melissa McEuen and Thomas H. Appleton Jr. (Athens: University of Georgia Press, 2015), 140–67.

15. Historians of southern women often suggest that very few women, especially women of the elite, worked. Although Lucy Cobb did not keep statistics on alumnae employment, individual accounts of alumnae suggest higher numbers of employment than normally assumed. Many if not most of these women worked temporarily or casually, and may not have self-identified as "career" women or even as employed.

16. Christie Anne Farnham, *The Education of the Southern Belle: Higher Education and Student Socialization in the Antebellum South* (New York: New York University Press, 1994), 97–98.

17. *Lucy Cobb Magazine*, December 1905, January 1907, 29, and June 1907, 61; unidentified newspaper clipping, June 1907, folder 15, box 30, Coulter Manuscripts, Hargrett Library.

18. Rutherford, "Early History of the Lucy Cobb," 12.

19. Mildred Rutherford spent forty-eight years at Lucy Cobb, Mary Ann eighteen, Bessie three years before she married, and Lollie only one, in the Domestic Science Department. List of Faculty, Lucy Cobb Institute File, Athens-Clarke County Heritage Foundation, Athens, Georgia (hereafter cited as Athens Heritage Foundation).

20. Newspaper clipping, "Rosa Woodberry Taken by Death," n.d., scrapbook, Lucy Cobb Alumnae Association, Lucy Cobb Institute Collection, box 4; "Alumnae List," in *Higher Education for Women in the South: A History of Lucy Cobb Institute, 1858–1994*, comp. and ed. Phinizy Spalding (Athens, Ga.: Georgia Southern Press, 1994), 17; List of Faculty, Lucy Cobb Institute File, Athens Heritage Foundation (indicates that she taught at Lucy Cobb 1899–1904).

21. Montgomery, *Politics of Education*, 47.

22. Several obituaries name her as the first female student at the University of Georgia. See the following newspaper clippings: "Rosa Woodberry Taken by Death" [1932]; "Federated Church Women Pay Tribute to Miss Rosa Woodberry," 1932; Mrs. F. R. Graham, "Federated Church Women Pay Tribute to Miss Rosa Woodberry" [1932]; "Miss Rosa Woodberry" [1932]; all in scrapbook, Lucy Cobb Alumnae Association, box 4, Lucy Cobb Institute Collection. Also "Miss Rosa Woodberry Dies: Southern Educator," *New York Times*, July 20, 1932.

23. Newspaper clipping, "Rosa Woodberry Taken by Death" [1932].

24. "For Lucy Cobb Educational Fund," file 2, box 1, Lucy Cobb Institute Collection.

25. Newspaper clipping, "Miss Rosa Woodberry."

26. "Rosa Woodberry Taken by Death"; "Federated Church Women Pay Tribute to Miss Rosa Woodberry," 1932; Mrs. F. R. Graham, "Federated Church Women Pay Tribute to Miss Rosa Woodberry"; "Miss Rosa Woodberry."

27. Obituary of Jennie Smith, *Athens Banner*, March 17, 1946, file 1, box 1, Jennie Smith Papers, Hargrett Library.

28. Phyllis Jenkins Barrow, "History of Lucy Cobb Institute, 1858–1950" (MA thesis, University of Georgia, 1951); reprinted in Spalding, comp. and ed., *Higher Education for Women in the South*, 44–45; Bessie Mell Lane, "Miss Jennie Smith and Lucy Cobb," in Spalding, *Higher Education*, 273–75.

29. Laurel Thatcher Ulrich, "'A Quilt unlike Any Other': Rediscovering the Work of Harriet Powers," in *Writing Women's History: A Tribute to Anne Firor Scott*, ed. Elizabeth Anne Payne (Jackson: University Press of Mississippi, 2011), 82–116; Catherine L. Holmes, "The Darling Offspring of her Brain: The Quilts of Harriet Powers," in *Georgia Quilts: Piecing Together a History*, ed. Anita Zaleski Weinraub (Athens: University of Georgia Press, 2006); "Harriet Powers's Bible Quilt," Treasures of American History online exhibition, National Museum of American History, http://american-history.si.edu/treasures.

30. Ulrich, "'A Quilt unlike Any Other,'" 86, 90–91.

31. Ulrich, "'A Quilt unlike Any Other,'" 87–88, 96, 100.

32. Ulrich, "'A Quilt unlike Any Other,'" 102–4; Theda Perdue, *Race and the Atlanta Cotton States Exposition of 1895* (Athens: University of Georgia Press, 2010).

33. Lane, "Miss Jennie Smith," 274; newspaper clipping and program, "Lucy Cobb Day, Alumnae Reunion, Cotton States and International Exposition, Auditorium Hall, Friday, Nov. 29th, 1895, 11am, Atlanta," folder 2, box 1, Lucy Cobb Institute Collection; Ulrich, "A Quilt Unlike Any Other," 99.

34. Johnson, *Southern Women at the Seven Sister Colleges*, 137; Gordon, *Gender and Higher Education*, 169.

35. James B. Nevins, ed., *Prominent Women of Georgia* (Atlanta: National Biographical Publishers, [1928?]), 63, 163; "Moina Michael, 74, Founded Poppy Day," *New York Times*, May 11, 1944; Alexander Watson, "A Holiday to End all Wars," *New York Times*, November 11, 2008; "Where did the idea to sell poppies come from?" *BBC News Magazine,* November 10, 2006, http://news.bbc.co.uk/2/hi/uk_news/magazine/6133312.stm.

36. Barrow, "History of Lucy Cobb Institute," 50; Thomas Dyer, *The University of Georgia: A Bicentennial History, 1785–1985* (Athens: University of Georgia Press, 1985), 179, 193; "Local Alumnae, Published by the Local Alumnae Association," 1919, folder 11, box 1, Mildred Lewis Rutherford Papers.

37. Lucy Cobb Institute Catalogue, 1918–19.

38. Or, more accurately, recognition for their training; Gerdine and Woodbury were among the women who took summer school courses and unofficial private lessons from university faculty, but could not get those courses to count towards a university degree. Sara Bertha Townsend, "The Admission of Women to the University of Georgia," *Georgia Historical Quarterly* 43, no. 2 (June 1959): 156–69.

39. "Lucy Cobb Institute, Athens, Georgia, Announcement," 1918–19, 3, Rare Books Collection, Hargrett Library; "Lucy Cobb Institute Announcement," 1923, 4; Thomas,

Portrait of Historic Athens, 177; Montgomery, *Politics of Education*, 35–37; Townsend, "The Admission of Women to the University of Georgia"; Anne Wallis Brumby, "Education of Women in the United States" (MA thesis, University of Georgia, 1925); Announcement of the University of Georgia for the Session 1921–22, With a Register of Officers and Students for the Session 1920–21 (Athens: University of Georgia, [1922]), 190.

40. *Minutes of the Fourth Annual Meeting of the United Daughters of the Confederacy*, 74.

41. Paul DeForest Hicks, "Caroline O'Day: The Gentlewoman from New York," *New York History* (Summer 2007): 287–305; Gladstone Williams, "Atlanta Women to Hear Address by Mrs. Caroline O'Day Tomorrow," newspaper clipping [1936]; Mary Mayo Crenshaw, "New York's Georgia Congresswoman," newspaper clipping [1934], both in scrapbook, Lucy Cobb Alumnae Association, box 4, Lucy Cobb Institute Collection.

42. Hicks, "Caroline O'Day," 291–92; Crenshaw, "New York's Georgia Congresswoman"; Office of History & Preservation, U.S. House of Representatives, "Caroline Love Goodwin O'Day," in *Women in Congress, 1917–2006* (Washington: Government Printing Office, 2006), 155–59.

43. "Mrs. O'Day, Ill, Won Solely on Record," *New York Times*, November 6, 1940. Hicks, Crenshaw, and other sources repeat this story.

44. Hicks, "Caroline O'Day," 292–93; Crenshaw, "New York's Georgia Congresswoman"; "Mrs. O'Day, Ill, Won Solely on Record"; House History Office, "Caroline Love Goodwin O'Day," 155.

45. Hicks, "Caroline O'Day," 293; House History Office, "Caroline Love Goodwin O'Day," 155; Blanche Wiesen Cook, *Eleanor Roosevelt, Vol. 1: 1884–1933* (New York: Penguin, 1992), 323–24; Robyn Muncy, *Creating a Female Dominion in American Reform, 1890–1935* (New York: Oxford University Press, 1991).

46. Hicks, "Caroline O'Day," 299–301; House History Office, "Caroline Love Goodwin O'Day," 156–57; Blanche Wiesen Cook, *Eleanor Roosevelt, Vol. 2: 1933–1938* (New York: Penguin, 1999), 221–22, 441–42.

47. Crenshaw, "New York's Georgia Congresswoman"; Williams, "Atlanta Women to Hear Address by Mrs. Caroline O'Day Tomorrow"; "Mrs. O'Day Will be Given Dinner by Democratic Luncheon Club May 24" [1936], "Mrs. Caroline O'Day, N.Y. Congresswoman, to Pay Visit to Athens," and "Lucy Cobb Dons New, White Gown to Welcome Celebrated Alumna," *Atlanta Constitution*, Oct. 24, 1937, all in scrapbook, Lucy Cobb Alumnae Association, box 4, Lucy Cobb Institute Collection.

48. Crenshaw, "New York's Georgia Congresswoman."

49. "Mrs. Caroline O'Day, N.Y. Congresswoman, to Pay Visit to Athens," first quote; "Lucy Cobb Dons New, White Gown to Welcome Celebrated Alumna," second quote.

50. "Carrie Love" to "Dear Lamar," [1936], file 1, box 1, Jennie Smith papers.

51. Barrow, "History of Lucy Cobb Institute," 37–41.

52. Letter to Judge Andrew Cobb from his brother [signature missing], October 16, 1907, folder 5, box 1, Lucy Cobb Institute Records, Hargrett Library.

53. Since catalogues for every year do not survive, it is not clear exactly which year the school shifted to the domestic science course, but it was listed by 1914. "Lucy Cobb Institute Annual Announcement, 1902–1903," 43; "Lucy Cobb Institute Annual Announcement, 1914–1915," 5–6 (the announcement for this year lists both a domestic science instructor and a married women in charge of the "domestic department"). Many schools introduced home economic courses after the Smith-Hughes Act provided funding for it in 1917; in this sense, Lucy Cobb Institute was ahead of a trend. Helen Lefkowitz Horowitz, *Alma Mater: Design and Experience in the Women's Colleges from Their Nineteenth Century Beginnings to the 1930s* (Amherst: University of Massachusetts Press, 1993 [second edition]), 296–97; Amy McCandless, *The Past in the Present: Women's Higher Education in the Twentieth-Century South* (Tuscaloosa: University of Alabama Press, 1999), 27.

54. Ruth Schwartz Cowan, "The 'Industrial Revolution' in the Home: Household Technology and Social Change in the Twentieth Century," *Technology and Culture* 17 (1976): 1–23. To some extent, the changes in education were catching up with changes that had begun in the immediate aftermath of the Civil War. Although southern black women had few employment opportunities outside of domestic service, they were successful in limiting the terms of their service, and as a result, white women took on more domestic responsibilities. Censer, *Reconstruction of White Southern Womanhood*, chapter 2, especially 64–69; Tera W. Hunter, *To 'Joy My Freedom: Southern Black Women's Lives and Labors after the Civil War* (Cambridge, Mass.: Harvard University Press, 1997).

55. "Lucy Cobb Institute Annual Announcement, 1918–1919," 6–8.

56. Colton called Agnes Scott the only "standard college for women" in Georgia. Mildred Lewis Rutherford, "Sketch of Lucy Cobb Institute," 77; "A Word to the Alumnae of Lucy Cobb and to the Citizens of Athens," 2, folder 9, box 2, Rutherford Papers. The report took Colton seven years, and was generally critical of the 142 institutions that it surveyed. McCandless, *Past in the Present*, 36–37; Elizabeth Avery Colton, "Standards for Southern Colleges for Women," *The School Review* 20, no. 7 (Sept. 1912): 458–75.

57. Barrow, "History of the Lucy Cobb," 45; Board of Trustees, Minutes, May 28, 1910, Lucy Cobb Institute, Stock Book and Minutes, Hargrett Library (hereafter Lucy Cobb Institute Stock Books).

58. Catalogue, 1917–18. On preparation for college, see p. 16.

59. Board of Trustees, Minutes, 9 April 1917, 5 July 1917, and 11 June 1918, Lucy Cobb Institute Stock Books; Margaret Anne Womack, "Mildred Lewis Rutherford: Exponent of Southern Culture" (MA thesis, University of Georgia, 1947), 113.

60. [No author], "Mrs. George A. Mell," and Williams Rutherford, "Life of Bessie Mell from her birth to her marriage to G. A. Mell," both in folder 1, box 1, Mell-Rutherford Family Papers, Hargrett Library.

61. "Augusta Amelia Wright Mell," *Prominent Women in Georgia* [1928], clipping in folder 1, box 1, Augusta Amelia Wright Mell Papers, Hargrett Library.

62. Bessie Mell Lane, "Mildred Rutherford Mell, 1889–1982" in Spalding, *Higher Education for Women in the South*, 257–59.

63. "Senior Notes," and "Commencement Notes," *Lucy Cobb Magazine* 2 (June 1907): 43, 58; *Lucy Cobb Magazine* 2 (January 1907): 20–21, 22, 26.

64. "Prizes Won by two Athens Girls at Lucy Cobb Institute this year," unidentified newspaper clipping, folder 9, box 2, Rutherford Papers; Mildred Mell, "Valedictory," *Lucy Cobb Magazine* 2 (June 1907): 26–28.

65. Mildred Mell to Annie Laurie Mell, May 31, 1910, folder 15; Mildred Mell to Rosa Smith, June 10, 1910, folder 17; Mildred Mell to George Mell, June 5, 1910, folder 18; Mildred Mell to George Mell, July 8, 1910, folder 19; Mildred Mell to Annie Laurie Mell, August 2, 1910, folder 20; Mildred Rutherford to Annie Laurie, August 13, 1910; Mildred Rutherford to "Papa," June 23, 1912, all box 2, Mell-Rutherford Family Papers. Mell is referring to the 1910 interracial "Fight of the Century" between the (previously) undefeated heavyweight James J. Jeffries and Jack Johnson, world heavyweight champion, which ended with the defeat of Jeffries. At the time, it was promoted as a fight that would demonstrate Anglo-Saxon superiority; after Johnson's victory, riots broke out across the country. Gail Bederman, *Manliness and Civilization: A Cultural History of Gender and Race in the United States, 1880–1917* (Chicago: University of Chicago Press, 1995), 1–5.

66. Lane, "Mildred Rutherford Mell," 257–59; Mildred Rutherford Mell, vita, prepared by Bessie Mell Lane, Mildred Mell folder, College Archives, McCain Library, Agnes Scott College, Decatur, Georgia.

67. Lynn Gordon, *Gender and Higher Education in the Progressive Era* (New Haven: Yale University Press, 1990), 35, 43.

68. Muncy, *Creating a Female Dominion*, 31.

69. Lane, "Mildred Rutherford Mell," 256; Mildred Rutherford Mell, vita; State of Georgia, County of Clarke, memorandum of an agreement between the Lucy Cobb Institute and Mildred Mell, president, February 1922, and Andrew Cobb from Mildred Mell, February 13, 1922, both in box 1, Lucy Cobb Institute Stock Books; "Report of Mildred Mell, President of Lucy Cobb Institute," folder 4, box 1, Rutherford Papers.

70. Board of Trustees to Mildred Mell, 7 February 1922; Board of Trustees to Mildred Rutherford, 7 February 1922; Mildred Mell to Andrew Cobb, 13 February 1922; Andrew Cobb to Mildred Mell, 14 February 1922; all in Lucy Cobb Institute Stock Books; William F. Holmes, "Part Five: 1890–1940" in *A History of Georgia*, ed. Kenneth Coleman (Athens: University of Georgia Press, 1977, 1991), 263.

71. "Lucy Cobb Annual Announcement," 1923, 4–5.

72. Beginning in 1918, women could enter the College of Education and the College of Agriculture (to study domestic science) and over the course of the next decade were able to enroll in some programs in the College of Arts and Sciences. Dyer, *History of the University of Georgia*, 172–73, 178–79; Thomas, *Portrait of Historic Athens*, 177; "Lucy Cobb Institute, Athens, Georgia, Sixty-Sixth Annual Announcement, 1858–1923," 1923, 15–16.

73. Lucy Cobb Institute Announcement, 1923, 15–16.

74. Wedding announcements often listed attendance or graduation from UGA. See "Stewart-Bird"; "Wedding of Miss Dorothy Watson, Mr. Locke Solemnized Thursday"; "Miss Flanagan Mr. Bostwick Take Vows"; "Miss Daisy Amanda Billups Becomes the Bride of Mr. Charles Brown Harrell, Jr."; "Mr. and Mrs. Sams Announce Marriage of Niece, Elizabeth Armstrong, to Eugene Edwin Traber," all newspaper clippings, scrapbook, Lucy Cobb Alumnae Association, box 4, Lucy Cobb Institute Collection.

75. "Address of Mrs. May Hull Pope" [1922], folder 4, box 1, Rutherford Papers (quotation p. 3). An early article made a similar observation. "What the Lucy Cobb Stands for in the State," *Lucy Cobb Dots* 1 (October 3, 1917): 1–2.

76. "Address of Mrs. May Hull Pope," [1922], 3.

77. "Tribute to Late Miss Carrie Walden," newspaper clipping, scrapbook, Lucy Cobb Alumnae Association, box 4, Lucy Cobb Institute Collection; "Miss Brooks Engaged to the Rev. Mr. Richardson," newspaper clipping, scrapbook, Lucy Cobb Alumnae Association, box 4, Lucy Cobb Institute Collection.

78. "Lucy Cobb Institute Annual Announcement, 1923–24," 21.

79. "Engagement of Miss Marie Lumpkin Upson to Mr. Joseph Orchard Foil of Concord and Greensboro, NC, Announced Today," 1937, newspaper clipping, scrapbook, Lucy Cobb Alumnae Association, box 4, Lucy Cobb Institute Collection; "Miss Mathilde Lumpkin Upson to Marry Mr. Paul DeForest Hicks Of Pittsburgh, Penn.," [1930], newspaper clipping, scrapbook, Lucy Cobb Alumnae Association, box 4, Lucy Cobb Institute Collection.

80. Johnson, *Southern Women at the Seven Sister Colleges*, 138.

81. "Lucy Cobb Catalogue, 1925"; John Drewry, "Possibilities for Journalistic Training at Lucy Cobb," *The Lightning Bug* 1, no. 5 (May 1926): 76–77.

82. Gary L. Whitby and Lynn K. Whitby, "John Drewry and Social Progress," in *Makers of the Media Mind: Journalism Educators and Their Ideas*, ed. Wm. David Sloan (New York: Routledge, 1990): 142–48; Robert Platt, *We Shall Not be Moved: The Desegregation of the University of Georgia* (Athens: University of Georgia Press, 2002), 33, 37–39.

83. Drewry, "Possibilities for Journalistic Training," 76.

84. *The Lightning Bug* 1, no. 2 (December 1925): 28. Merry later experienced mental instability, leading to the couple's divorce, her attempted murder of her ex-husband and his new finacée, and a sensational trial, which may have cost Drewry the chance to become UGA president. "Dean's Ex Guilty in Shooting Rival," *The Pittsburgh Press*, April 22, 1950; "Court Upholds Conviction of Drewry Shooting," *The Tuscaloosa News*, February 1, 1951; "Finding Aid for the John E. Drewry Papers," Hargrett Library, http://www.libs.uga.edu/hargrett/archives/uga04-026.html.

85. Nevin, *Prominent Women of Georgia*, 45. As Polly Peachtree, she famously described the young Margret Mitchell as having had "more men really, truly 'dead in love' with her, more honest-to-goodness suitors than almost any other girl in

Atlanta." Margret Ripley Wolfe, *Daughters of Canaan: A Saga of Southern Women* (Lexington: The University Press of Kentucky, 1995), 149.

86. Lamar Rutherford Lipscomb, *Essays Wise and Otherwise* (Mildred Seydell Publishing Company, 1957). She was the daughter of John Rutherford and married Andrew A. Lipscomb.

87. "Mildred Seydell," New Georgia Encyclopedia, http://www.georgiaencyclopedia .org/articles/arts-culture/mildred-seydell-1889–1988; Mary Elizabeth Holcomb, "Mildred Seydell: The Road from Southern Belle to Feminist Journalist" (MA thesis, Georgia State University, 1997).

88. "Student Handbook of Rules and Regulations, 1925–26," 1, 6, 7, folder 7, box 1, Rutherford Scrapbooks.

89. "Memories of Lucy Cobb Girlhood," *Athens Observer*, 23 October 1986, Lucy Cobb Institute File, Athens Heritage Foundation.

90. Clare, *Thunder and Stars*, 222.

91. "Athens Remembers," *Athens Banner-Herald*, unidentified newspaper clipping, folder 3, box 1; "Athens UDC Chapter Celebrates 118 Anniversary of Miss Millie," *Athens Daily News*, unidentified newspaper clipping, 16 July 1969, folder 4, box 1; both in Rutherford Scrapbooks. Southern Baptists generally regarded dancing as particularly sinful; Rufus B. Spain, *At Ease in Zion: A Social History of Southern Baptists, 1865–1900* (Tuscaloosa: University of Alabama Press, 2003 [Vanderbilt University Press, 1967]), 198–99.

92. "Student Handbook of Rules and Regulations, 1925–26," 11–12; "Memories of Lucy Cobb Girlhood"; John Toon, "Lucy Cobb [remainder of title obscured by mailing label]," *Athens Observer*, 28 December 1978, Lucy Cobb Institute File, Athens-Clarke County Library.

93. "Bessie Mell Lane," 267 (first quotation), 269 (second quotation); Toon, "Lucy Cobb"; Clare, *Thunder and Stars*, 222.

94. Minutes, June 21, 1926, minute book, box 1, Lucy Cobb Institute Stock Books.

95. "Report of Miss Mildred Mell, President Lucy Cobb Institute" [1923], 3–4, folder 4, box 1, Rutherford Papers; Mildred Mell to Andrew Cobb, May 1, 1923, Lucy Cobb Institute Stock Books; Bartley, *Creation of Modern Georgia*, 169.

96. Mildred Mell to Andrew Cobb, March 13, 1923; Mildred Mell to Andrew Cobb, May 1, 1923; Mildred Mell to Andrew Cobb, minutes of May 10, 1923; all in box 1, Lucy Cobb Institute Stock Books; "Report of Miss Mildred Mell, President Lucy Cobb Institute" [1923], 3–4, folder 4, box 1, Rutherford Papers.

97. Lucy Cobb Institute Alumnae Association Minutes book, 1902, folder 2, box 1, Lipscomb-Lucy Cobb Institute Collection.

98. Proposition, Board of Education, Athens, Georgia, 1925; T. J. Woofter to Board of Trustees, 6 February 1925; and Anne Billup to Board of Trustees, 6 March 1925, all Lucy Cobb Institute Stock Books; Andrew Cobb to Mildred Lewis Rutherford, 1925, folder 15, box 30, Coulter Manuscripts. See the several articles in the fundraising circular, "A Word to the Alumnae of Lucy Cobb and to the Citizens of Athens."

99. Womack, "Mildred Lewis Rutherford," 131–33; *The Lightning Bug* (November 1925); George Mell to Annie Laurie Poats, 15 April 1926, folder 12, box 2, Mell-Rutherford Family Papers, Hargrett Library.

100. Barrow, "History of Lucy Cobb Institute," 28.

101. Katherine Trussell Wilson, LaGrange Trussell DuPree, and Phyllis Jenkins Barrow, comps., "Interview with Bessie Mell Lane," in Spalding, *Higher Education for Women in the South*, 265.

102. George Mell to Annie Laurie Mell, April 20, 1926, folder 12, box 2, Mell-Rutherford Family Papers.

103. Censer, *Reconstruction of Southern Womanhood*, 30–41; George Mell to Annie Laurie Mell, February 9, 1922, folder 8, box 2; George Mell to Annie Laurie Mell, April 22, 1924, folder 10, box 2; George Mell to Annie Laurie Mell, November 22, 1926, folder 11, box 2; George Mell to Annie Laurie Mell, April 20, 1926, folder 12; Mildred Mell to Annie Laurie Mell, June 18, 1910, folder 15; Mildred Mell to Annie Laurie Mell, August 26, 1910, folder 20, box 2; all Mell-Rutherford Papers, Hargrett Library.

104. Lane, "Mildred Rutherford Mell," 256–57; Mell, vita. Odum worked at UGA from 1912 to 1919. Lynn Moss Sanders, *Howard W. Odum's Folklore Odyssey: Transformation to Tolerance through African American Folk Studies* (Athens: University of Georgia Press, 2003).

105. Morton Sosna, *In Search of the Silent South: Southern Liberals and the Race Issue* (New York: Columbia University Press, 1977): 57; Mildred Mell, "A Definitive Study of Poor Whites in the South" (PhD dissertation, University of North Carolina, 1938). Mell published an article in *Social Forces*, a journal edited by Odum targeting both an academic and public audience, summarizing the major themes of her dissertation. Mell, "Poor Whites of the South," *Social Forces* 17 (December 1938): 153–67. The dissertation was cited extensively and treated as the definitive source on the topic in a 1940 review article, W. O. Brown, "Role of Poor Whites in Race Contacts of the South," *Social Forces* 19, no. 2 (December 1940): 258–68.

106. Sosna, *In Search of the Silent South*, 45.

107. Mell, vita, 2.

108. Muncy, *Creating a Female Dominion*.

109. Sarah Wilkerson-Freeman, "The Creation of a Subversive Feminist Dominion: Interracialist Social Workers and the Georgia New Deal," *Journal of Women's History* 13 (Winter 2002): 132–154, especially 138–40.

110. She did write during the 1960s about trade with Europe and other matters. Mildred Mell, "Trade Relations of the United States with the New Europe," *West Georgia College Studies in the Social Sciences* 3, no. 1 (June 1964).

111. Mildred Mell to Phinizy Spalding, May 13, 1978, Lucy Cobb Institute File, Athens Heritage Foundation.

112. Turner M. Heirs, "Lucy Cobb Institute, Now Dormitory for University Co-eds, Formerly Finishing School for 'Cream of Old South,'" unidentified newspaper clipping, [1931], Lucy Cobb Institute Folder, Georgiana Vertical Files, Hargrett Library; Womack, "Mildred Lewis Rutherford," 143; Toon, "Lucy Cobb"; Phinizy Spalding,

"Introduction," in Spalding, *Higher Education for Women in the South*, 4; Phinizy Spalding to Robert Woodruff, November 11, 1980, Lucy Cobb Institute File, Athens Clarke County Heritage Foundation; Robert G. Stephens Jr., "Lucy Cobb: Send Money," *Athens Observer*, February 1, 1990, in Lucy Cobb Institute File, Athens Clarke County Heritage Foundation; Tommie Lacavera, "The Spirit of Lucy Cobb," *Athens Magazine*, October 1992, Lucy Cobb Institute File, Athens-Clarke County Library.

Chapter 3. Training "Leaders of Their Own Race"

1. Evelyn Brooks Higginbotham, *Righteous Discontent: The Women's Movement in the Black Baptist Church, 1880–1920* (Cambridge, Mass.: Harvard University Press, 1993), 22–23; Stephanie J. Shaw, *What a Women Ought to Be and Do: Black Professional Women Workers During the Jim Crow Era* (Chicago: University of Chicago Press, 1996); Victoria W. Wolcott, *Remaking Respectability: African American Women in Interwar Detroit* (Chapel Hill: University of North Carolina Press, 2001); Alison Dorsey, *To Build Our Lives Together: Community Formation in Black Atlanta, 1875–1906* (Athens: University of Georgia Press, 2004); Joan Marie Johnson, *Southern Ladies, New Women: Race, Region, and Clubwomen in South Carolina, 1890–1930* (Gainesville: University Press of Florida, 2004); Michele Mitchell, *Righteous Propagation: African Americans and the Politics of Racial Destiny after Reconstruction* (Chapel Hill: University of North Carolina Press, 2004).

2. Florence Matilda Read, *The Story of Spelman College* (Atlanta: United Negro College Fund with Princeton University Press, 1961), 1–2, 7–8.

3. "In Loving Remembrance," *Spelman Messenger*, May 1893, 2–3; Read, *Story of Spelman*, 1–4; Dr. Morehouse, "Miss Harriet E. Giles," Cora L. P. Laster, "Miss Giles in the Home," Claudia T. White, "Miss Giles—A Character Sketch," "From Our Dear Mrs. Reynolds," and "Extracts from Letters," *Spelman Messenger*, January 1910, 2–3, 6–7. A note on the *Messenger*: several articles are not identified in the paper by title or author; others have a byline, but no title.

4. Harriet Giles Diaries (microfilm), reel 2, July 2, 1891; reel 3, January 26, 1896, April 11, 1896, Spelman College Archives, Spelman College, Atlanta, Georgia (hereafter Spelman College Archives).

5. Read, *Story of Spelman*, 4, 7, 11, 13.

6. Personal writings suggest that they may have shared a more intimate relationship, as was common among highly educated professional women of their time. In their journals, the two called each other "dear" or "darling" and frequently referred to their love for each other. Sophia Packard Diaries (microfilm), February 4, 1882, February 16, 1882, Spelman College Archives; Giles Diaries, reel 1, March 21, 1890; reel 2, June 21, 1891, June 23, 1895; reel 3, January 3, 1896.

7. Read, *Story of Spelman*, 15–16, 19, 28–30; Isabella Webb Parks, "A Noble Life Work After Fifty-Seven," *Spelman Messenger*, May 1893, 1–2.

8. Read, *Story of Spelman*, 31; Parks, "A Noble Life Work After Fifty-Seven," 1–2.

9. Paul Harvey, *Freedom's Coming: Religious Culture and the Shaping of the South from the Civil War through the Civil Rights Era* (Chapel Hill: University of North Carolina Press, 2005), 6, 25.

10. According to James McPherson, Northern postwar reformers, often children of anti-slavery activists themselves, sought to extend the values of abolitionism by influencing the education and religious training of the recently freedmen and women. James M. McPherson, *The Abolitionist Legacy, from Reconstruction to the NAACP* (Princeton: Princeton University Press, 1975). On the ABHMS, see Sandy Dwayne Martin, "The American Baptist Home Mission Society and Black Higher Education in the South, 1865–1920," *Foundations* 24 (1981): 310–27; Daniel W. Stowell, *Rebuilding Zion: The Religious Reconstruction of the South, 1863–1877* (New York: Oxford University Press, 1998), 130–42.

11. McPherson, *Abolitionist Legacy*, 75 (quotation); Martin, "The American Baptist Home Mission Society," 311, 318–320; Stowell, *Rebuilding Zion*, 141. Creating an educated ministry was a concern of Baptists generally in the nineteenth century. William H. Brackney, *A Genetic History of Baptist Thought: With Special Reference to Baptists in Britain and North America* (Macon, Ga.: Mercer University Press, 2004), 251–3.

12. Peggy Pascoe, *Relations of Rescue: The Search for Female Moral Authority in the American West, 1874–1939* (New York: Oxford University Press, 1990); Robyn Muncy, *Creating a Female Dominion in American Reform, 1890–1935* (New York: Oxford University Press, 1991); Linda Gordon, *Pitied But Not Entitled: Single Mothers and the History of Welfare* (Cambridge: Harvard University Press, 1994); Gwendolyn Mink, *The Wages of Motherhood: Inequality in the Welfare State, 1917–1942* (Ithaca: Cornell University Press, 1995); Georgina Hickey, *Hope and Danger in the New South City: Working-Class Women and Urban Development in Atlanta, 1890–1940* (Athens: University of Georgia Press, 2003); Yolanda L. Watson and Sheila T. Gregory, *Daring to Educate: The Legacy of Early Spelman College Presidents* (Sterling, Va.: Stylus Publishing, 2005).

13. Read, *Story of Spelman*, 35–42; Packard Diaries, February 17, 1880, February 20, 1880; Giles Diaries, reel 1, March 24, 1881, April 4, 1881.

14. Harold H. Martin, *Georgia: A Bicentennial History* (Nashville, Tenn.: American Association of State and Local History, 1977), 81–82, 123, 128; Numan V. Bartley, *The Creation of Modern Georgia* (Athens: University of Georgia Press, 1983), 54–55, 108–12, 139; Gary M. Pomeranz, *Where Peachtree Meets Sweet Auburn: A Saga of Race and Family* (New York: Penguin Books, 1996), 60, 72–77; Tera W. Hunter, *To 'Joy My Freedom: Southern Black Women's Lives and Labors after the Civil War* (Cambridge, Mass.: Harvard University Press, 1997), 45, 49, 100; Ronald H. Bayor, *Race and the Shaping of Twentieth-Century Atlanta* (Chapel Hill: University of North Carolina Press, 1996), 6–7; Hickey, *Hope and Danger*, 54, 57; William A. Link, *Atlanta, Cradle of the New South: Race and Remembering in the Civil War's Aftermath* (Chapel Hill: University of North Carolina Press, 2013).

15. Bayor, *Race and the Shaping of Twentieth-Century Atlanta*, 3–12; Dorsey, *To Build Our Lives Together*, 35–37, 128–29, 150–51; David Fort Godshalk, *Veiled Visions: The 1906 Atlanta Race Riot and the Reshaping of American Race Relations* (Chapel Hill: University of North Carolina Press, 2005); Rebecca Burns, *Rage in the Gate City: The Story of the 1906 Atlanta Race Riot* (Athens: University of Georgia Press,

2006); Gregory Mixon, *The Atlanta Riot: Race, Class, and Violence in a New South City* (Gainesville: University Press of Florida, 2005).

16. Dorsey, *To Build Our Lives Together*, 1–13, 53 (quotation). Dorsey makes a distinction between "class" and "status," noting that accomplishment and education rather than income levels determined status in the postwar black community (p. 9).

17. Ann Short Chirhart, *Torches of Light: Georgia Teachers and the Coming of the Modern South* (Athens: University of Georgia Press, 2005), 24–25, 93, 96; Bayor, *Race and the Shaping of Twentieth Century Atlanta*, 7, 10–11, 197–205.

18. Heather Andrea Williams, *Self-Taught: African American Education in Slavery and Freedom* (Chapel Hill: University of North Carolina Press, 2005); James D. Anderson, *The Education of Blacks in the South, 1860–1935* (Chapel Hill: University of North Carolina Press, 1988), 4–7, 16–19 (quotation p. 17); Higginbotham, *Righteous Discontent*, 19–20; Dorsey, *To Build Our Lives Together*, chapter 4; Chirhart, *Torches of Light*, 22–25.

19. Ron E. Butchart, *Schooling the Freedpeople: Teaching, Learning, and the Struggle for Black Freedom, 1861–1876* (Chapel Hill: University of North Carolina Press, 2010), xii, 18–19, 54, 79–81.

20. Jacqueline Jones, *Soldiers of Light and Love: Northern Teachers and Georgia Blacks, 1865–1873* (Chapel Hill: University of North Carolina Press, 1980); Johnetta Cross Brazzell, "Bricks without Straw: Missionary-Sponsored Black Higher Education in the Post-Emancipation Era," *Journal of Higher Education* 63 (January/February 1992): 26–49.

21. Giles diaries, April 3 and April 4, 1881.

22. Chirhart, *Torches of Light*, 22.

23. Dorsey, *To Build Our Lives Together*, 57–62, 70–71.

24. Parks, "A Noble Life Work After Fifty-Seven," 1–2; Read, *Story of Spelman*, 42–47; Martin, "The American Baptist Home Mission Society," 312; Higginbotham, *Righteous Discontent*, 22–23; Jacqueline Jones Royster, *Traces of a Stream: Literacy and Social Change Among African American Women* (Pittsburgh: University of Pittsburgh Press, 2000), 155–56; Harvey, *Freedom's Coming*, 18.

25. Read, *Story of Spelman*, 42–43, appendix III, 379; V. W. Maddox, "The Good Old Times," *Spelman Messenger*, April 1887, 1.

26. Maddox, "The Good Old Times," 1 (quotation); "Spelman's Birthday," *Spelman Messenger*, May 1888, 2; "In Loving Remembrance," 2–3.

27. Read, *Story of Spelman*, 53. Supporting the Sunday school movement became a major focus of Baptists in the later nineteenth century. Robert G. Torbet, *A History of the Baptists* (Valley Forge, Penn.: The Judson Press, 1963 [1950]), 327.

28. The women of the ABHMS in Boston, on the other hand, believed the school's course of study to be too ambitious and even temporarily cut funding. Read, *Story of Spelman*, 54–55, 60–61.

29. Read, *Story of Spelman*, 70–71, 77–79, 64–65, 81–84; Taylor Branch, *Parting the Waters: America in the King Years* (New York: Touchstone, 1988), 27–29; Johnetta Brazzell, "Education as a Tool of Socialization: Agnes Scott Institute and Spelman

Seminary, 1881–1910" (PhD dissertation, University of Michigan, 1991), 169; "Dedication of Giles Hall, Spelman Seminary," *Spelman Messenger*, January 1894, 1–3, 5, donations detailed on 2; Harriet Giles and Lucy Upton, "Annual Report, Spelman Seminary," *Spelman Messenger*, March 1898, supplemental pages.

Although later sources suggest that the school was named for Rockefeller's wife, Laura Spelman Rockefeller, the 1883–84 catalogue stated that the school was named for Rockefeller's father-in-law, "the firm friend of the colored race." "Third Annual Catalogue of the Spelman Baptist Seminary for Women and Girls, in Atlanta, Georgia, 1883–84"; see also "Our Name," *Spelman Messenger*, April 1885, 1; Read, *Story of Spelman*, 81–84.

30. "Rockefeller Hall," *Spelman Messenger*, May 1886; "Giles Hall," *Spelman Messenger*, June 1893, 1; "Dedication of Giles Hall, Spelman Seminary," *Spelman Messenger*, January 1894, 1; Harriet Giles and Lucy Upton, "Annual Report: To the Trustees of Spelman Seminary," *Spelman Messenger*, March 1901, 1–2.

31. Branch, *Parting the Waters*, 29.

32. Harriet Giles and Lucy Upton, "Annual Report, Spelman Seminary," *Spelman Messenger*, March 1898, supplemental pages; Harriet Giles and Lucy Upton, "Annual Report," *Spelman Messenger*, March 1899, 1–2; "Annual Report," *Spelman Messenger*, June 1900, 5; Harriet E. Giles and Lucy H. Upton, "Annual Report," *Spelman Messenger*, March 1903, 1–2.

33. Helen Lefkowitz Horowitz, *Alma Mater: Design and Experience in the Women's Colleges from Their Nineteenth Century Beginnings to the 1930s* (Amherst: University of Massachusetts Press, 1993 [second edition]), 4–5. Horowitz emphasized that by the turn of the century, the seminary model lost favor among northern white women's colleges. Harriet E. Giles and Lucy H. Upton, "Annual Report," *Spelman Messenger*, March 1901, 1–2 (quotation). See similar statements in "A Description of Spelman Seminary," *Spelman Messenger*, May 1898, 1–2; Harriet Giles, "Spelman Seminary," *Spelman Messenger*, November 1908, 1–2; Lucy H. Upton, "Spelman's Educational Plant," *Spelman Messenger*, April 1911, 2–3.

34. M. E. R., "Our Family Life," *Spelman Messenger*, February 1914, 5.

35. Lucy Hale Tapley and Edith V. Brill, "Annual Report to the Trustees of Spelman Seminary, 1916–1917," *Spelman Messenger*, April 1917, 2–3; "A Wonderful Week," *Spelman Messenger*, April 1919, 1–3; Branch, *Parting the Waters*, 33.

36. Henry Allan Bullock, *A History of Negro Education in the South: From 1619 to the Present* (Cambridge, Mass.: Harvard University Press, 1967), 142.

37. Branch, *Parting the Waters*, 28–29 (quotation p. 29).

38. Mrs. Adeline J. Smith, "My Early Life," *Spelman Messenger*, May 1901, 6. Similar stories are reported in "Sketches of Graduates," *Spelman Messenger*, May 1901, 2–3, 5; "Sketches of Spelman Graduates," *Spelman Messenger*, October 1901, 2–3; *Spelman Messenger*, October 1901, 4; "Mattie Brookins Johnson," *Spelman Messenger*, October 1902, 3; E. O. W., "Emma S. DeLamotta," *Spelman Messenger*, November 1903, 1–2.

39. Mrs. A. DeLamotta, "At School," *Spelman Messenger*, April 1891, 2.

40. "In Memorandum," *Spelman Messenger*, March 1885.

41. Mary L. Shepard, "Spring Days at Spelman Seminary," *Spelman Messenger*, May 1894, 2.

42. *Spelman Messenger*, December 1888, 6. Giles mentioned the poverty and poor clothing of students in her diary: Giles Diaries, reel 1, December 4, 1882, and in a letter to "Lizzie," March 14, 1884, Giles letters, box 5, Lucy Hale Tapley Collection, Spelman Seminary.

43. On the importance of Christian instruction to the principals, see "Spelman Seminary," *Spelman Messenger*, April 1885, 1; Harriet Giles and Lucy Upton, "Sixteenth Annual Report of the Principals of Spelman Seminary," *Spelman Messenger*, April 1897, 1–3; Watson and Gregory, *Daring to Educate*, 69–70.

44. Packard Diaries, March 12, 1882 and January 1, 1883; Giles Diaries, reel 1, October 30, 1887, reel 3, February 4, 1896 (quotation).

45. "Catalogue, 1883–84," 21; "Twentieth Annual Circular and Catalogue, of Spelman Seminary for Women and Girls in Atlanta, Georgia, 1900–01," 32–34.

46. "Christian Endeavor at Spelman," *Spelman Messenger*, March 1891, 9; Giles Diaries, reel 1 (journal at end of reel), December 3, 1882; reel 3, January 4, 1897.

47. Dorsey, *To Build Our Lives Together*, 70–71.

48. *Spelman Messenger*, November 1886, 2; *Spelman Messenger*, November 1889, 4; *Spelman Messenger*, December 1889, 4; *Spelman Messenger*, June 1890, 4.

49. Giles Diaries, reel 1, October 12, October 18, October 30, and November 15, 1887.

50. "The Faculty," *Spelman Messenger*, March 1885; "Seventh Annual Catalogue, Spelman Seminary, 1887–88," 7; "Eighth Annual Catalogue, Spelman Seminary, 1889–90"; Harriet Giles and Lucy Tapley, "Annual Report of the Principals of Spelman Seminary," *Spelman Messenger*, April 1895, 5–6; "Twenty-fifth Annual Catalogue, Spelman Seminary, 1905–6"; Watson and Gregory, *Daring to Educate*, 69, 77.

51. *Spelman Messenger*, January 1892, 2; *Spelman Messenger*, May 1894, 4; S. Frances Wingfield, "The Negro Woman in the Church and Other Missionary Activities," *Spelman Messenger*, May 1902, 1–3; Harriet E. Giles and Lucy H. Upton, "Annual Report," *Spelman Messenger*, March 1903, 1–2; Harriet E. Giles and Lucy H. Upton, "President's Annual Report," *Spelman Messenger*, March 1905, 1–2; E. O. W., "Y.W.C.A. at Spelman," *Spelman Messenger*, December 1905, 4; Susie E. Jones, "Societies of Spelman," *Spelman Messenger*, April 1906, 2–3; Mamie L. Strong, "The Young Women's Christian Association," *Spelman Messenger*, November 1908, 5.

52. Ella Knox, "Prayer," *Spelman Messenger*, January 1890, 3; A. H. M., "A Visit to Spelman," *Spelman Messenger*, January 1892, 1. *The Messenger* often dedicated the April and December issues to discussing the Easter or Christmas story, or chronicling how the holidays were spent around the world.

53. Read, *Story of Spelman*, 124, 165–67.

54. Beginning in 1893, annual reports report a steady decline throughout the 1890s, attributing it primarily to low cotton prices. In 1900, enrollment began to rise again. *Spelman Messenger*, April 1891, 3; "Annual Meeting of Spelman Trustees," *Spelman Messenger*, April 1893, 2–3; *Spelman Messenger*, June 1893, 4; *Spelman Messenger*, November 1894, 4; Harriet Giles and Lucy Tapley, "Annual Report of the Principals

of Spelman Seminary," *Spelman Messenger*, April 1895, 5–6; "Annual Report," *Spelman Messenger*, June 1900, 5; Harriet E. Giles and Lucy H. Upton, "Twenty-Six Annual Report of the President of Spelman Seminary," *Spelman Messenger*, April 1907, 5–6; Harriet E. Giles, "Annual Report to the Trustees of Spelman Seminary," *Spelman Messenger*, April 1908, 5–6; "Spelman Seminary Statistics Prepared for the Thirtieth Anniversary," *Spelman Messenger*, May 1911, 3; Lucy H. Tapley and Edith V. Brill, "Annual Report, April 8, 1921," *Spelman Messenger*, April 1921, 5–7; Lucy Hale Tapley and Edna E. Lamson, "Annual Report," *Spelman Messenger*, April 1923, 2–3. On problems faced by other missionary schools, see Anderson, *Education of Blacks in the South*, 248–49.

55. *Spelman Messenger*, May 1909, 4; "Spelman Seminary Statistics Prepared for the Thirtieth Anniversary," *Spelman Messenger*, May 1911, 3.

56. "Catalogue, 1883–84," 17.

57. Royster, *Traces of a Stream*, 155–57.

58. Watson and Gregory, *Daring to Educate*, 72.

59. Harriet Giles and Lucy Upton, "Annual Report of the Principals of Spelman Seminary," *Spelman Messenger*, April 1894, 1–3; "Eighteenth Annual Circular and Catalogue of Spelman Seminary for Women and Girls in Atlanta, Georgia for the Academic Year 1898–99," 39; "Twenty-Fourth Annual Circular and Catalogue of Spelman Seminary for Women and Girls in Atlanta, Georgia for the Academic Year 1904–05," 16–17.

60. "Eleventh Annual Circular and Catalogue of Spelman Seminary, for Women and Girls in Atlanta, Georgia, 1891–92"; "Annual Meeting of Spelman Trustees," *Spelman Messenger*, April 1893, 2–3; "Catalogue, 1898–99," 31, 38.

61. "Annual Report," *Spelman Messenger*, June 1900, 5; "Summary of Attendance, Spelman Seminary, 1919–1920," *Spelman Messenger*, May 1920, 7. By 1920, however, much larger numbers of students took the high school and professional courses.

62. The national average for students studying precollegiate curricula in institutions of higher education was 25 percent. Anderson, *Education of Blacks in the South*, 249.

63. Harriet Giles and Lucy Upton, "Sixteenth Annual Report of the Principals of Spelman Seminary," *Spelman Messenger*, April 1897, 1–3; "Catalogue, 1898–99," 30, 33–36; Anderson, *Education of Blacks in the South*, 241, 249. Board president Henry Morehouse had requested funds in 1894 for college-level study from Rockefeller but was denied. Watson and Gregory, *Daring to Educate*, 74.

64. Harriet Giles and Lucy Upton, "Annual Report," *Spelman Messenger*, March 1901, 1–2; "Spelman Seminary Statistics Prepared for the Thirtieth Anniversary," *Spelman Messenger*, May 1911, 3.

65. "Spelman Seminary Statistics Prepared for the Thirtieth Anniversary," *Spelman Messenger*, May 1911, 3.

66. Speech by Henry Morehouse, reprinted in "Dedication of Giles Hall, Spelman Seminary," *Spelman Messenger*, January 1894, 2; Harriet Giles and Lucy Upton, "Sixteenth Annual Report of the Principals of Spelman Seminary," *Spelman Messenger*,

April 1897, 1–3; "Catalogue, 1898–99," 33–36; Mary A. Speer, "The Study of English," *Spelman Messenger*, February 1899, 6; *Spelman Messenger*, February 1899, 4.

67. "Spelman Seminary, Atlanta, Ga.," [reprinted from the *Independent*], *Spelman Messenger*, May 1892, 5; "Printing Department, Spelman Seminary" [reprinted from the *Boonville Herald*], *Spelman Messenger*, November 1893, 3, 7; Morehouse, in "Dedication of Giles Hall, Spelman Seminary," 2; [Henry Morehouse], "The Worth of Spelman Seminary to the World," *Spelman Messenger*, June 1896, 2; Rev. T. J. Morgan, "What Spelman Stands For," *Spelman Messenger*, December 1901, 4; Shaw, *What a Women Ought to Be and Do*, 70.

68. Horowitz, *Alma Mater*, 17–19, 25–27.

69. Horowitz, *Alma Mater*, 29, 33, 40–41.

70. *Spelman Messenger*, December 1895, 4.

71. In 1910, Giles died after a brief illness, and after directing the school alone for a year, Upton, then sixty-three, chose to retire. "Principals' Annual Report," *Spelman Messenger*, March 1892, 1; "Spelman Seminary Trustees' Meeting," *Spelman Messenger*, March 1892, 2; *Spelman Messenger*, November 1909, 4; *Spelman Messenger*, March 1910, 4.

72. White, "Miss Giles—A Character Sketch," 3 (quotation); Lucy Hale Tapley and Edith V. Brill, "Thirty-Second Annual Report of the President of Spelman Seminary to the Board of Trustees," *Spelman Messenger*, April 1913, 1–3; "Annual Report of Spelman Seminary for the Year 1915–1916," *Spelman Messenger*, April 1915, 5; Lucy Hale Tapley and Edith V. Brill, "Annual Report to the Trustees of Spelman Seminary, 1916–17," *Spelman Messenger*, April 1917, 2–3; Lucy Hale Tapley and Edith V. Brill, "Annual Report," *Spelman Messenger*, April 1923, 2–3; Read, *Story of Spelman*, 127, 187–88, 199–200; Watson, *Daring to Educate*, 83–88.

73. Watson, *Daring to Educate*, 89–91.

74. Lucy Hale Tapley and Edith V. Brill, "Annual Report," *Spelman Messenger*, April 1923, 2–3; Edna E. Lamson, "Spelman College," *Spelman Messenger*, April 1923, 3, 7; Spelman Seminary Catalog, 1923–1924, and Spelman College Bulletin, 1924–1925, Atlanta, Georgia [1923], 47–61; Read, *Story of Spelman*, 196–203.

75. Lucy Hale Tapley and Edna E. Lamson, "Annual Report," *Spelman Messenger*, May 1926, 1–3, 8. The school granted its last certificates for industrial courses in 1926.

76. Lucy Hale Tapley and Edith V. Brill, "Annual Report," *Spelman Messenger*, April 1924, 1–2, (quotation p. 1).

77. Anderson, *Education of Blacks in the South*, 243; David Spivey, *Schooling for the New Slavery* (Westport, Conn.: Greenwood Press, 1978).

78. August Meier, *Negro Thought in America, 1880–1915: Racial Ideologies in the Age of Booker T. Washington* (Ann Arbor: University of Michigan Press, 1963), 95; Elizabeth Jacoway, *Yankee Missionaries in the South: The Penn School Experiment* (Baton Rouge: Louisiana State University Press, 1980), 5; Cynthia Neverdon-Morton, *Afro-American Women of the South and the Advancement of the Race* (Knoxville: University of Tennessee Press, 1989), 14; Shaw, *What a Woman Ought to Be and Do*, 93.

79. "Catalogue, 1883–84," 23.

80. Horowitz, *Alma Mater*, 205, 224–27; The Woman in Grey, "This is Spelman," *Spelman Messenger*, May 1923, 5–6.

81. "Catalogue, 1891–92"; Mabel H. Parsons, "A Day at Spelman," *Spelman Messenger*, November 1908, 3.

82. Harriet E. Giles and Florence B. Cordo, "Annual Report of Spelman Seminary for the School Year 1908–09," *Spelman Messenger*, May 1909, 1–3, 7.

83. Lucy Hale Tapley, "An Appeal," *Spelman Messenger*, November 1912, 1–2.

84. Horowitz, *Alma Mater*, 17–19, 25–27.

85. "How We Spend Our Time," *Spelman Messenger*, March 1885; Harriet Giles and Lucy Upton, "Sixteenth Annual Report of the Principals of Spelman Seminary," *Spelman Messenger*, April 1897, 1–3.

86. Mink, *The Wages of Motherhood*; Muncy, *Creating a Female Dominion in American Reform*; Marilyn Irvin Holt, *Linoleum, Better Babies, and the Modern Farm Woman, 1890–1930* (Albuquerque: University of New Mexico Press, 1995); Sarah Stage and Virginia B. Vincenti, *Rethinking Home Economics: Women and the History of a Profession* (Ithaca: Cornell University Press, 1997).

87. Minnie Lee Thomas, "The Work of the Industrial Department of Spelman Seminary," *Spelman Messenger*, April 1896, 5 (first and third quotation); Carrie Bailey, "Our Sewing Department," *Spelman Messenger*, May 1893, 7 (second quotation); Maggie Roundtree, *Spelman Messenger*, March 1893, 3; "Echoes from the Spelman Dress-Makers," *Spelman Messenger*, June 1890, 5; Susie A. Carter, *Spelman Messenger*, March 1893, 3.

88. Trudie Houser, "The Essentials of an Ideal Home," *Spelman Messenger*, December 1898, 7.

89. Maggie Roundtree, *Spelman Messenger*, March 1893, 3; other essays echo this theme.

90. Mitchell, *Righteous Propagation*, 135–37.

91. The number of articles discussing how the industrial training would educate housewives far exceeds references to alumnae engaging in domestic service. Harriet Giles and Lucy Tapley, "Annual Report of the Principals of Spelman Seminary," *Spelman Messenger*, May 1896, 1–3.

92. "A Revolution," *Spelman Messenger*, November 1896, 5.

93. John Hope, "Spelman's Twenty-Fifth Anniversary," *Spelman Messenger*, May 1906, 1–2.

94. "Catalogue, 1898–99"; "Laundry Work," and "Cooking," *Spelman Messenger*, January 1908, 6; Lucy Hale Tapley and Edna E. Lamson, "Annual Report," April 1926, *Spelman Messenger*, 1–3, 6.

95. Bayor, *Race and the Shaping of Twentieth Century Atlanta*, 8.

96. Meier, *Negro Thought in America*, 197.

97. Audrey Thomas McCluskey, *A Forgotten Sisterhood: Pioneering Black Women Educators in the Jim Crow South* (Lanham, Md.: Rowman and Littlefield, 2014).

98. Bullock, *History of Negro Education in the South*, 164–65.

99. "Printing," *Spelman Messenger*, March 1885; "Printing Department, Spelman Seminary" [reprinted from the *Boonville Herald*], *Spelman Messenger*, November 1893, 3, 7.

100. Founded in 1882 by John Fox Slater of Connecticut, the Slater Fund was fundamental in promoting industrial training and the primary model for southern black education. "Printing"; Anderson, *Education of Blacks in the South*, 66; Meier, *Negro Thought in America*, 95; Roy E. Finkenbine, "'Our Little Circle': Benevolent Reformers, the Slater Fund, and the Argument for Black Industrial Education, 1882–1908," in *African Americans and Education in the South, 1865–1900*, ed. Donald G. Nieman (New York: Garland Publishing, Inc., 1994), 70–86 (reprinted from *Hayes Historical Journal* 6 [1986], 6–22).

101. "Printing Department, Spelman Seminary," 3 (quotation), 7.

102. *Spelman Messenger*, December 1889, 4; letter from Emma Sinkfield Anderson, *Spelman Messenger*, February 1893, 7; "Printing Department, Spelman Seminary," 3, 7.

103. Read, *Story of Spelman*, 86–87; Higginbotham, *Righteous Discontent*, 34.

104. Darlene Clark Hine, *Black Women in White: Racial Conflict and Cooperation in the Nursing Profession, 1890–1950* (Bloomington: Indiana University Press, 1989), xviii, 13, 89, 101, 188–89.

105. Untitled article on closing exams, *Spelman Messenger*, May 1886; Narcissa West, "Nursing," *Spelman Messenger*, January 1890, 2; Harriet Giles and Lucy Tapley, "Annual Report of the Principals of Spelman Seminary," *Spelman Messenger*, May 1896, 1–3; Harriet Giles and Lucy Upton, "Sixteenth Annual Report of the Principals of Spelman Seminary," *Spelman Messenger*, April 1897, 1–3; "Catalogue, 1898–99," 40.

106. Lucy Upton, "Our Nurses and their Need," *Spelman Messenger*, November 1899, 1–2; Hunter, *To 'Joy My Freedom*, 113.

107. J. Elmer Dellinger, M.D., "Hospital Work for Negro Women," *Spelman Messenger*, March 1902, 1–3, 6–7.

108. Harriet Giles and Lucy Upton, "Annual Report, Spelman Seminary," *Spelman Messenger*, March 1898, supplemental pages; Lucy Upton, "Our Nurses and their Need," *Spelman Messenger*, November 1899, 1–2; Harriet Giles and Lucy Upton, "Annual Report," *Spelman Messenger*, March 1901, 1–2. Spelman closed its nursing program in 1927, because, according to president Florence Read, its small hospital, lack of sophisticated equipment, and limited funds prevented the school from offering a top-flight program. Hine, *Black Women in White*, 8–9.

109. Watson and Gregory, *Daring to Educate*, 74.

110. "Spelman Seminary, Atlanta, Georgia, 1891–1892"; "Principals' Annual Report," *Spelman Messenger*, March 1892, 1.

111. "Catalogue, 1898–99."

112. Ruth Ramsey and Hattie Phinney, Letter from Ragoon, Burma, May 13, 1893, *Spelman Messenger*, November 1893, 5; Florence Anthony, Anadarko, Oklahoma Territory, February 15, 1895, *Spelman Messenger*, May 1895, 7.

113. Robert Edgerton, *The Troubled Heart of Africa: A History of the Congo* (New York: St. Martin's Press, 2002), chapter 4; Pagan Kennedy, *Black Livingstone: A True Tale of Adventure in the Nineteenth-Century Congo* (New York: Viking, 2002).

114. Harriet E. Giles and Lucy H. Upton, "Annual Report," *Spelman Messenger*, March 1901, 1–2; "Catalogue, 1900–1901," 13; Harriet Giles, "Spelman Seminary," *Spelman Messenger*, November 1908, 1–2.

115. James Anderson notes that most schools for African Americans in the New South viewed teacher training as their chief mission. *Education of Blacks in the South*, 253.

116. *Spelman Messenger*, December 1896, 6; Harriet Giles and Lucy Upton, "Sixteenth Annual Report of the Principals of Spelman Seminary," *Spelman Messenger*, April 1897, 1–3; E. V. Griffin, "Our Normal Work," *Spelman Messenger*, January 1899, 1–2.

117. Griffin, "Our Normal Work," 1–2; "Catalogue, 1898–99"; "Catalogue, 1904–05," 17–19.

118. "Spelman Normal Training School," *Spelman Messenger*, February 1893, 2; E. V. Griffin, "Our Normal Work," *Spelman Messenger*, January 1899, 1–2.

119. "Twenty-Third Annual Report, Spelman Seminary, 1904," *Spelman Messenger*, March 1904, 1, 7.

120. "From a Graduate," *Spelman Messenger*, December 1894, 5.

121. Harriet Giles and Lucy Tapley, "Annual Report of the Principals of Spelman Seminary," *Spelman Messenger*, May 1896, 1–3.

122. Fannie S. Wingfield, *Spelman Messenger*, February 1893, 3 and 5 (first quotation); Mary M. Gordon, *Spelman Messenger*, February 1893, 3 (second quotation); James L. Leloudis, *Schooling the New South: Pedagogy, Self, and Society in North Carolina, 1880–1920* (Chapel Hill: University of North Carolina Press, 1996), 29–33.

123. "Education of the Negroes: Mrs. Scott, at Fifth Avenue Baptist Church, Appeals for Patience and Help on Their Behalf," *New York Times*, January 14, 1899.

124. Chirhart, *Torches of Light*, introduction; quotation p. 5.

125. Lucy Hale Tapley and Edith V. Brill, "President's Annual Report to the Trustees of Spelman Seminary, 1918," *Spelman Messenger*, April 1918, 2–3; Lucy Hale Tapley, "Home Economics at Spelman," *Spelman Messenger*, May 1918, 3; Lucy Hale Tapley and Edith V. Brill, "Annual Report of Spelman Seminary," *Spelman Messenger*, April 1922, 5–6.

126. Lucy Hale Tapley, "President's Annual Report," *Spelman Messenger*, March 1912, 1–2; Lucy Hale Tapley and Edith V. Brill, "Thirty-Second Annual Report of the President of Spelman Seminary to the Board of Trustees," *Spelman Messenger*, April 1913, 1–3; Lucy Hale Tapley and Edith V. Brill, "Annual Report to the Trustees of Spelman Seminary, 1916–1917," *Spelman Messenger*, April 1917, 2–3.

127. Brazzell, "Bricks without Straw," 32; Jacoway, *Yankee Missionaries*, 5; Shaw, *What a Women Ought to Be and Do*, 73–75; Glenda Gilmore, *Gender and Jim Crow: Women and the Politics of White Supremacy in North Carolina, 1896–1920* (Chapel Hill: University of North Carolina Press, 1996), 140.

128. *Spelman Messenger*, January 1887, 4; *Spelman Messenger*, May 1887, 4; "Sixth Annual Circular and Catalogue, Spelman Seminary, 1887–88," 33 (quotation), 36; "Principals' Annual Report," *Spelman Messenger*, March 1892, 1; Morehouse, in "Dedication of Giles Hall, Spelman Seminary," 2; Speech by Rev. T. J. Morgan, reprinted in "Dedication of Giles Hall, Spelman Seminary," *Spelman Messenger*, January 1894, 5; [Morehouse], "The Worth of Spelman Seminary to the World," 1–3, 5–6; Rev. T. J. Morgan, "For the Negroes of America," *Spelman Messenger*, April 1897, 4–5.

129. [Morehouse], "The Worth of Spelman Seminary to the World," 1.

130. *Spelman Messenger*, June 1889, 7. Other examples expressing this idea include "Catalogue, 1883–84," 23, and "Principals' Annual Report," *Spelman Messenger*, March 1892, 1.

131. Giles Diaries, reel 1, March 6 and March 8, 1889; reel 2, March 26, 1896, January 4, 1897.

132. *Spelman Messenger*, May 1887, 4.

133. Linda R. Buchanan and Philip A. Hutchenson, "Reconsidering the Washington-Du Bois Debate: Two Black Colleges in 1910–11," in *Essays in Twentieth-Century Southern Education: Exceptionalism and Its Limits*, ed. Wayne J. Urban (New York: Garland Publishing, 1999), 77–99; Shaw, *What a Woman Ought to Be and Do*, 80; Frankenbine, "Our Little Circle," 72; Jacqueline M. Moore, *Booker T. Washington, W. E. B. Du Bois, and the Struggle for Racial Uplift* (Wilmington, Del.: Scholarly Resources, Inc., 2003), 30–32.

134. Wayne J. Urban, "Educational Reform in a New South City: Atlanta, 1890–1925," in *Education and the Rise of the New South*, eds. Ronald K. Goodenow and Arthur O. White (Boston: G.K. Hall & Co., 1981), 114–30.

135. Link, *Hard Country and Lonely Place*, 177–79; Chirhart, *Torches of Light*, 89.

136. Leloudis, *Schooling the New South*, 100.

137. Pascoe, *Relations of Rescue*; Mink, *Wages of Motherhood*; Meier, *Negro Thought in America*, 89–91; Jacoway, *Yankee Missionaries*, 10–14; Eric Anderson and Alfred A. Moss Jr., *Dangerous Donations: Northern Philanthropy and Southern Black Education, 1902–1930* (Columbia: University of Missouri Press, 1999), 201.

138. Jacoway, *Yankee Missionaries*, 13–14; Pascoe, *Relations of Rescue*, especially chapter 3; Mink, *Wages of Motherhood*.

139. As this suggests, Spelman faculty could be quite critical of the parents of students, especially those who drank or otherwise did not conform to respectable behavior. Giles Diaries, reel 1, November 15, 1887, journal (end of reel 1), April 18, 1883; reel 2, April 1, 1896, January 12, 1897.

140. [Morehouse], "The Worth of Spelman Seminary to the World," 3; Morgan, "What Spelman Stands For," (first quotation p. 7; second quotation p. 6); Higginbotham, *Righteous Discontent*, 26, 40.

141. Audrey Thomas McCluskey, "'We Specialize in the Wholly Impossible': Black Women School Founders and their Mission," *Signs* 22, no. 2 (Winter 1997): 403–26; Sharon Harley, "Nannie Helen Burroughs: 'The Black Goddess of Liberty'" *The Journal*

of Negro History 81, no. 1–4 (Winter-Autumn 1996): 62–71; Ann Short Chirhart, "'Gardens of Education': Beulah Rucker and African-American Culture in the Twentieth-Century Georgia Upcountry," *Georgia Historical Quarterly* 82 no. 4 (Winter 1998); 829–47; Shaw, *What a Woman Ought to Be and Do*.

142. McCluskey, "Black Women School Founders," 423–24.

143. McCluskey, "Black Women School Founders," 422; Gilmore, *Gender and Jim Crow*, 179–83.

144. William H. Watkins, *The White Architects of Black Education: Ideology and Power in America, 1865–1954* (New York: Teachers College, Columbia University, 2001), 118–25.

145. Brazzell, "Education as a Tool of Socialization," 158–59, 169.

146. Brazzell, "Education as a Tool of Socialization," 150–85.

147. Brazzell, "Education as a Tool of Socialization," 150–85; Read, *Story of Spelman*, 151–54, 212–14; Watkins, *White Architects of Black Education*, 127–29.

148. Watkins, *White Architects of Black Education*, 120, 129–35.

149. Beverly Guy-Sheftall, "Black Women in Higher Education: Spelman and Bennett Colleges Revisited," *Journal of Negro Education* 51 (1982): 279–289; Shaw, *What a Woman Ought to Be and Do*, 76, 90.

150. "Spelman Seminary Incorporated," *Spelman Messenger*, April 1888, 1; Read, *Story of Spelman*, 103–4, 145–48; "Annual Meeting of the Board of Trustees, Spelman Seminary," *Spelman Messenger*, April 1894, 1; Alice Coleman, "Our Ideals or Spelman's Aims," *Spelman Messenger*, December 1901, supplement, 1–3.

151. "Twelfth Annual Circular and Catalogue, Spelman Seminary 1892–93"; Read, *Story of Spelman*, 145; Anderson, *Education of Blacks in the South*, 68–69, 243.

152. Read, *Story of Spelman*, 146; Anderson, *Education of Blacks in the South*, 68–69.

153. "Negroes of the South: American Baptist Home Mission Society and Its Efforts for Their General Education," *New York Times*, April 11, 1897.

154. [Morehouse], "The Worth of Spelman Seminary to the World," 3 (quotations); Lucy H. Upton, "Signs of Progress of the Negro," *Spelman Messenger*, October 1906, 1–3.

155. Morehouse, in "Dedication of Giles Hall, Spelman Seminary," 2.

156. Rev. H. L. Morehouse, "General Survey of Spelman's Twenty Years," *Spelman Messenger,* January 1902, supplement, 1–2.

157. Anderson, *Education of Blacks in the South*, 252–53.

158. Morgan, "For the Negroes of America," 5.

159. Morgan, "What Spelman Stands For," 6.

160. Morgan, "For the Negroes of America," 5.

161. For the clearest statement of this sentiment, see Rev. T. J. Morgan, "What the American Baptist Home Missionary Society Has Done for the Negroes," *Spelman Messenger*, March 1901, 2–3, 7. On white northern attitudes towards black education, see Jennings L. Wagoner Jr., "The American Compromise: Charles W. Eliot, Black Education, and the New South," in Goodenow and White, *Education and the Rise of the New South*, 26–41; Anderson, *Education of Blacks in the South*, 241–42.

162. "Catalogue, 1887–88."

163. Jacqueline Jones found a similar emphasis on the reform of black character in her study of white teachers who flocked to Georgia during Reconstruction. As she pointed out, this overemphasis on character de-emphasized some of the real needs and hope of the freedpeople themselves. Jones, *Soldiers of Light and Love,* 207; Shaw, *What a Woman Ought to Be and Do,* 80–82.

164. Morgan called slavery a "monstrosity" that nonetheless taught slaves civilization, Christianity, and "habits of industry." Morgan, "For the Negroes of America," 4. See also Morehouse, "The Worth of Spelman Seminary to the World," 2, and "General Survey of Spelman's Twenty Years"; and Morgan, "What Spelman Stands For."

165. "A Sunday Service at Spelman," *Spelman Messenger,* April 1895, 1–2; Read, *Story of Spelman,* 147.

166. Harry G. Lefever, *Undaunted by the Fight: Spelman College and the Civil Rights Movement, 1957–67* (Macon, Ga.: Mercer University Press, 2005), 5; Brazzell, "Bricks without Straw."

167. Giles's only mention of the violence is the sentence "Great riot in Atlanta tonight." Giles Diaries, September 22, 1906, September 23, 1906; Watson, *Daring to Educate,* 76; Mixon, *Atlanta Riot,* 106.

168. Higginbotham, *Righteous Discontent,* 26–27 (quotation p. 27).

169. George M. Fredrickson, *The Black Image in the White Mind: The Debate on Afro-American Character and Destiny, 1817–1914* (New York: Harper & Row, 1971), 262–82; Joel Williamson, *Rage for Order: Black-White Relations in the American South Since Emancipation* (New York: Oxford University Press, 1986), 78–116.

170. Read, *Story of Spelman,* 148; Link, *Hard Country and Lonely Place,* 84; Anderson, *Education of Blacks in the South,* 86; Brazzell, "Education as a Tool of Socialization," 136–45; *Spelman Messenger,* January 1889, 4; Claudia T. White, "Report of Dr. Curry's Address," and Emma Z. Youngblood, "Dr. Curry's Talk," *Spelman Messenger,* December 1890, 1–2; *Spelman Messenger,* November 1892, 4.

171. Anderson, *Education of Blacks in the South,* 86–90.

172. Watkins, *White Architects of Black Education,* 161–77; Meier, *Negro Thought in America,* 95–96; Anderson, *Education of Blacks in the South,* 66; Dan Frost, *Thinking Confederates: Academia and the Idea of Progress in the New South* (Knoxville: University of Tennessee Press, 2000), 76; "Catalogue, 1887–88," 34, 40; *Spelman Messenger,* November 1892, 4; "Dedication of Giles Hall, Spelman Seminary," *Spelman Messenger,* January 1894, 1.

173. *Spelman Messenger,* November 1892, 4; "Annual Meeting of Spelman Trustees," *Spelman Messenger,* April 1893, 2–3; "Dedication of Giles Hall, Spelman Seminary," *Spelman Messenger,* January 1894, 1.

174. Lucy Hale Tapley, "Industrial Work in the Teachers' Professional Department," *Spelman Messenger,* January 1908, 2–3, 6 (quotation 2).

175. Brazzell, "Bricks without Straw," 41–44.

176. Watkins, *The White Architects of Black Education,* 177.

177. Anderson, *Education of Blacks in the South,* 80–81; Link, *Hard Country and Lonely Place,* 84–91; Leloudis, *Schooling the New South,* 70–71, 113, 140–41, 145–46, 148, 181–84.

178. Watkins, *The White Architects of Black Education*, 175–76.

179. Read, *Story of Spelman*, 148; Link, *Hard Country and Lonely Place*, 84; Anderson, *Education of Blacks in the South*, 84; Finkenbine, "Our Little Circle," 80 (quotation).

180. Link, *Hard Country and Lonely Place*, 174–77; Anderson, *Education of Blacks in the South*, 79–81, 94–96, 97–102; Leloudis, *Schooling the New South*, 178–80, 185. For hints of opposition to Spelman, see *Spelman Messenger*, January 1893, 4; Morehouse, "General Survey of Spelman's Twenty Years," 1–2; "Our Thirtieth Anniversary," *Spelman Messenger*, May 1911, 1.

181. *Spelman Messenger*, March 1887, 2; "Splendid Exhibition of Skill by Pupils of Spelman Seminary," *Spelman Messenger*, February 1888, 5; *Spelman Messenger*, January 1890, 4; Harriet Giles and Lucy Tapley, "Annual Report of the Principals of Spelman Seminary," *Spelman Messenger*, May 1896, 1–3; *Spelman Messenger*, May 1896, 5; Harriet Giles and Lucy Upton, "Sixteenth Annual Report of the Principals of Spelman Seminary," *Spelman Messenger*, April 1897, 1–3; *Spelman Messenger*, November 1900, 3; *Spelman Messenger*, December 1900, 2; G. R. Glenn, "The Work of Negro Women in the Public Schools," *Spelman Messenger*, January 1902, 1–2 (quotation 2). The *Constitution* continued to endorse Spelman after Grady's death. *Spelman Messenger*, May 1896, 4–5.

182. Sidney Root, "Memorandum of My Life," 14 September 1893, mss 293 f, Atlanta History Center, Atlanta, Georgia; *Spelman Messenger*, March 1897, 4.

183. Root, "Memorandum of My Life," 14.

184. *Spelman Messenger*, October 1902, 7; Urban, "Educational Reform in a New South City," 117–19; Dewey Grantham, *Hoke Smith and the Politics of the New South* (Baton Rouge: Louisiana State University Press, 1967 [1958]), 31, 122, 148. Smith could be inconsistent; he also stated that "the uneducated Negro is a good Negro; he is contented to occupy the natural status of his race, the position of inferiority." Mixon, *Atlanta Riot*, 41.

185. Glenn, "The Work of Negro Women in the Public Schools," 2.

186. Gilmore, *Gender and Jim Crow*, 138–40.

187. August Meier and David Lewis, "History of the Negro Upper Class in Atlanta, Georgia, 1890–1958," *Journal of Negro Education* 28 (Spring 1958): 128–39; Bartley, *Creation of Modern Georgia*, 135–36; Pomeranz, *Where Peachtree Meets Sweet Auburn*, 65, 70–71; Branch, *Parting the Waters*, 42, 54 (quotation); Hunter, *To 'Joy My Freedom*, 100–1; Dorsey, *To Build Our Lives Together*, 6–9, 35, 116–17; Mixon, *The Atlanta Riot*, 38–40.

188. The paper's outspoken editor, J. Max Barber, was forced to leave Atlanta in 1906 after anonymously publishing a letter in the New York *World* accusing whites aligned with gubernatorial candidate Hoke Smith of perpetrating in blackface the alleged rapes that sparked the Atlanta Race Riot. Barber published the paper from Chicago for only one year more. Kevin K. Gaines, *Uplifting the Race: Black Leadership, Politics, and Culture in the Twentieth Century* (Chapel Hill: University of North Carolina Press, 1996), 65–66; Mixon, *The Atlanta Riot*, 120–22.

189. A few examples include, "The Supreme Court and the Negro" and "Is it Ignorance or Slander? The Answer to Thomas Nelson Page," *Voice of the Negro*, June 1904, 217, 228–33; "A Rebuke to Jimcrowism," *Voice of the Negro*, August 1904, 302; Emma F. G. Merritt, "American Prejudice—Its Cause, Effect and Possibilities," *Voice of the Negro*, July 1905, 466–69. See also Gaines, *Uplifting the Race*, 60–66.

190. Booker T. Washington, "The Negro's Part in the South's Upbringing," *Voice of the Negro*, January 1904, 28–29; W. E. Burghardt Du Bois, "The Atlanta Conference," *Voice of the Negro*, March 1904, 85–90; Mary Church Terrell, "The Progress of Negro Women," *Voice of the Negro*, July 1904, 291–94. Washington, however, chafed at what he perceived to be a critique of his leadership by Barber, and viewed the publication as a threat to his control of black public opinion. Indeed, after unsuccessfully pressuring the editor, Washington succeeded in shutting down the paper and ultimately ending Barber's career in journalism. Louis R. Harlan, "Booker T. Washington and the Voice of the Negro, 1904–1907," *Journal of Southern History*, 45, no. 1 (Feb. 1979): 45–62.

191. John Hope, "Our Negro Schools," *Voice of the Negro*, January 1904, 10–16; Lewis B. Moore, "Education of Negro Teachers," *Voice of the Negro*, April 1904, 157–59; J. W. E. Bowen, "Doing Things at Tuskegee Institute," *Voice of the Negro*, April 1905, 249–53; Anna H. Jones, "A Century's Progress for the American Colored Woman," *Voice of the Negro*, September 1905, 631–33.

192. Moore, "Education of Negro Teachers," 159.

193. Mary Church Terrell, "The Progress of Colored Women," Josephine B. Bruce, "What Has Education Done for Colored Women," and Sylvanie Francaz Williams, "The Social Status of the Negro Woman," *Voice of the Negro*, July 1904, 291–94, 294–98, 298–300.

194. A few examples include Hope, "Our Negro Schools"; "Two Great Schools: Spellman [sic] Seminary and Tuskegee Institute," *Voice of the Negro*, April 1906, 289; "Spelman's Twenty-fifth Anniversary," *Voice of the Negro*, May 1906, 322–23. For Spelman advertisements in the paper, see for example January 1904 and July 1905.

195. John R. L. Diggs, "Negro Church Life," and Kelly Miller, "The Negro as a Political Factor," *Voice of the Negro*, February 1904, 46–50, 59–60; Williams, "The Social Status of the Negro Woman"; "Shall We Materialize the Negro," *Voice of the Negro*, 194–96.

196. Higginbotham, *Righteous Discontent*, 186–87, 191–205; Leloudis, *Schooling the New South*, 199, 203–206; Link, *Hard Country and Lonely Place*, 180–84; Johnson, *Southern Ladies, New Women*, 194–98; Mixon, *Atlanta Riot*, 40; Katharine Capshaw Smith, "Childhood, the Body, and Race Performance: Early Twentieth-Century Etiquette Books for Black Children," *African-American Review* 40 no. 1 (Winter 2006): 795–811; David H. Jackson Jr., *Booker T. Washington and the Struggle Against White Supremacy: The Southern Educational Tours, 1908–1912* (New York: Palgrave Macmillan, 2008), 178–80. Glenda Gilmore termed this same process the "Best Man" idea, and argued that by the time of disenfranchisement, its promise proved hollow. Gilmore, *Gender and Jim Crow*, 62–93, 75–77, 115–16, 160, especially chapter 4.

197. Mitchell, *Righteous Propagation*, 78–86, quotation p. 80. Mitchell uses "aspiring" rather than "middle class" to underline their differences from the white middle class. See "Note on Usage and Terminology," xx.

198. Hickey, *Hope and Danger*, 58–59.

199. Higginbotham, *Righteous Discontent*, 95–96; Mitchell, *Righteous Propagation*, 108–16; Johnson, *Southern Ladies, New Women*, 195–97.

200. *Spelman Messenger*, February 1887; *Spelman Messenger*, March 1888; W. J. White, "D.D. to Miss Giles," *Spelman Messenger*, December 1891, 4; "Spelman Seminary, Atlanta, Ga.," [reprinted from the *Independent*], *Spelman Messenger*, May 1892, 5; *Spelman Messenger*, June 1898, 4; John Hope, "Spelman's Twenty-Fifth Anniversary," *Spelman Messenger*, May 1906, 1–2; Rev. James M. Nabrit, "Emancipation Day Address Delivered at Spelman Seminary, Jan. 1, 1913," *Spelman Messenger*, February 1913, 4–8.

201. Rev. E. K. Love, "Extracts from Emancipation Oration," *Spelman Messenger*, February 1888, 2.

202. Benjamin Hubert, "The Larger Freedom of the Negro," *Spelman Messenger*, February 1921, 2–3, 5.

203. "Donations for Spelman," *Spelman Messenger*, November 1890, 7; "Dedication of Giles Hall, Spelman Seminary," *Spelman Messenger*, January 1894, 3; "Donations for Spelman," *Spelman Messenger,* November 1899, 7; "Donations for Spelman," *Spelman Messenger*, February 1900, 5; "Donations for Spelman," *Spelman Messenger*, May 1902, 7; "Contributions to Spelman," *Spelman Messenger*, November 1902, 7; "Contributions for Spelman from Negroes," *Spelman Messenger*, October 1903, 7; "Unreported Contributions From Negroes," *Spelman Messenger*, October 1907, 4; "Negro Donors to March 1, 1910," *Spelman Messenger*, March 1910, 7; "Donations from Negroes, May 1 to October 1, 1910," *Spelman Messenger*, October 1910, 7; Royster, *Traces of a Stream*, 156.

204. Rev. P. J. Bryant, "Now and Then, or the To-Day and To-Morrow of the Negro Race in America," *Spelman Messenger*, February 1902, 2–3, 7 (quotation p. 2).

205. Read, *Story of Spelman*, 147–48; Bartley, *Creation of Modern Georgia*, 143; Harvey, *Freedom's Coming*, 10–12; Bobby J. Donaldson, "Standing on a Volcano: The Leadership of William Jefferson White," in Edward J. Cashin and Glenn T. Eskew, *Paternalism in a Southern City: Race, Religion and Gender in Augusta, Georgia* (Athens: University of Georgia Press, 2001), 135–176, quotation 143.

206. Jaqueline Anne Rouse, *Lugenia Burns Hope: Black Southern Reformer* (Athens: University of Georgia Press, 1989), 42–48; Mixon, *Atlanta Riot*, 106. The closeness of Hope and Read's relationship sparked rumors of a romantic affair, but a Hope biographer found little concrete evidence to back up such beliefs. Leroy Davis, *A Clashing of the Soul: John Hope and the Dilemma of African American Leadership and Black Higher Education in the Early Twentieth Century* (Athens: University of Georgia Press, 1998), 326–28.

207. Meier, *Negro Thought in America*, 193, 195, 198–200; McPherson, *Abolitionist Legacy*, 361–62, 368.

208. August Meier, *Negro Thought in America*, 95; Buchanan and Hutchenson, "Reconsidering the Washington-Du Bois Debate"; Moore, *Booker T. Washington,*

W.E.B. Du Bois, and the Struggle for Racial Uplift; W. Fitzhugh Brundage, *Booker T. Washington and Black Progress: Up From Slavery 100 Years Later* (Gainesville: University Press of Florida, 2003); Jackson, *Booker T. Washington and the Struggle Against White Supremacy*. For the traditional view see Spivey, *Schooling for the New Slavery*, and Anderson, *Education of Blacks in the South*.

209. *Spelman Messenger*, April 1890, 7; *Spelman Messenger*, November 1895, 5 (quotation).

210. Article reprinted from *Young Men's Era*, *Spelman Messenger*, April 1892, 5; *Spelman Messenger*, April 1896, 4; *Spelman Messenger*, April 1897, 4; *Spelman Messenger*, April 1901, 4; J. W. E. Bowen, "Doing Things at Tuskegee Institute," *Voice of the Negro*, April 1905, 249–53.

211. W. E. Burghardt Du Bois, "The Work of Negro Women in Society," *Spelman Messenger*, February 1902, 1–3.

212. Mitchell, *Righteous Propagation*, 136–37. Mitchell identifies the emphasis on homemaking with a turning away from, even mocking of, electoral politics.

213. Du Bois, "The Work of Negro Women in Society," 2.

Chapter 4. Respectability and Reform

1. Melissa Rose to Selena Sloan Butler, February 15, 1957, Selena Sloan Butler File, Spelman College Archives, Spelman College, Atlanta, Georgia (hereafter Spelman College Archives).

2. Jacqueline Jones Royster, *Traces of a Stream: Literacy and Social Change Among African American Women* (Pittsburgh: University of Pittsburgh Press, 2000), especially 109–10, 177–78.

3. "Twenty-Third Annual Report, Spelman Seminary, 1904," *Spelman Messenger*, March 1904, 1, 7; "Graduates' Corner," *Spelman Messenger*, October 1912, 8; "Graduates' Corner," *Spelman Messenger*, November 1912, 4; "Graduates' Corner," *Spelman Messenger*, January 1916, 8; Angie E. Kendall, "Spelman Graduates," *Spelman Messenger*, February 1919, 5; "Graduates' Corner," *Spelman Messenger*, February 1920, 5; Lucy Hale Tapley and Edith V. Brill, "Annual Report, April 8, 1921," *Spelman Messenger*, April 1921, 5; "Graduates' Corner," *Spelman Messenger*, March 1922, 8; *Spelman Messenger*, January 1923, 4; "Graduates' Corner," *Spelman Messenger*, January 1923, 8; "Graduates' Corner," *Spelman Messenger*, October 1923, 4.

4. Minnie Lee Thomas, "The Work of the Industrial Department of Spelman Seminary," *Spelman Messenger*, April 1896, 5; Mrs. A. L. Klugh, "A Tribute to Spelman," *Spelman Messenger*, October 1901, 6 (quotation).

5. *Spelman Messenger*, December 1884; Carrie Walls, "The Duty of the Hour," *Spelman Messenger*, June 1888; Minnie C. Berry, "Emancipation," *Spelman Messenger*, February 1889; Laura Kent, "The Macedonian Cry," *Spelman Messenger*, February 1890, 5; Hattie White, "What I Wish my Character to Be Twenty Years Hence," *Spelman Messenger*, January 1891, 2; Della M. Richardson, "Practical Ways to Help Ourselves," *Spelman Messenger*, December 1894, 2; Sarah Mahardy, "How Success is Won," *Spelman Messenger*, February 1889, 6; Esther L. Garrison, "Self Help," *Spelman Messenger*, May 1905, 1–2.

6. V. W. Maddox, *Spelman Messenger*, February 1893, 2.

7. Viola L. F. Chaplain, "The Duties of a Citizen to His Community," *Spelman Messenger*, October 1909, 3, 7; Ida B. Davis, "The Duties of an American Citizen," *Spelman Messenger*, February 1911, 1–2.

8. "Spelman Seminary Statistics Prepared for the Thirtieth Anniversary," *Spelman Messenger*, May 1911, 3; "Graduates' Corner," *Spelman Messenger*, March 1917, 6–7; "Graduates' Corner," *Spelman Messenger*, April 1917, 7 (quotation); "Graduates' Corner," *Spelman Messenger*, February 1918, 3; "Graduates' Corner," *Spelman Messenger*, January 1920, 6.

9. "Mrs. Victoria Maddox Simmons," *Spelman Messenger*, December 1898, 3; *Spelman Messenger*, January 1900, 3 (on Sallie Addams); "Sketches of Graduates," *Spelman Messenger*, May 1901, 2–3, 5; "Sketches of Spelman Graduates," *Spelman Messenger*, October 1901, 2–3; "Twenty-Third Annual Report, Spelman Seminary, 1904," *Spelman Messenger*, March 1904, 1, 7; "Graduates' Corner," *Spelman Messenger*, October 1909, 6; "Graduates' Corner," *Spelman Messenger*, October 1911, 4; "Graduates' Corner," *Spelman Messenger*, November 1923, 4.

10. "Visit to Graduates in Florida," *Spelman Messenger*, May 1909, 6; "Granddaughters' Club," *Spelman Messenger*, May 1910, 5; "Graduates' Corner," *Spelman Messenger*, February 1918, 3; "Graduates' Corner," *Spelman Messenger*, October 1920, 5; "Graduates' Corner," *Spelman Messenger*, May 1924, 7.

11. "From the Spelman Mail," *Spelman Messenger*, January 1919, 6; "Graduates' Corner," *Spelman Messenger*, December 1920, 6; "Graduates' Corner," *Spelman Messenger*, January 1921, 6.

12. "Spelman Seminary Statistics Prepared for the Thirtieth Anniversary," *Spelman Messenger*, May 1911, 3; "Graduates' Corner," *Spelman Messenger*, November 1911, 4; "Contributions to Rally Fund," *Spelman Messenger*, May 1912, 7; "Contributions," *Spelman Messenger*, April 1913, 1–3; "Contributions," *Spelman Messenger*, May 1914, 5; "Founders' Day," *Spelman Messenger*, May 1919, 5; "Summary of Founders Day Rally—April 1920," *Spelman Messenger*, May 1920, 4; "Summary of Founders Day Rally, April 11, 1922," *Spelman Messenger*, May 1922, 3; "Summary of Founders Day Rally, April 11, 1924," *Spelman Messenger*, May 1924, 4.

13. Letter from Clara Bynes, *Spelman Messenger*, May 1883, 5; *Spelman Messenger*, May 1904, 6.

14. "From Our Letter File," *Spelman Messenger*, April 1904, 5; Harriet E. Giles, "Annual Report to the Trustees of Spelman Seminary," *Spelman Messenger*, April 1908, 5–6; "From the Spelman Mail-Bag," *Spelman Messenger*, April 1914, 8.

15. Giles Diaries, reel 3, February 24, 1897; reel 5, March 21, 1907.

16. Lucy Hale Tapley and Edith Villora Brill, "Annual Report to the Trustees of Spelman Seminary," *Spelman Messenger*, April 1920, 2, (quotation). For evidence of students living outside of the South, see "Twenty-Third Annual Report, Spelman Seminary, 1904," *Spelman Messenger*, March 1904, 1, 7; "Graduates' Corner," *Spelman Messenger*, February 1920, 5; "Graduates' Corner," *Spelman Messenger*, March 1920, 6; "Graduates' Corner," *Spelman Messenger*, November 1921, 6; "Graduates' Corner,"

Spelman Messenger, February 1922, 8; "Graduates' Corner," *Spelman Messenger*, April 1922, 8; "Graduates' Corner," *Spelman Messenger*, May 1922, 3–4; "Graduates' Corner," *Spelman Messenger*, February 1924, 8.

17. "Spelman Seminary Statistics Prepared for the Thirtieth Anniversary," *Spelman Messenger*, May 1911, 3.

18. Raymond Wolters, *The New Negro on Campus: Black College Rebellions of the 1920s* (Princeton: Princeton University Press, 1975).

19. Margaret A. Lowe, *Looking Good: College Women and Body Image, 1875–1930* (Baltimore: Johns Hopkins University Press, 2003), 125–31.

20. Florence Matilda Read, *The Story of Spelman College* (Atlanta, Ga.: United Negro Fund with Princeton University Press, 1961), 188.

21. Lowe, *Looking Good*, 128; Read, *Story of Spelman*, 195–96.

22. V. M. S. to Miss Tapley Sept. 7, 1923; My dear Mrs. Simmons from Lucy Tapley, Sept 11, 1923; V. M. Simmons to Miss Tapley, Aug. 7, 1925 (quotations); My dear Mrs. Simmons from Lucy Tapley, August 12, 1925, all in Victoria Maddox Simmons File, Spelman College Archives. These are the only letters I found from alumnae to Spelman administrators that stated that alumnae and current students complained openly about the school. Simmons wrote that she was very concerned as a loyal alumna and recruiter for the school about rumors circulating about Spelman. In her replies, Tapley strongly defended Lamson. Simmons was one of the original students, in the basement school of 1881, and among its first graduates. She remained a regular correspondent and addressed graduates and alumnae in 1948 on the sixtieth anniversary of her graduation. Simmons, Address to "Mrs. Borders, National President of Spelman Alumnae Association, President Read, Alumnae, 1948 Graduating Class, and Visitors," also in Simmons File, Spelman College Archives.

23. My dear Mrs. Simmons from Lucy Tapley, August 12, 1925.

24. Hortense Powdermaker, *After Freedom: A Cultural Study of the Deep South* (New York: Viking Press, 1939); August Meier and David Lewis, "History of the Negro Upper Class in Atlanta, Georgia, 1890–1958," *Journal of Negro Education* 28 (Spring 1958): 128–39; Taylor Branch, *Parting the Waters: America in the King Years* (New York: Touchstone, 1988), 54; Alison Dorsey, *To Build Our Lives Together: Community Formation in Black Atlanta, 1875–1906* (Athens: University of Georgia Press, 2004).

25. Dorsey, *To Build Our Lives Together*, 6–10.

26. Giles Diaries (at end of reel 1), December 4, 1882; *Spelman Messenger*, December 1888, 6.

27. Kevin K. Gaines, *Uplifting the Race: Black Leadership, Politics, and Culture in the Twentieth Century* (Chapel Hill: University of North Carolina Press, 1996), especially xiv–v, 1–10; Dorsey, *To Build Our Lives Together*, 104.

28. Darlene Clark Hine, "'We Specialize in the Wholly Impossible': The Philanthropic Work of Black Women," in *Hine Sight: Black Women and the Re-Construction of American History*, comp. Hine (Brooklyn, N.Y.: Carlson Publishing, 1994), 109–28, especially 112–13; Anne Firor Scott, "Most Invisible of All: Black Women's Voluntary Associations," *Journal of Southern History* 56 (February 1990), 3–22; Evelyn Brooks Higginbotham,

Righteous Discontent: The Women's Movement in the Black Baptist Church, 1880–1920
(Cambridge, Mass.: Harvard University Press, 1993), 186–87, 191–205; Linda Gordon,
Pitied But Not Entitled: Single Mothers and the History of Welfare, 1890–1935 (Cambridge,
Mass.: Harvard University Press, 1994), 129–35; Elizabeth Lasch-Quinn, *Black Neighbors:
Race and the Limits of Reform in the American Settlement House Movement, 1890–1945*
(Chapel Hill: University of North Carolina Press, 1993), 117–19; Georgina Hickey, *Hope
and Danger in the New South City: Working-Class Women and Urban Development in
Atlanta, 1890–1940* (Athens: University of Georgia Press, 2003), 96–102; Victoria W.
Wolcott, *Remaking Respectability: African American Women in Interwar Detroit* (Chapel
Hill: University of North Carolina Press, 2001); Joan Marie Johnson, *Southern Ladies,
New Women: Race, Region, and Clubwomen in South Carolina, 1890–1930* (Gainseville:
University Press of Florida, 2004).

29. Jacqueline Anne Rouse, *Lugenia Burns Hope: Black Southern Reformer* (Athens:
University of Georgia Press, 1989), 89–90; Scott, "Most Invisible of All," 20; Gordon,
Pitied But Not Entitled, 112–13; Hine, "We Specialize in the Wholly Impossible," 126–28;
Ronald H. Bayor, *Race and the Shaping of Twentieth-Century Atlanta* (Chapel Hill:
University of North Carolina Press, 1996), 6; Hickey, *Hope and Danger*, 101–2; Michele
Mitchell, *Righteous Propagation: African Americans and the Politics of Racial Destiny
after Reconstruction* (Chapel Hill: University of North Carolina Press, 2004), 9–15;
Dorsey, *To Build Our Lives Together*, 1–5; Johnson, *Southern Ladies, New Women*,
171, 173–75.

30. David Fort Godshalk, *Veiled Visions: The 1906 Atlanta Race Riot and the Reshaping of American Race Relations* (Chapel Hill: University of North Carolina Press,
2005).

31. Lowe, *Looking Good*, 39–41.

32. Patricia K. Hunt, "Clothing as an Expression of History: The Dress of African
American Women in Georgia, 1880–1915," in *"We Specialize in the Wholly Impossible":
A Reader in Black Women's History*, eds. Darlene Clark Hine, Wilma King, and Linda
Reed (Brooklyn, N.Y.: Carlson Publishing, 1995), 393–404.

33. Higginbotham, *Righteous Discontent*, 172–79, 187, 191–94; Patricia A. Schechter,
Ida B. Wells-Barnett and American Reform, 1880–1930 (Chapel Hill: University of
North Carolina Press, 2001), 3, 12–13; 67–69; Mitchell, *Righteous Propagation*, 108–16,
141–48, 173–77; "Spelman Seminary, Atlanta, Ga." *Spelman Messenger*, May 1892, 5
(reprinted from the *Atlanta Independent*). The *Independent* was a conservative, pro-
Washington paper. Bobby J. Donaldson, "Standing on a Volcano: The Leadership
of William Jefferson White," in *Paternalism in a Southern City: Race, Religion, and
Gender in Augusta, Georgia* (Athens: University of Georgia Press, 2001), 135–76, esp.
164.

34. Johnetta Cross Brazzell, "Bricks without Straw: Missionary-Sponsored Black
Higher Education in the Post-Emancipation Era," *Journal of Higher Education* 63, no. 1
(January/February 1992): 46–47; Glenda Gilmore, *Gender and Jim Crow: Women and
the Politics of White Supremacy in North Carolina, 1896–1920* (Chapel Hill: University
of North Carolina Press, 1996), 75–77, 140. On African American parents' concern

about their daughters' modesty generally, see Stephanie J. Shaw, *What a Women Ought to Be and Do: Black Professional Women Workers During the Jim Crow Era* (Chicago: University of Chicago Press, 1996), 83–90.

35. *Spelman Messenger*, May 1896.

36. Susie Ford Bailey to "My Dear Daughter" [Sue Bailey], January 2, 1918; Susie Ford Bailey to "Dear Little Daughter" [Sue Bailey], October 28, 1921, both in box 3, Bailey/Thurman Family Papers, Special Collections, Robert W. Woodruff Library, Emory University, Atlanta, Georgia.

37. [Henry Morehouse], "The Worth of Spelman Seminary to the World," *Spelman Messenger*, June 1896, 1–3, 5–6; quote page 3.

38. In publications, faculty generally referred to students as "Spelman women" or "girls" rather than "ladies," but they did use titles ("Miss and Mrs.") when discussing them. One editorial reprinted in the *Messenger* from the African American publication *Georgia Baptist* did call Spelman "the best school for young ladies of color in the South." *Spelman Messenger,* March 1891.

39. Hine, "We Specialize in the Wholly Impossible," 126–28; Higginbotham, *Righteous Discontent*, 189–91; Johnson, *Southern Ladies, New Women*, 196.

40. Shaw, *What a Woman Ought to Be and Do*, 2, 7–8.

41. Estelle Ivey and Ethel E. Hudson, "The Spelman Graduates Club," *Spelman Messenger*, February 1921, 7.

42. "Spelman College Bulletin, Directory of Graduates and Former Students, 1881–1930," Spelman College, 1930. Catalogues routinely listed names, marital status, and addresses of graduates, indicating that a majority married. Gordon contrasts this to the choice of many white social welfare leaders to remain single; *Pitied But Not Entitled*, 120–21. The faculty themselves primarily were single white women.

43. For some of many examples, see "Sketches of Graduates," *Spelman Messenger*, May 1901, 2–3, 5; "Graduates' Corner," *Spelman Messenger*, April 1914, 4 (quotation).

44. Claudia T. White, "Spelman Field Notes," *Spelman Messenger*, October 1911, 2–3, 8; H. R. Watson, "From the College Department," *Spelman Messenger*, November 1914, 6; Myrtle Dona Hull, "The College Woman of To-Day," *Spelman Messenger*, December 1921, 8.

45. For some examples, see "Personals," *Spelman Messenger*, March 1897, 6; "Personals," *Spelman Messenger*, November 1899, 7; "Sketches of Graduates," *Spelman Messenger*, May 1901, 2–3, 5; "Twenty-Third Annual Report, Spelman Seminary, 1904," *Spelman Messenger*, March 1904, 1, 7; "Graduates' Corner," *Spelman Messenger*, March 1912, 5; "Graduates' Corner," *Spelman Messenger*, April 1912, 3; "Graduates' Corner," *Spelman Messenger*, October 1912, 6; "Graduates' Corner," *Spelman Messenger*, April 1918, 8; "Graduates' Corner," *Spelman Messenger*, October 1923, 4.

46. "Sketches of Graduates," *Spelman Messenger*, May 1901, 2–3, 5; Carrie Walls Gassaway, "One Graduate's Work," *Spelman Messenger*, May 1914, 8.

47. "Sketches of Graduates," *Spelman Messenger*, May 1901, 2–3, 5; "Mattie Brookins Johnson," *Spelman Messenger*, October 1902, 3; "Twenty-Third Annual Report, Spelman Seminary, 1904," *Spelman Messenger*, March 1904, 1, 7; "Graduates'

Corner," *Spelman Messenger*, April 1912, 3; "Graduates' Corner," *Spelman Messenger*, May 1913, 7.

48. "Personals," *Spelman Messenger*, March 1897, 6; "Mrs. Victoria Maddox Simmons," *Spelman Messenger*, December 1898, 3; Rev. C. N. Hampton, "Hattie Bryant Hampton," *Spelman Messenger*, February 1902, 6; Ida Burton Jones, "A Spelman's Girl's Work," *Spelman Messenger*, November 1902, 6–7; E. O. W., "Emma S. DeLamotta," *Spelman Messenger*, November 1903, 1–2; "From the Spelman Mail-Bag," *Spelman Messenger*, April 1914, 4–8; *Spelman Messenger*, October 1916, 8; Angie E. Kendall, "Spelman Graduates," *Spelman Messenger*, February 1919, 5; "Graduates' Corner," *Spelman Messenger*, November 1920, 6; *Spelman Messenger*, March 1922, 5.

49. *Spelman Messenger*, November 1886, 5; M. J. Watson, "A True Woman," *Spelman Messenger*, December 1889, 2; Jessie Milton, "Our Mistakes," *Spelman Messenger*, January 1891, 3; Selena Sloan Butler, "Woman's Highest Calling," *Spelman Messenger*, November 1904, 1–2; [E. Leola Hudson], "The Development of Negro Home Life," *Spelman Messenger*, January 1914, 1–2 (Hudson is identified as the author of the article in "Graduates' Corner," *Spelman Messenger*, March 1914, 8); Selena Sloan Butler, "The Model Homemaker's Part in the Uplift of the Community," *Spelman Messenger*, October 1916, 5; Mitchell, *Righteous Propagation*, chapter 5.

50. Jacqueline Jones, *Labor of Love, Labor of Sorrow: Black Women, Work, and the Family, From Slavery to the Present* (New York: Vintage, 1985), 4, 78, 95; Sharon Harley, "For the Good of Family and Race: Gender, Work, and Domestic Roles in the Black Community, 1880–1930" *Signs* 15 (Winter 1990): 336–49, especially 337, 346; Sharon Harley, "When Your Work is Not Who You Are: The Development of a Working-Class Consciousness among Afro-American Women," in Hine, King, and Reed, *"We Specialize in the Wholly Impossible,"* 25–37.

51. Nora Gordon, "Influence of Woman on National Character," *Spelman Messenger*, November 1888, 1–2 (first quotation); *Spelman Messenger*, November 1886, 5 (second quotation).

52. R. S. Jones, "Every Woman Should Have a Trade," *Spelman Messenger*, February 1890, 3.

53. Mrs. M. W. Reddick, "The Awakened Woman," *Spelman Messenger*, March 1915, 7–8; Ruth Lois Murden, "Women in Industry," *Spelman Messenger*, October 1919, 3; "Women in the New Era," *Spelman Messenger*, January 1921, 2; Sarah Williams, "Woman in Professions," *Spelman Messenger*, November 1922, 102.

54. In 1880, 98 percent of wage-earning black women worked in domestic service; by 1920, the number had fallen to 75 percent. Tera W. Hunter, *To 'Joy My Freedom: Southern Black Women's Lives and Labors after the Civil War* (Cambridge, Mass.: Harvard University Press, 1997), 242. Atlanta had more per capita domestics than any other American city in this period. Tera W. Hunter, "Domination and Resistance: The Politics of Wage Household Labor in New South Atlanta," in Hine, King, and Reed, *"We Specialize in the Wholly Impossible,"* 343–57.

55. "Graduates Corner," *Spelman Messenger*, December 1911, 4; Angie E. Kendall, "Spelman Graduates," *Spelman Messenger*, February 1919, 5; "Graduates' Corner," *Spelman Messenger*, November 1920, 6.

56. "Graduates' Corner," *Spelman Messenger*, October 1918, 7.

57. "Graduates Corner," *Spelman Messenger*, February 1913, 4; Angie E. Kendall, "Spelman Graduates," *Spelman Messenger*, February 1919, 5; "An Appreciation," *Spelman Messenger*, May 1924, 5–6; Harley, "For the Good of Family and Race," 341.

58. Shaw, *What a Woman Ought to Be and Do*, 2–3, 7–8, 211–13.

59. Harriet Giles, "President's Annual Report Spelman Seminary, Atlanta, Georgia," *Spelman Messenger*, April 1906, 1–2; Lucy Hale Tapley and Edith V. Brill, "Annual Report, April 8, 1921," *Spelman Messenger*, April 1921, 6. In 1912, the number reached 94 percent. Lucy Hale Tapley, "An Appeal," *Spelman Messenger*, November 1912, 1–2.

60. Every catalogue and edition of the *Messenger* indicate the high numbers of students who became teachers. A few examples include *Spelman Messenger*, January 1888, 7; *Spelman Messenger*, May 1890, 6; *Spelman Messenger*, January 1891, 4; "Fifteenth Annual Circular and Catalogue of Spelman Seminary for Women and Girls in Atlanta, Georgia for the Academic Year 1895–96," 9–12; "Personals," *Spelman Messenger*, March 1897, 6; "Our Last Year's Graduates," *Spelman Messenger*, January 1905, 1; "Graduates' Corner," *Spelman Messenger*, April 1913, 5; H. R. Watson, "From the College Department," *Spelman Messenger*, November 1914, 6; "Graduates' Corner," *Spelman Messenger*, April 1917, 6–7; "Graduates' Corner," *Spelman Messenger*, October 1917, 6; "Graduates' Corner," *Spelman Messenger*, February 1918, 3; "Graduates' Corner," *Spelman Messenger*, February 1919, 6; "Graduates' Corner," *Spelman Messenger*, March 1923, 8.

61. Letter from Sallie Waugh, *Spelman Messenger*, May 1883, 5; letter from "Cousin Carrie" [Carrie P. Walls], *Spelman Messenger*, November 1886, 5; *Spelman Messenger*, June 1887; R. E. Humpreys, "Dear Friends," and C. A. Howard, "Dear Readers of the Messenger," *Spelman Messenger*, November 1887, 2; Nora Gordon, "Letter to Messenger," *Spelman Messenger*, December 1887; Harriet Giles and Lucy Tapley, "Annual Report of the Principals of Spelman Seminary," *Spelman Messenger*, April 1894, 1–3; Hannah Howell, "The Influence of Normal Training," *Spelman Messenger*, January 1897, 1–2; Penelope Burwell, "The Responsibility and Opportunity of the Teacher," *Spelman Messenger*, February 1911, 7; Camilla Weens, "The Relation of the Rural School to the Community," *Spelman Messenger*, May 1912, 2–3; "Graduates' Corner," *Spelman Messenger*, January 1913, 7; Isabelle Tolbert, "The Teacher's Opportunity for Service," *Spelman Messenger*, January 1920, 2–3.

62. *Spelman Messenger*, November 1896, 6; "Personals," *Spelman Messenger*, November 1897, 5; "Mrs. Victoria Maddox Simmons," *Spelman Messenger*, December 1898, 3; "Personals," *Spelman Messenger*, October 1902, 5; E. O. W., "Emma S. DeLamotta," *Spelman Messenger*, November 1903, 1–2; "Graduates' Corner," *Spelman Messenger*, November 1909, 6; "Graduates' Corner," *Spelman Messenger*, October 1911, 4; "Miss Mattie C. Durham," *Spelman Messenger*, January 1913, 5; "Graduates' Corner," *Spelman Messenger*, December 1923, 8.

63. *Spelman Messenger*, November 1889, 5; "Graduates' Corner," *Spelman Messenger*, December 1912, 4.

64. Jennifer Lund Smith, "Ties that Bind: Educated African American Women in Post-Emancipation Atlanta," in John C. Inscoe, *Georgia in Black and White:*

Explorations in the Race Relations of a Southern State, 1865–1950 (Athens: University of Georgia Press, 1994), 91–105, especially 97.

65. M. H. P., "Our Influence," *Spelman Messenger*, February 1914, supplement, 1; "Mrs. Sylvia C.J. Bryant, B.Th.," *Spelman Messenger*, February 1920, 4.

66. "Personals," *Spelman Messenger*, May 1898, 7 (quotation); "Graduates' Corner," *Spelman Messenger*, February 1922, 8.

67. For examples see "Graduates' Corner," *Spelman Messenger*, March 1912, 5; "Graduates' Corner," *Spelman Messenger*, April 1912, 3; Ophelia G. Strobert, "From an Old Spelman Student," *Spelman Messenger*, October 1913, 3, 7; "From the Spelman Mail-Bag," *Spelman Messenger*, April 1914, 4–8; Carrie Walls Gassaway, "One Graduate's Work," *Spelman Messenger*, May 1914, 8; "Graduates' Corner," *Spelman Messenger*, January 1916, 8; "Graduates' Corner," *Spelman Messenger*, December 1916, 7; Wilhelmina Johnson, "Providence Industrial School, De Land, Fla.," *Spelman Messenger*, April 1920, 2; "Graduates' Corner," *Spelman Messenger*, November 1920, 6; "Graduates' Corner," *Spelman Messenger*, April 1922, 8; "Graduates' Corner," *Spelman Messenger*, May 1922, 4–5.

68. Untitled note and "Personals," *Spelman Messenger*, March 1900, 4; J. H. Brown, "Jeruel Academy," *Spelman Messenger*, May 1901, 1–2; "Sketches of Graduates," *Spelman Messenger*, May 1901, 2–3, 5; "Graduates' Corner," *Spelman Messenger*, December 1908, 6; "News of Graduates," *Spelman Messenger*, December 1911, 8; "Miss Mattie C. Durham," *Spelman Messenger*, January 1913, 5; "Graduates' Corner," *Spelman Messenger*, January 1921, 7; "Graduates' Corner," *Spelman Messenger*, February 1918, 3; "Graduates' Corner," *Spelman Messenger*, March 1921, 8; "Graduates' Corner," *Spelman Messenger*, February 1922, 8; Monica Dellengerber Knight, "Seeking Education for Liberation: The Development of Black Schools in Athens, Georgia, from Emancipation Through Desegregation" (Ph.D. dissertation, University of Georgia, 2007), 50–51.

69. *Spelman Messenger*, October 1911, 7; "Graduates' Corner," *Spelman Messenger*, November 1912, 4; "Graduates' Corner," *Spelman Messenger*, October 1918, 7; "Graduates' Corner," *Spelman Messenger*, January 1919, 7; *Spelman Messenger*, February 1919, 4; "Graduates' Corner," *Spelman Messenger*, March 1922, 8; "Graduates' Corner," *Spelman Messenger*, April 1923, 8; Angie E. Kendall, "Attending Convention," *Spelman Messenger*, December 1923, 7; "Graduates' Corner," *Spelman Messenger*, December 1923, 8; "Graduates' Corner," *Spelman Messenger*, March 1924, 8.

70. "The Americus Institute," *Spelman Messenger*, October 1901, 1–2; "Sketches of Spelman Graduates," *Spelman Messenger*, October 1901, 2–3; "Personals," *Spelman Messenger*, October 1902, 5; "From the Spelman Mail-Bag," *Spelman Messenger*, April 1914, 4.

71. Angie E. Kendall, "Attending Convention," *Spelman Messenger*, December 1923, 7.

72. *Spelman Messenger*, June 1887, 4.

73. Yolanda L. Watson and Sheila T. Gregory, *Daring to Educate: The Legacy of Early Spelman College Presidents* (Sterling, Va.: Stylus Publishing, 2005), 87.

74. R. E. Humpreys, "Dear Friends," *Spelman Messenger*, November 1887, 2 (quotation); Nora Gordon, "Letter to *Messenger*" *Spelman Messenger*, December 1887, 4.

75. C. A. Howard, "Dear Readers of the *Messenger*," *Spelman Messenger*, November 1887, 2; Nora Gordon, "Letter to *Messenger*," *Spelman Messenger*, December 1887; "Twenty-Third Annual Report, Spelman Seminary, 1904," *Spelman Messenger*, March 1904, 1, 7.

76. "Our County Work," *Spelman Messenger*, February 1914, supplement, 1–2; Camilla Weems, "Supervising Rural S.C.," *Spelman Messenger*, November 1915, 6; Camilla Weems, "Report of Work Done in the Colored Public Schools of the Fulton County System for 1917," *Spelman Messenger*, February 1918, 3; "Graduates' Corner," *Spelman Messenger*, November 1920, 6; Annie C. Latimer, "Spelman Girl in Arkansas," *Spelman Messenger*, December 1921, 1–2.

77. "Graduates' Corner," *Spelman Messenger*, March 1912, 5; "From the Spelman Mail-Bag," *Spelman Messenger*, April 1914, 4–8; "Graduates' Corner," *Spelman Messenger*, January 1919, 7; Lucy Hale Tapley and Edith V. Brill, "Annual Report to the Trustees of Spelman Seminary," *Spelman Messenger*, April 1919, 5; "Graduates' Corner," *Spelman Messenger*, November 1922, 8; "Graduates' Corner," *Spelman Messenger*, October 1923, 4; "Graduates' Corner," *Spelman Messenger*, November 1923, 4.

78. William A. Link, *A Hard Country and Lonely Place: Schooling, Society, and Reform in Rural Virginia* (Chapel Hill: University of North Carolina Press, 1986), 183–85; James Anderson, *The Education of Blacks in the South, 1860–1935* (Chapel Hill: University of North Carolina Press, 1988), 86, 156; James L. Leloudis, *Schooling the New South: Pedagogy, Self, and Society in North Carolina, 1880–1920* (Chapel Hill: University of North Carolina Press, 1996), 202–4; Gilmore, *Gender and Jim Crow*, 161–65.

79. Henry Allan Bullock, *A History of Negro Education in the South: From 1619 to the Present* (Cambridge, Mass.: Harvard University Press, 1967), 162; Leloudis, *Schooling the New South*, 216, 217; Link, *Hard Country and Lonely Place*, 180, 182–84.

80. Hine, "We Specialize in the Wholly Impossible," 126–28; Lasch-Quinn, *Black Neighbors*, 76–78, 88–90, 109.

81. Darlene Clark Hine, *Black Women in White: Racial Conflict and Cooperation in the Nursing Profession, 1890–1950* (Bloomington: Indiana University Press, 1989), xvii (quotation), 188; Darlene Clark Hine, "'They Shall Mount Up with Wings as Eagles': Historical Images of Black Nurses, 1890–1950," in Hine, *Hine Sight*, 163–81.

82. Hine, *Black Women in White*, 8–9. Many Spelman-trained nurses did work in private service; see "Graduates' Corner," *Spelman Messenger*, March 1913, 8; Angie E. Kendall, "Spelman Graduates," *Spelman Messenger*, February 1919, 5.

83. E. O. Werden, "From Hospital to Hospital," March 1909, 2–3; "Graduates' Corner," *Spelman Messenger*, December 1912, 4; "Graduates' Corner," *Spelman Messenger*, February 1915, 7; "Graduates' Corner," *Spelman Messenger*, October 1915, 8; Angie E. Kendall, "Spelman Graduates," *Spelman Messenger*, February 1919, 5; "Graduates' Corner," *Spelman Messenger*, March 1920, 5.

84. Mrs. Ludie Andrews, "The Trained Nurse," *Spelman Messenger*, May 1916, 3; "Graduates' Corner," *Spelman Messenger*, February 1918, 3; Hine, *Black Women in*

White, xxi, 93; Florence Fleming Corley, "Higher Education For Southern Women: Four Church-Related Women's Colleges in Georgia, Agnes Scott, Shorter, Spelman, and Wesleyan, 1900–1920" (Ph.D. dissertation, Georgia State University, 1985), 409–15.

85. *Spelman Messenger*, January 1887, 4; "Farewell Services," *Spelman Messenger*, March 1890, 1; L. C. Fleming, "Congo Women," *Spelman Messenger*, December 1891, 4; Mary L. Shepard, "Spring Days at Spelman Seminary," *Spelman Messenger*, May 1894, 2.

86. Sallie Robinson, "Africa," *Spelman Messenger*, March 1893, 2.

87. Robert Edgerton, *The Troubled Heart of Africa: A History of the Congo* (New York: St. Martin's Press, 2002), chapter 4.

88. "Reception," *Spelman Messenger*, March 1889, 2; *Spelman Messenger*, November 1889, 6; Sylvia M. Jacobs, "Three African American Missionaries in the Congo, 1887–1899: The Confluence of Race, Culture, Identity, and Nationality," in Barbara Reeves-Ellington, Kathryn Kish-Sklar, and Connie A. Shemo, *Competing Kingdoms: Women, Mission, Nation, and the American Protestant Empire, 1812–1960* (Durham, N.C.: Duke University Press, 2010), 318–41.

89. Jacobs, "Three African American Missionaries in the Congo," 326 (quotation), 329.

90. Lena Clark, "From Africa," Ikoko, Congo, *Spelman Messenger*, March 1896, 5; Margaret G. Rattray, "From Congo," *Spelman Messenger*, January 1903, 6.

91. Edgerton, *The Troubled Heart of Africa*, chapter 3 and 4; Adam Hochschild, *King Leopold's Ghost: A Story of Greed, Terror and Heroism and Colonial Africa* (Boston: Houghton Mifflin, 1998); Jacobs, "Three African American Missionaries in the Congo," 320–21.

92. Nora A. Gordon "Some Characterizations of the Heathen," *Spelman Messenger*, May 1895, 2.

93. Lena Clark, "From Ikoko Station, Congo, S.W. Africa," *Spelman Messenger*, May 1899, 7.

94. Nora A. Gordon, *Spelman Messenger*, April 1890, 5 (quotation); Lucy R. Gates, "Letter from Greytown, Natal, November 13, 1893," *Spelman Messenger*, February 1894, 5; Nora A. Gordon, "Some Characteristics of the Heathen," *Spelman Messenger*, May 1895; "Extracts from Letters from Africa," *Spelman Messenger*, January 1897, 5; "From Africa," *Spelman Messenger*, February 1897, 4; Emma B. Delaney, "Why I Go as a Foreign Missionary," *Spelman Messenger*, February 1902, 5; Clara A. Howard, "American Baptist Mission Stations on the Congo," *Spelman Messenger*, November 1904, 5; Emma Delaney, "The Story of Anna Ruth Malekebu," *Spelman Messenger*, March 1906, 1–2.

95. Nora A. Gordon, "Notes on the Congo," *Spelman Messenger*, February 1894, 2.

96. Letter from Clara A. Howard, *Spelman Messenger*, February 1892, 4–5; Nora A. Gordon, "Some Characteristics of the Heathen," *Spelman Messenger*, May 1895; Clara Howard, "My Lukungu Children," *Spelman Messenger*, January 1896, 5; "From Miss Delaney," *Spelman Messenger*, November 1902, 4.

97. Nora A. Gordon, "Notes on the Congo," *Spelman Messenger*, March 1894, 4–5; Rev. S. C. Gordon, "Congo Customs," *Spelman Messenger*, April 1901, 5; Suluka M.

Gardner, "The Responsibility of a Medical Missionary," and following untitled note, *Spelman Messenger*, October 1904, 3; Emma B. Delaney, "News From Africa," *Spelman Messenger*, January 1905, 7.

98. Margaret G. Rattray, "From Congo," *Spelman Messenger*, January 1903, 6.

99. M. I. W., "Spelman and the Congo," *Spelman Messenger*, June 1893, 7; *Spelman Messenger*, February 1894, 4; Lena F. Clark, "An Autobiography," *Spelman Messenger*, May 1895, 2 (quote); Lena Clark, "From Africa," Ikoko, Congo, *Spelman Messenger*, March 1896, 5; Margaret Rattray, "From Congo," *Spelman Messenger*, March 1902, [9].

100. L. C. Fleming, "Congo Women," *Spelman Messenger*, December 1891, 4; Clara A. Howard, "Letter from Lukungu," June 9, 1893, *Spelman Messenger*, February 1894, 5; Nora Gordon, "Notes on the Congo," *Spelman Messenger*, March 1894, 4–5; Lena Clark, "To A Teacher," *Spelman Messenger*, May 1897, 5; "Three Letters from One of Our Missionaries [Lena F. Clark]," *Spelman Messenger*, February 1900, 5; Emma B. Delaney, "From the Zambesi," *Spelman Messenger*, January 1903, 7; "From Miss Delaney," *Spelman Messenger*, January 1904, 7; Clara A. Howard, "American Baptist Mission Stations on the Congo," *Spelman Messenger*, November 1904, 5. Like Spelman missionaries to the Congo, African American missionaries in southern Africa studied by Sylvia M. Jacobs emphasized their duty to Africans and their difference from them. Sylvia M. Jacobs, "Give a Thought to Africa: Black Women Missionaries in Southern Africa" in Hine, King, and Reed, "*We Specialize in the Wholly Impossible*," 103–23.

101. Antoinette Burton, *Burdens of History: Feminists, Indian Women, and Imperial Culture, 1865–1915* (Chapel Hill: University of North Carolina Press, 1994); Jacobs, "Three African American Missionaries in the Congo," 328–29.

102. Hine, "'We Specialize in the Wholly Impossible': The Philanthropic Work of Black Women," especially 112–13; Higginbotham, *Righteous Discontent*; Gordon, *Pitied But Not Entitled*, 129–35; Lasch-Quinn, *Black Neighbors*, 117–19; Jacobs, "Three African American Missionaries in the Congo," 330–31.

103. Jacobs, "Three African American Missionaries in the Congo," 323.

104. Edgerton, *The Troubled Heart of Africa*, 114. Michele Mitchell found that black men in the 1890s connected their support for or participation in imperial and missionary ventures of the United States, especially as soldiers, to a defense of their own masculinity. She found African American men to be much more vocal than women on the subject of imperialism. Mitchell, *Righteous Propagation*, 52–56, 74–75.

105. "News from Miss Delaney," *Spelman Messenger*, May 1902, 4.

106. Kathleen C. Berkeley, "'Colored Ladies Also Contributed': Black Women's Activities from Benevolence to Social Welfare, 1866–1896," in *The Web of Southern Social Relations: Women, Family, and Education*, eds. Walter J. Fraser Jr., R. Frank Saunders Jr., and Jon L. Wakelyn (Athens: University of Georgia Press, 1985), 181–203; Rouse, *Lugenia Burns Hope*, 4–6; Scott, "Most Invisible of All," 5–6, 8; Hine, "We Specialize in the Wholly Impossible"; Stephanie Shaw, "Black Club Women and the Creation of the National Association of Colored Women," in Hine, King, and Reed, "*We Specialize in the Wholly Impossible*," 433–47; Hunter, *To 'Joy My Freedom*, 136–37;

Cynthia Neverdon-Morton, *Afro-American Women of the South and the Advancement of the Race* (Knoxville: University of Tennessee Press, 1989), 1–9; Dorsey, *To Build Our Lives Together*, 110–11; Johnson, *Southern Ladies, New Women*, esp. chapters 2 and 6; Robyn Muncy, *Creating a Female Dominion in American Reform, 1890–1935* (New York: Oxford University Press, 1991).

107. "Personals," *Spelman Messenger*, March 1904, 5–6; "From Our Letter File," *Spelman Messenger*, March 1906, 7; "Graduates' Corner," *Spelman Messenger*, May 1913, 7; Virginia Hulsey Brown, "The Religious Influence of Spelman," *Spelman Messenger*, November 1916, 7.

108. "Twenty-Third Annual Report, Spelman Seminary, 1904," *Spelman Messenger*, March 1904, 1, 7.

109. "Sketches of Graduates," *Spelman Messenger*, May 1901, 2–3, 5; Ida Burton Jones, "A Spelman's Girl's Work," *Spelman Messenger*, November 1902, 6–7; "Personals," *Spelman Messenger*, March 1904, 5–6; "Grad's Directory," *Spelman Messenger*, March 1905, 3, 5–7; "From Our Letter File," *Spelman Messenger*, March 1906, 7; "A Home Mission," *Spelman Messenger*, October 1913, 3.

110. Angie E. Kendall, "Spelman Graduates," *Spelman Messenger*, February 1919, 5; Corley, "Higher Education For Southern Women," 315–16; Lasch-Quinn, *Black Neighbors*, 131–50; Nancy Marie Robertson, *Christian Sisterhood, Race Relations, and the YWCA, 1906–46* (Urbana: University of Illinois Press, 2007).

111. Frances Sanders Taylor, "'On the Edge of Tomorrow': Southern Women, the Student YWCA, and Race, 1920–1944" (PhD dissertation, Stanford University, 1984); Helen Laville, "'If the Time is Not Ripe, Then it is Your Job to Ripen the Time!': The Transformation of the YWCA in the USA from Segregated Association to Interracial Organization," *Women's History Review* 15, no. 3 (July 2006): 359–83.

112. Hunter, *To 'Joy My Freedom*, 130; Georgina Hickey, "Disease, Disorder, and Motherhood: Working-Class Women, Social Welfare, and the Process of Urban Development in Atlanta," in *Before the New Deal: Social Welfare in the South, 1830–1930*, ed. Elna Green (Athens: University of Georgia Press, 1999), 181–207, especially 196, 200.

113. Mattie P. Williams, "City Missions," *Spelman Messenger*, November 1903, 3; S. C. J. Bryant, "Mission Work Done by the Colored Women of Atlanta," Lugenia Hope, "Kindergartens," and Selena Sloan Butler, "Atlanta Women's Club," *Spelman Messenger*, February 1906, 2–4, 6; Scott, "Most Invisible of All," 16–17; Gordon, *Pitied But Not Entitled*, 112, 114–15; Neverdon-Morton, *Afro-American Women of the South*, especially chapter 7 on Atlanta; Shaw, *What a Woman Ought to Be and Do*, chapter 6; Hunter, *To 'Joy My Freedom*, 130, 136; Johnson, *Southern Ladies, New Women*, 169–72.

114. *Spelman Messenger*, January 1912, 4; Lucy Hale Tapley and Edith V. Brill, "Thirty-Second Annual Report of the President of Spelman Seminary to the Board of Trustees," *Spelman Messenger*, April 1913, 1–3.

115. Claudia White Harreld to Amy Chadwick, 19 April 1937, Claudia White Harreld File, Spelman College Archives; Lugenia Hope, "Kindergartens," *Spelman Messenger*, February 1906, 2–3; "The Leonard Street Orhpans' Home," *Spelman Messenger*, February 1908, 1–2.

116. "The Constitution of the Neighborhood Union, 1908," box 2, Neighborhood Union Collection, Special Collections, Robert W. Woodruff Library, Atlanta University Center (hereafter Neighborhood Union Collection); Rouse, *Lugenia Burns Hope*, 65–66; Corley, "Higher Education For Southern Women," 318–19; Lasch-Quinn, *Black Neighbors*, 120–26. Hope became president of Atlanta University in 1929.

117. Rouse, *Lugenia Burns Hope*, 17.

118. Hattie Rutherford Watson, "Work of the Neighborhood Union," *Spelman Messenger*, November 1912, 6–7; Rouse, *Lugenia Burns Hope*, 67.

119. Hattie Rutherford Watson, untitled essay, later printed in *Messenger*, April 1928, in Hattie Rutherford Watson file, Spelman College Archives; Fon Gordon, "'A Generous and Exemplary Womanhood': Hattie Rutherford Watson and NYA Camp Bethune in Pine Bluff, Arkansas," in *The Southern Elite and Social Change: Essays in Honor of Willard B. Gatewood, Jr.*, eds. Randy Finley and Thomas A. DeBlack (Fayetteville: University of Arkansas Press, 2002).

120. NU Minute Book 1908–1918, box 4, folder 1, September 3, 1908; folder 2, November 9, 1911.

121. H. L. Morehouse to Mrs. H.R. Watson, Aug 11, 1915, box 2, Neighborhood Union Collection; "Our Thirty-Fifth Anniversary," *Spelman Messenger*, April 1916, 2–4, 7; Lucy Hale Tapley and Edith V. Brill, "Annual Report of Spelman Seminary for the Year 1915–1916," *Spelman Messenger*, April 1916, 6; Hattie Rutherford Watson, "The Opening of the Neighborhood House," *Spelman Messenger*, May 1916, 2–3; "Graduates' Corner," *Spelman Messenger*, December 1916, 7; Carrie L. Dukes, "The Neighborhood House," *Spelman Messenger*, December 1917, 7.

122. Goldshalk, *Veiled Visions*, chapter 10.

123. Watson, "Work of the Neighborhood Union"; Rouse, *Lugenia Burns Hope*, 69, 71, 90; Hunter, *To 'Joy My Freedom*, 136–43; Hickey, *Hope and Danger*, 96–102, 154.

124. Lasch-Quinn, *Black Neighbors*, 120; Numan V. Bartley, *The Creation of Modern Georgia* (Athens: University of Georgia Press, 1983), 149.

125. "Children's Survey," [1911], "School Survey," [1911], "School Survey," [1911], all box 9, Neighborhood Union Collection; Members of the Neighborhood Union to Mayor Walter Sims and Members of the City Council, Hon. W. W. Gaines, President and Members of Board of Education, and Prof. W. A. Sutton, Superintendent of Public Schools, 1914, box 6, Neighborhood Union Collection; "Survey of Clored [sic] Public Schools (1913–14)," box 7, Neighborhood Union Collection; Rouse, *Lugenia Burns Hope*, 74–79.

126. Typewritten note on success of street light campaign, [1913], box 6, Neighborhood Union Collection; Lugenia Hope to "Mayor," February 24, 1932, and "Mayor and Council Build a Wall around Neighborhood Center as Requested," both box 3, Neighborhood Union Collection; Louise Delphia Davis Shivery, "The History of Organized Social Work Among Atlanta Negroes, 1890–1935" (M.A. thesis, Atlanta University, 1936), 100–101.

127. Mayor Walter Sims to "Whom it may concern" [letter of appreciation of Neighborhood Union], December 30, 1926, Lugenia Burns Hope to Mayor Sims

(handwritten draft), [1926], both box 2, Neighborhood Union Collection; Lugenia Hope to "Mayor," February 24, 1932, and "Mayor and Council Build a Wall around Neighborhood Center as Requested," both box 3, Neighborhood Union Collection. James L. Key served as mayor from 1919 to 1923 and from 1931 to 1937, and Sims served from 1923 to 1927. African Americans were instrumental in defeating a recall of Key in 1932. Bayor, *Race and the Shaping of Twentieth Century Atlanta*, 17–19.

128. Read, *Story of Spelman*, 208.

129. "Organizing Negroes for Law Enforcement," *Spelman Messenger*, May 1920, 7; "Leading White Women Pledge Racial Good Will," *Spelman Messenger*, January 1923, 8–9.

130. Ella Barksdale Brown Papers, biographical guide; "National Council on Lynching" pamphlet [n.d.], folder 65, box 5; receipt, NAACP Anti-Lynching Fund, folder 80, box 2, all Beinecke Rare Book and Manuscript Library, Yale University, New Haven, Connecticut (hereafter EBB Papers).

131. Brown, "The Negro's Burden," [n.d.], folder 163, box 6, EBB Papers, pp. 9–10. Throughout she stresses good character and behavior as a way to combat disparaging stereotypes. Language denouncing alcohol would seem to indicate that it was written before Prohibition, pp. 18–19.

132. Ella Barksdale Brown to Lucy Tapley, October 24, 1914, folder 55, box 1; C. A. Howard to "Alumna," January 31, 1914, folder 87, box 2; Ella Barksdale Brown to Florence Read, March 21, 1951 (quotation), folder 1, box 1, all EBB Papers.

133. *Spelman Messenger*, November 1889, 4; "Spelman Seminary Catalogue, 1888–89"; "Eleventh Annual Circular and Catalogue of Spelman Seminary, for Women and Girls in Atlanta Georgia, 1891–92"; "Spelman Seminary, Atlanta, Georgia, 1891–1892"; *Spelman Messenger*, June 1891, 5; *Spelman Messenger*, March 1893, 5; *Spelman Messenger*, May 1900, 2; "From the Spelman Mail-Bag," *Spelman Messenger*, April 1914, 5–6; Dr. H. R. Butler, "Louisville, Ky., and Some of Her People," *Independent,* August 22, 1929, and "Mrs. H. R. Butler: Our Founder," *Our National Family,* December 1964, both from Selena Sloan Butler File, Spelman College Archives; "Selena Sloan Butler," *New Georgia Encyclopedia*, http://www.georgiaencyclopedia.org/nge/Article .jsp?id=h-2508.

134. Examples include Sloan to Lucy Tapley, Dec. 3, 1910, folder 1, box 1; Butler to J. Louise Fowler, June 3, 1949, folder 3, box 4 (this folder also contains commencement programs, fund-raising appeals, alumnae association meeting programs, and other Spelman information), Selena Sloan Butler Papers, Auburn Avenue Research Library on African American Culture and History, Atlanta, Georgia.

135. Selena Sloan Butler, "Woman's Highest Calling," *Spelman Messenger*, November 1904, 1–2.

136. Lucy Hale Tapley, president of Spelman Seminary, to Mrs. John D. Rockefeller, Jr., 17 April 1924; Mrs. H. R. Butler, "The Rise and Growth of the National Congress of Colored Parents and Teachers," January 1929; Mrs. H. R. Butler to Miss Edith Glode, January 22, 1930; Selena Sloan Butler to Florence Read, April 29, 1930; newspaper clipping, "Colored YWCA Branch Plans Splendid Program For Its Annual Meeting";

newspaper clipping, "Mrs. Butler Asked By Sec'y Ickes to Attend Education Conference," *Atlanta World*, April 29, 1934; Newspaper clipping, "Hundreds Attend Annual 'Y' Meeting; Progress is Lauded," *Atlanta World*, February 1, 1935; "Mrs. H. R. Butler: Our Founder," *Our National Family* December 1964; all from Selena Sloan Butler File, Spelman College Archives.

137. "Graduates' Corner," *Spelman Messenger*, April 1924, 8; form updating alumnae records, April 20, 1943; Selena Sloan Butler to Miss Read, April 20, 1943; Newspaper clipping, "Atlanta Physician is Army Specialist" *Atlanta World*, January 9, 1944; newspaper clipping "Troops Get Best of Medical Attention at Fort Huachuca," *Arizona Star*, December 15, 1943; Selena Sloan Butler to Florence Read, April 9, 1945; "Mrs. H. R. Butler: Our Founder"; all in Selena Sloan Butler File, Spelman College Archives.

138. "Annual Convention National Congress of Colored Parents and Teachers. Charles Young School, Washington, D.C. June 27–29, 1948"; newspaper clipping, *Atlanta World*, June 4, 1958; Albert E. Manley to Mrs. Selena S. Butler, May 10, 1960; all Selena Sloan Butler File, Spelman College Archives.

139. Form for alumnae records, undated, Selena Sloan Butler File, Spelman College Archives.

140. Donaldson, "Standing on a Volcano: The Leadership of William Jefferson White," quote p. 139; Gilmore, *Gender and Jim Crow*, 62.

141. Untitled typewritten manuscript, and "Claudia White Harreld," (quotation) both in Claudia White Harreld File, Spelman College Archives; Read, *Story of Spelman*, 204; Corley, "Higher Education For Southern Women," 399–404; Claudia White, "Spelman Field Notes," *Spelman Messenger*, October 1911, 2–3, 5.

142. Claudia T. White, *Spelman Messenger*, June 1897, 2.

143. "Mrs. Claudia White Harreld's Passing is Great Loss to Atlanta; Deceased was Distinguished Spelman Graduate"; untitled typewritten manuscript; Will W. Alexander to Harreld, 19 July 1927, all in Claudia White Harreld File, Spelman College Archives; Corley, "Higher Education For Southern Women," 403–6.

144. Claudia White Harreld to Amy Chadwick, April 19, 1937, and Claudia White Harreld to Rev. Harold B. Ingalls, September 25, 1937, Claudia White Harreld File, Spelman College Archives; Corley, "Higher Education For Southern Women," 406.

145. "Mrs. Claudia White Harreld's Passing"; untitled typewritten manuscript; poems including "Julius Caesar," "Miss 'Liza," "Johnnie," and "Mystic, the Detroit Hospital Maid"; all in Claudia White Harreld File, Spelman College Archives.

146. "Mystic, the Detroit Hospital Maid," Claudia White Harreld File, Spelman College Archives.

147. "Mrs. Thurman to Tour for Derricotte Fund," newspaper clipping, 1937, Ken Oilschlager-Juliette Derricotte Collection, box 4, folder 26, University of Mississippi Library Archives and Special Collections, Oxford, Mississippi.

148. "Class Roll, 1920," *Spelman Messenger*, May 1920, 8; finding guide, Bailey/Thurman Family Papers; "Baby" [Sue Bailey] to "Dear Darling Mother" [Susie Ford Bailey], April 5, 1926, and "Baby" [Sue Bailey] to "Mother dearest" [Susie Ford Bailey], October 9, 1928, box 2, Bailey/Thurman Family Papers; Trudi Smith, *Building Bridges*

to Common Ground (Boston, Mass.: The Thurman Center, Boston University, 1985), 5, in box 5, Bailey/Thurman Family Papers; William H. Brackney, *A Genetic History of Baptist Thought: With Special Reference to Baptists in Britain and North America* (Macon, Ga.: Mercer University Press, 2004), 438–44.

149. National Council of Negro Women, Inc., *The Historical Cookbook of the American Negro*, compiled and edited by Sue Bailey Thurman, reprinted edition (Boston: Beacon Press, 2000).

150. Finding guide, Bailey/Thurman Family Papers; "Baby" [Sue Bailey] to "Darling, Dearest Mama" [Susie Ford Bailey], November 28 [1945], and "Baby" [Sue Bailey] to "My Dearest, Darling Mama" [Susie Ford Bailey], August 10, 1946, box 2, Bailey/Thurman Family Papers; Smith, *Building Bridges to Common Ground*, 12–13, 16, 21.

151. Smith, *Building Bridges to Common Ground*, 4.

152. Harley, "For the Good of Family and Race," 343–44; Shaw, *What a Woman Ought to Be and Do*, chapter 5; Gilmore, *Gender and Jim Crow*, 186.

153. Harry G. Lefever, *Undaunted by the Fight: Spelman College and the Civil Rights Movement, 1957–1967* (Macon: Mercer University Press, 2005).

Conclusion

1. Victoria E. Bynum, *Unruly Women: The Politics of Social and Sexual Control in the Old South* (Chapel Hill: University of North Carolina Press, 1992).

2. Mildred Lewis Rutherford, *Civilization of the Old South: What Made It; What Destroyed It; What Has Replaced It* (Athens, Ga.: McGregor Co., 1917), 39–40.

3. Deborah Gray White, *Ar'n't I a Woman?: Female Slaves in the Plantation South* (New York: W. W. Norton, 1985); Thelma Jennings, "'Us Colored Women Had to Go Through a Plenty': Sexual Exploitation of African American Slave Women," *Journal of Women's History* 1, no. 3 (Winter 1990): 45–74.

4. Evelyn Brooks Higginbotham, *Righteous Discontent: The Women's Movement in the Black Baptist Church, 1880–1920* (Cambridge: Harvard University Press, 1993), 190.

5. Donald Spivey, *Schooling for the New Slavery: Black Industrial Education, 1868–1915* (Westport, Conn.: Greenwood Press, 1978).

6. Turner M. Hiers, "Lucy Cobb Institute, Now Dormitory for University Co-eds, Formerly Finishing School for 'Cream of the Old South'" [c. 1931], unidentified newspaper clipping in Lucy Cobb Institute File, Athens-Clarke County Heritage Foundation, Athens, Georgia.

7. Lucy Hale Tapley and Edith V. Brill, "Annual Report," *Spelman Messenger*, April 1923, 2–3; Edna E. Lamson, "Spelman College," *Spelman Messenger*, April 1923, 3, 7; Spelman Seminary Catalogue, 1923–1924, and Spelman College Bulletin, 1924–1925, Atlanta Georgia [1923], 47–61; Florence Matilda Read, *The Story of Spelman College* (Atlanta: United Negro College Fund with Princeton University Press, 1961), 196–203, 209–17; Yolanda L. Watson and Sheila T. Gregory, *Daring to Educate: The Legacy of the Early Spelman College Presidents* (Sterling, Va.: Stylus Publishing, LLC, 2005).

Bibliography

Primary Sources

ARCHIVES

Athens, Georgia
    Athens-Clarke County Heritage Foundation
        Lucy Cobb Institute File
    Athens-Clarke County Library
        Athens Woman's Club Minutes
        Lucy Cobb Institute File
    Hargrett Library, University of Georgia
        Bower Family Papers
        E.M. Coulter Manuscripts
        John E. Drewry Papers
        Irene Felker Scrapbook
        Friends of Lucy Cobb and Seney-Stovall Collection
        Harden-Jackson-Carithers Collection
        Mary Ann Rutherford Lipscomb Family Papers
        Lipscomb-Lucy Cobb Institute Collection
        Lucy Cobb Institute Collection
        Lucy Cobb Institute Grade Books
        Lucy Cobb Institute Photographs
        Lucy Cobb Institute Records
        Lucy Cobb Institute Stock Books and Minutes
        Lucy Cobb Institute Trustees Extract
        Sarah A. McElmurray Scrapbook
        Augusta Amelia Wright Mell Papers
        Mell-Rutherford Family Papers

Edna Pope Diary
Mildred Lewis Rutherford Notebooks
Mildred Lewis Rutherford Papers
Jennie Smith Papers
State Normal School Records, University Archives
Atlanta, Georgia
  Agnes Scott College Library
    Mildred Mell File
  Atlanta History Center
    Grace Towns Hamilton Papers
    Millie J. McCreary Diary
    Sidney Root Memoirs
  Auburn Avenue Research Library on African American Culture and History
    Selena Sloan Butler Papers
  Georgia State Archives
    Atlanta Normal Schools Minute Books
    Georgia Federation of Women's Clubs Collection
  Special Collections, Robert W. Woodruff Library, Atlanta University Center
    John Hope and Lugenia Burns Hope Papers
    Neighborhood Union Collection
  Special Collections, Robert W. Woodruff Library, Emory University
    Bailey/Thurman Family Papers
  Spelman College Archives
    Ella Barksdale Brown File
    Selena Sloan Butler File
    Harriet Giles Diaries
    Claudia White Harreld File
    Sophia Packard Diaries
    Victoria Maddox Simmons File
Chapel Hill, North Carolina
  Southern Historical Collection, University of North Carolina
    Howard Odum Papers
Columbia, South Carolina
  South Caroliniana Library, University of South Carolina
    Columbia Female College Papers
New Haven, Connecticut
  Beinecke Rare Book and Manuscript Library, Yale University
    Ella Barksdale Brown Papers
Oxford, Mississippi
  University of Mississippi Library Archives and Special Collections
    Ken Oilschlager—Juliette Derricotte Collection
Richmond, Virginia
  American Civil War Museum, Eleanor S. Brockenbough Library
    Mildred Lewis Rutherford Scrapbooks

United Daughters of the Confederacy Collection
Virginia State Library and Archives
    Hill's Richmond City Directory 1894–1898 and 1900–1906

PERIODICALS

Athens Banner
Athens Daily News
Athens Magazine
Athens Observer
The Atlanta Constitution
The Lightning Bug
The Mountain Star
Lucy Cobb Dots
Lucy Cobb Magazine
New York Times
Mildred Rutherford's *Scrapbook*
Spelman Messenger
Voice of the Negro

PUBLISHED SOURCES

Confederate Records of the State of Georgia, Compiled and Published under Authority of the Legislature by Allen D. Candler, A. M., L.L.D. Vol. 1. Atlanta: Chas. P. Byrd, State Printer, 1909.

DuBois, W. E. B. *The College-Bred Negro*. Atlanta: Atlanta University Press, 1900.

Johnstone, H. W. *Truth of the War Conspiracy of 1861*. Athens, Ga.: McGregor Co., 1921.

Lipscomb, Lamar Rutherford. *Essays Wise and Otherwise,* [Atlanta?]: Mildred Seydel Publishing, 1957.

Mell, Mildred. "Economic Problems are with Us Always." *Agnes Scott Alumnae Quarterly* 32 (Winter 1954): 3–5.

———. "Economic Signposts for a Post-War World." *Agnes Scott Alumnae Quarterly* 18 (April 1942): 3–5.

———. "Poor Whites of the South." *Social Forces* 17 (December 1938): 153–67.

———. "The Sociologist Outside the Ivory Tower." *The Alpha Kappa Delta Quarterly* 11 (March 1951): 10–16.

———. "Some of the Characteristics of the Population of the Atlanta Area." In *Report on Health and Welfare in DeKalb & Fulton Counties*, Social Planning Council, 33–94. Atlanta: Social Planning Council, 1943.

———. "The Southern Poor White: Myth, Symbol, and Reality of A Nation." *The Saturday Review of Literature* 26 (January 23, 1943): 3–5.

———. *Taxes, Taxes, Still More Taxes*. Atlanta: League of Women Voters of Georgia, 1949.

———. "Trade Relations of the United States with the New Europe." *West Georgia College Studies in the Social Sciences* 3 (June 1964): 55–68.

Minutes of the Fourth Annual Meeting of the United Daughters of the Confederacy, Nov. 10–12, 1897. Nashville, Tenn.: Press of Foster and Webb, 1898.

Odum, Howard. *Social and Mental Traits of the Negro.* New York: AMS Press, [1910] 1968.

Rutherford, Mildred Lewis. *Southern Regions of the United States.* Chapel Hill: The University of North Carolina Press, 1936.

——. *American Authors.* Atlanta: Franklin Printing and Publishing Co., 1894.

——. *Bible Questions With Reference in the Old Testament.* Athens, Ga.: McGregor Co. [?], 1890.

——. *Civilization of the Old South: What Made It: What Destroyed It; What Has Replaced It.* Athens, Ga.: McGregor Co., 1917.

——. *English Authors: A Handbook of English Literature from Chaucer to Living Writers.* Atlanta: Constitutional Book Company, 1890.

——. *Four Addresses by Mildred Lewis Rutherford.* Birmingham, Ala.: Mildred Lewis Rutherford Historical Circle Printers, 1922.

——. *French Authors.* Atlanta: Franklin Printing and Publishing Co., 1906.

——. *Georgia: The Empire State of the South.* Athens, Ga.: McGregor Co., 1914.

——. "Historical Sins of Omission and Commission" (1915) in Rutherford, *Four Addresses by Mildred Lewis Rutherford.* Birmingham, Ala.: Mildred Lewis Rutherford Historical Circle Printers, 1922.

——. *A Measuring Rod to Test Text Books, and Reference Books in Schools, Colleges and Libraries.* Athens, Ga.: The McGregor Co., 1919.

——. *The South in History and Literature: A Hand-book of Southern Authors from the Settlement of Jamestown, 1607, to Living Writers.* Atlanta: Franklin Printing and Publishing Co., 1906.

——. "The South in the Building of the Nation" (1912), in Rutherford, *Four Addresses by Mildred Lewis Rutherford.* Birmingham, Ala.: Mildred Lewis Rutherford Historical Circle Printers, 1922.

——. *The South Must Have Her Rightful Place in History.* Athens, Ga.: McGregor Co., 1923.

——. "Thirteen Periods of United States History" (1912) in Rutherford, *Four Addresses by Mildred Lewis Rutherford.* Birmingham, Ala.: Mildred Lewis Rutherford Historical Circle Printers, 1922.

——. *Truths of History: A Fair, Unbiased, Impartial, Unprejudiced, and Conscientious Study of History.* Athens, Ga.: McGregor Co., nd.

——. *What the South May Claim.* Athens, Ga., 1916 [?].

——. *Where the South Leads and Where Georgia Leads.* Athens, Ga.: McGregor Co., 1917.

——. "Wrongs of History Righted" (1914) in Rutherford, *Four Addresses by Mildred Lewis Rutherford.* Birmingham, Ala.: Mildred Lewis Rutherford Historical Circle Printers, 1922.

Social Planning Council. *A Report on Health and Welfare in DeKalb & Fulton Counties: The Health and Welfare Problems and the Programs to Meet Them, with an*

Analysis of the General Setting Out of Which These Problems Arise. Atlanta: Social Planning Council, 1943.

Underwood, Rev. J.L. *The Women of the Confederacy.* New York and Washington: The Neale Publishing Company, 1906.

Washington, Booker T. *Character Building: Being Addresses Delivered on Sunday Evenings to the Students of Tuskegee Institute.* New York: Doubleday, Page & Company, 1902.

INTERNET SOURCES

Georgia Humanities Council and the University of Georgia Press. *New Georgia Encyclopedia.* http://www.georgiaencyclopedia.org/.

Kathryn Kish Sklar and Thomas Dublin, eds., *Women and Social Movements in the United States, 1600–2000.* Document Project: Bonnie Laughlin Schultz, editor, "How did Susanna Rowson and Other Reformers Promote Higher Education as an Antidote to Women's Sexual Vulnerability, 1780–1820?"

Treasures of American History online exhibition, National Museum of American History. http://americanhistory.si.edu/treasures.

Secondary Sources

BOOKS

Allitt, Patrick. *The Conservatives: Ideas and Personalities Throughout American History.* New Haven: Yale University Press, 2009.

Anderson, Eric, and Alfred A. Moss, Jr. *Dangerous Donations: Northern Philanthropy and Southern Black Education, 1902–1930.* Columbia: University of Missouri Press, 1999.

Anderson, James D. *The Education of Blacks in the South, 1860–1935.* Chapel Hill: University of North Carolina Press, 1988.

Armstrong, Zella, and Janie Preston Collup French. *Notable Southern Families.* Chattanooga, Tenn.: Lookout Publishing Co., 1918.

Ayers, Edward L. *The Promise of the New South: Life After Reconstruction.* New York: Oxford University Press, 1992.

———, and John C. Willis, eds. *The Edge of the South: Life in Nineteenth-Century Virginia.* Charlottesville: University Press of Virginia, 1991.

Bartley, Numan V. *The Creation of Modern Georgia.* Athens: University of Georgia Press, 1983.

Batteau, Allan. *The Invention of Appalachia.* Tucson: University of Arizona Press, 1990.

Bayor, Ronald H. *Race and the Shaping of Twentieth-Century Atlanta.* Chapel Hill: University of North Carolina Press, 1996.

Bederman, Gail. *Manliness and Civilization: A Cultural History of Gender and Race in the United States 1880–1917.* Chicago: University of Chicago Press, 1995.

Berkin, Carol. *Revolutionary Mothers: Women in the Struggle for America's Independence.* New York: Knopf, 2005.

Blee, Kathleen. *Women of the Klan: Racism and Gender in the 1920s*. Berkeley: University of California Press, 1991.

Blesser, Carol, ed. *In Joy and in Sorrow: Women, Family, and Marriage in the Victorian South*. New York: Oxford University Press, 1991.

Blight, David W. *Race and Reunion: The Civil War in American Memory*. Boston: Harvard University Press, 2001.

Bond, Horace Mann. *The Education of the Negro in the American Social Order*. New York: Prentice-Hall, Inc., 1934.

Brackney, William H. *A Genetic History of Baptist Thought: With Special Reference to Baptists in Britain and North America*. Macon, Ga.: Mercer University Press, 2004.

Branch, Taylor. *Parting the Waters: America in the King Years*. New York: Touchstone, 1988.

Brundage, W. Fitzhugh. *Booker T. Washington and Black Progress: Up From Slavery 100 Years Later*. Gainesville: University Press of Florida, 2003.

Bullock, Henry Allen. *A History of Negro Education in the South: From 1619 to the Present*. Cambridge, Mass.: Harvard University Press, 1967.

Burns, Rebecca. *Rage in the Gate City: The Story of the 1906 Atlanta Race Riot*. Athens: University of Georgia Press, 2006.

Burton, Antoinette. *Burdens of History: Feminists, Indian Women, and Imperial Culture, 1865–1915*. Chapel Hill: University of North Carolina Press, 1994.

Butchart, Ron E. *Northern Schools, Southern Blacks, and Reconstruction: Freedmen's Education, 1862–1875*. Westport, Conn.: Greenwood Press.

———. *Schooling the Freedpeople: Teaching, Learning, and the Struggle for Black Freedom, 1861–1876*. Chapel Hill: University of North Carolina Press, 2010.

Bynum, Victoria E. *Unruly Women: The Politics of Social and Sexual Control in the Old South*. Chapel Hill: University of North Carolina Press, 1992.

Camhi, Jane Jerome. *Women Against Women: American Anti-Suffragism, 1880–1920*. Brooklyn: Carlson Publishing, 1994.

Campbell, Edward D. C., Jr., and Kym S. Rice, eds. *A Woman's War: Southern Women, Civil War, and the Confederate Legacy*. Richmond: The Museum of the Confederacy, 1996.

Cashin, Edward J., and Glenn T. Eskew. *Paternalism in a Southern City: Race, Religion and Gender in Augusta, Georgia*. Athens: University of Georgia Press, 2001.

Censer, Jane Turner. *The Reconstruction of White Southern Womanhood, 1865–1895*. Baton Rouge: Louisiana State University Press, 2003.

Chirhart, Ann Short. *Torches of Light: Georgia Teachers and the Coming of the Modern South*. Athens: University of Georgia Press, 2005.

———, and Betty Wood, eds., *Georgia Women, Their Lives and Times, Vol. 1*. Athens: University of Georgia Press, 2009.

Cimbala, Paul and Barton C. Shaw. *Making a New South: Race, Leadership, and Community after the Civil War*. Gainesville: University Press of Florida, 2007.

Clare, Virginia. *Thunder and Stars: The Life of Mildred Rutherford*. Oglethorpe, Ga.: Oglethorpe University Press, 1941.

Clayton, Bruce L., and John A. Salmond, eds. *"Lives Full of Struggle and Triumph"*: *Southern Women, Their Institutions, and Their Communities*. Gainesville: University Press of Florida, 2003.

Clinton, Catherine. *The Other Civil War: American Women in the Nineteenth Century United States*. New York: Hill and Wang, 1984.

————. *The Plantation Mistress: Woman's World of the Old South*. New York: Pantheon Books, 1982.

Cobb, James C. *Away Down South: A History of Southern Identity*. New York: Oxford University Press, 2006.

————. *Georgia Odyssey: A Short History of the State*. Athens: University of Georgia Press, 2008.

————, and Michael V. Namoto, eds. *The New Deal and the South*. Jackson: University Press of Mississippi, 1984.

Coleman, Kenneth. *Confederate Athens*. Athens: University of Georgia Press, 1967.

————, general editor. *A History of Georgia*. Athens: University of Georgia Press, 1977, 1991.

Cook, Blanche Wiesen. *Eleanor Roosevelt, Vol. 1: 1884–1933*. New York: Penguin, 1992.

Connelly, Thomas L. and Barbara L. Bellows. *God and General Longstreet: The Lost Cause and the Southern Mind*. Baton Rouge: Louisiana State University Press, 1982.

Cox, Karen L. *Dixie's Daughters: The United Daughters of the Confederacy and the Preservation of Southern Culture*. Gainesville: University Press of Florida, 2003.

Cuthbert, Marion. *Juliette Derricotte*. New York: The Woman's Press, 1933.

Dabney, Charles. *Universal Education in the South*, 2 vols. Chapel Hill: University of North Carolina Press, 1936.

Dailey, Jane, Glenda Elizabeth Gilmore, and Bryant Simon, eds. *Jumpin' Jim Crow: Southern Politics from Civil War to Civil Rights*. Princeton, N.J.: Princeton University Press, 2000.

Daniels, Pete. *Breaking the Land: The Transformation of Cotton, Tobacco, and Rice Cultures Since 1880*. Urbana: University of Illinois Press, 1985.

Davenport, F. Garvin, Jr. *The Myth of Southern History: Historical Consciousness in Twentieth-Century Southern Literature*. Nashville: Vanderbilt University Press, 1970.

Davidson, Cathy. *Revolution and the Word: The Rise of the Novel in America*, expanded edition. Oxford: Oxford University Press, 2004.

Davis, Alison, Burleigh Gardner, and Mary Gardner. *Deep South: An Anthropological Study of Caste and Class*. Chicago: University of Chicago Press, 1941.

Davis, Leroy. *A Clashing of the Soul: John Hope and the Dilemma of African American Leadership and Black Higher Education in the Early Twentieth Century*. Athens: University of Georgia Press, 1998.

Denton, Virginia Lantz. *Booker T. Washington and the Adult Education Movement*. Gainesville: University Press of Florida, 1993.

Dittmer, John. *Black Georgia in the Progressive Era, 1900–1920*. Urbana: University of Illinois Press, 1977.

Dollard, John. *Caste and Class in a Southern Town*. New Haven: Yale University Press, 1937.

Dorsey, Alison. *To Build Our Lives Together: Community Formation in Black Atlanta, 1875–1906*. Athens: University of Georgia Press, 2004.

DuBois, W. E. B. *The Education of Black People*, edited by Herbert Aptheker. Amherst: University of Massachusetts Press, 1973.

Dyer, Thomas. *The University of Georgia: A Bicentennial History, 1785–1985*. Athens: University of Georgia Press, 1985.

Edgerton, Robert. *The Troubled Heart of Africa: A History of the Congo*. New York: St. Martin's Press, 2002.

Edwards, Laura. *Scarlett Doesn't Live Here Anymore: Southern Women in the Civil War Era*. Urbana: University of Illinois Press, 2000.

Fahs, Alice, and John Waugh. *The Memory of the Civil War in American Culture*. Chapel Hill: University of North Carolina Press, 2004.

Fairclough, Adam. *A Class of their Own: Black Teachers in the Segregated South*. Cambridge, Mass.: Harvard University Press, 2007.

———. *Teaching Equality: Black Schools in the Age of Jim Crow*. Athens: University of Georgia Press, 2001.

Faragher, John Mack, and Florence Howe, eds. *Women and Higher Education in American History*. New York: Norton, 1988.

Farnham, Christie Anne. *The Education of the Southern Belle: Higher Education and Student Socialization in the Antebellum South*. New York: New York University Press, 1994.

———, ed. *Women of the American South: A Multicultural Reader*. New York: New York University Press, 1997.

Faust, Drew Gilpin. *Mothers of Invention: Women of the Slaveholding South in the American Civil War*. Chapel Hill: University of North Carolina Press, 1996.

Fisher, Bernice M. *Industrial Education: American Ideas and Institutions*. Madison: University of Wisconsin Press, 1967.

Flynn, Charles L., Jr. *White Land, Black Labor: Caste and Class in Late Nineteenth Century Georgia*. Baton Rouge: Louisiana State University Press, 1983.

Fosdick, Raymond B. *Adventure in Giving: The Story of the General Education Board, A Foundation Established by John D. Rockfeller*. New York: Harper & Row, 1962.

Foster, Gaines M. *Ghosts of the Confederacy: Defeat, the Lost Cause, and the Emergence of the New South, 1865 to 1913*. New York: Oxford University Press, 1987.

Fox-Genovese, Elizabeth. *Within the Plantation Household: Black and White Women of the Old South*. Chapel Hill: University of North Carolina Press, 1988.

Franklee, Noralee, and Nancy Dye. *Gender, Class, Race, and Reform in the Progressive Era*. Lexington: University Press of Kentucky, 1991.

Franklin, V. P., and James D. Anderson, eds. *New Perspectives on Black Educational History*. Boston: G. K. Hall, 1978.

Fraser, Walter J., Jr., R. Frank Saunders, Jr., and Jon L. Wakelyn, eds. *The Web of Southern Social Relations: Women, Family, and Education*. Athens: University of Georgia Press, 1985.

Frederickson, George. *The Black Image in the White Mind: The Debate on Afro-American Character and Destiny, 1817–1914*. New York: Harper & Row, 1971.

Friedman, Jean E. *The Enclosed Garden: Women and Community in the Evangelical South, 1830–1900*. Chapel Hill: University of North Carolina Press, 1985.

Frost, Dan R. *Thinking Confederates: Academia and the Idea of Progress in the New South*. Knoxville: University of Tennessee Press, 2000.

Gaines, Kevin K. *Uplifting the Race: Black Leadership, Politics, and Culture in the Twentieth Century*. Chapel Hill: University of North Carolina Press, 1996.

Gardner, Sarah E. *Blood and Irony: Southern White Women's Narratives of the Civil War, 1861–1937*. Chapel Hill: University of North Carolina Press, 2004.

Gaston, Paul M. *The New South Creed: A Study in Southern Mythmaking*. New York: Random House, 1970.

Gatewood, Willard B. *Aristocrats of Color: The Black Elite, 1880–1920*. Bloomington: Indiana University Press, 1990.

Gerster, Patrick, and Nicholas Cords, eds. *Myth and Southern History: Volume 1: The Old South*. Urbana: University of Illinois Press, 1989.

———, eds. *Myth and Southern History: Volume 2: The New South*. Urbana: University of Illinois Press, 1989.

Gillis, John, ed. *Commemorations: The Politics of National Identity*. Princeton: Princeton University Press, 1994.

Gilmore, Glenda. *Gender and Jim Crow: Women and the Politics of White Supremacy in North Carolina, 1896–1920*. Chapel Hill: University of North Carolina Press, 1996.

Glassberg, David. *American Historical Pagenatry: The Uses of Tradition in the Early Twentieth Century*. Chapel Hill: University of North Carolina Press, 1990.

Glatthaar, Joseph T. *The March to the Sea and Beyond: Sherman's Troops in the Savannah and Carolinas Campaigns*. New York: New York University Press, 1985.

Godshalk, David Fort. *Veiled Visions: The 1906 Atlanta Race Riot and the Reshaping of American Race Relations*. Chapel Hill: University of North Carolina Press, 2005.

Goodenow, Ronald K., and Arthur O. White, eds. *Education and the Rise of the New South*. Boston, Mass.: G. K. Hall, 1981.

Gordon, Ann D., with Bettye Collier-Thomas, John H. Bracey, Arlene Voski Avakian, and Joyce Avrech Berkman, eds. *African-American Women and the Vote, 1837–1965*. Amherst: University of Massachusetts Press, 1997.

Gordon, Lynn D. *Gender and Higher Education in the Progressive Era*. New Haven: Yale University Press, 1990.

Grantham, Dewey W. *Hoke Smith and the Politics of the New South*. Baton Rouge: Louisiana State University Press, 1956.

———. *The South in Modern America: A Region at Odds*. New York: HarperCollins, 1994.

———. *Southern Progressivism: The Reconciliation of Progress and Tradition*. Knoxville: University of Tennessee Press, 1983.

Green, Elna, ed. *Before the New Deal: Social Welfare in the South, 1830–1930*. Athens: University of Georgia Press, 1999.

———. *Southern Strategies: Southern Women and the Woman Suffrage Question.* Chapel Hill: University of North Carolina Press, 1997.

Guy-Sheftall, Beverly, and Jo Moore Stewart. *Spelman: A Centennial Celebration, 1881–1981.* Charlotte, N.C.: Delmar, 1981.

Hale, Grace Elizabeth. *Making Whiteness: The Culture of Segregation in the South, 1890–1940.* New York: Pantheon, 1998.

Hancock, Carol Stevens. *The Light in the Mountains: A History of Tallulah Falls School.* Toccoa, Ga.: Commercial Printing Company, 1975.

Handlin, Oscar. *John Dewey's Challenge to Education.* New York: Harper & Row, 1950.

Harlan, Louis R. *Separate and Unequal: Public School Campaigns and Racism in the Southern Seaboard States, 1901–1915.* New York: Atheneum, [1958] 1968.

———, ed. *Booker T. Washington: The Wizard of Tuskegee, 1901–1915.* New York: Oxford University Press, 1983.

Harvey, Paul. *Freedom's Coming: Religious Culture and the Shaping of the South from the Civil War through the Civil Rights Era.* Chapel Hill: University of North Carolina Press, 2005.

———. *Redeeming the South: Religious Cultures and Racial Identities among Southern Baptists, 1865–1925.* Chapel Hill: University of North Carolina Press, 1997.

Hayes-Turner, Elizabeth. *Women, Culture, and Community: Religion and Reform in Galveston, 1880–1920.* New York: Oxford University Press, 1997.

Hewitt, Nancy A., and Suzanne Lebsock, eds. *Visible Women: New Essays on American Activism.* Chicago: University of Illinois Press, 1993.

Hickey, Georgina. *Hope and Danger in the New South City: Working-Class Women and Urban Development in Atlanta, 1890–1940.* Athens: University of Georgia Press, 2003.

Higginbotham, Evelyn Brooks. *Righteous Discontent: The Women's Movement in the Black Baptist Church, 1880–1920.* Cambridge, Mass.: Harvard University Press, 1993.

Hine, Darlene Clark. *Black Women in White: Racial Conflict and Cooperation in the Nursing Profession, 1890–1950.* Bloomington: Indiana University Press, 1989.

———. *Hine Sight: Black Women and the Re-Construction of American History.* Brooklyn, N.Y.: Carlson Publishing, 1994.

———, Wilma King, and Linda Reed, eds. *"We Specialize in the Wholly Impossible": A Reader in Black Women's History.* Brooklyn, N.Y.: Carlson Publishing, 1995.

Hobbs, Catherine, ed. *Nineteenth-Century Women Learn to Write.* Charlottesville: University of Virginia Press, 1995.

Hochschild, Adam. *King Leopold's Ghost: A Story of Greed, Terror and Heroism and Colonial Africa.* Boston: Houghton Mifflin, 1998.

Horowitz, Helen Lefkowitz. *Alma Mater: Design and Experience in the Women's Colleges from Their Nineteenth Century Beginnings to the 1930s.* Amherst: University of Massachusetts Press, 1993 [second edition].

Hunter, Tera W. *To 'Joy My Freedom: Southern Black Women's Lives and Labors after the Civil War.* Cambridge, Mass.: Harvard University Press, 1997.

Hyde, Anne Bachman. *An Historical Account of the United Daughters of the Confederacy: Origin, Objects and Purposes.* Little Rock: Democrat Printing and Lithographing Co., 1911.

Hynds, Ernest C. *Antebellum Athens and Clarke County, Georgia*. Athens: University of Georgia Press, 1974.

Inscoe, John C., ed. *Appalachians and Race: The Mountain South From Slavery to Segregation*. Lexington: University Press of Kentucky, 2001.

——, ed. *Georgia in Black and White: Explorations in the Race Relations of a Southern State, 1865–1950*. Athens: University of Georgia Press, 1994.

Jablonsky, Thomas J. *The Home, Heaven, and Mother Party: Female Anti-Suffragists in the United States, 1868–1920*. Brooklyn, N.Y.: Carlson Publishing, 1994.

Jackson, Jr., David H. *Booker T. Washington and the Struggle Against White Supremacy: The Southern Educational Tours, 1908–1912*. New York: Palgrave Macmillan, 2008.

Jacoway, Elizabeth. *Yankee Missionaries in the South: The Penn School Experiment*. Baton Rouge: Louisiana State University Press, 1980.

Janney, Caroline. *Burying the Dead but Not the Past: Ladies' Memorial Associations and the Lost Cause*. Chapel Hill: University of North Carolina Press, 2007.

Johnson, Guy. *Research in Service to Society: The First Fifty Years of the Institute for Research in Social Science*. Chapel Hill: University of North Carolina Press, 1980.

Johnson, Joan Marie. *Southern Ladies, New Women: Race, Region, and Clubwomen in South Carolina, 1890–1930*. Gainesville: University Press of Florida, 2004.

——. *Southern Women at the Seven Sister Colleges: Feminist Values and Social Activism, 1875–1915*. Athens: University of Georgia Press, 2008.

Jones, Jacqueline. *Labor of Love, Labor of Sorrow: Black Women, Work, and the Family, From Slavery to the Present*. New York: Vintage, 1985.

——. *Soldiers of Light and Love: Northern Teachers and Georgia Blacks, 1865–1873*. Chapel Hill: University of North Carolina Press, 1980.

Jones, Thomas. *Negro Education: A Study of the Private and Higher Schools for Colored People in the United States*, 2 vol. Washington, D.C.: GPO, 1917.

Kammen, Michael. *Mystic Chords of Memory: The Transformation of Tradition in American Culture*. New York: Knopf, 1991.

Kelley, Mary. *Learning to Stand and Speak: Women, Education, and Public Life in America's Republic*. Chapel Hill: University of North Carolina Press, 2006.

Kennedy, Pagan. *Black Livingstone: A True Tale of Adventure in the Nineteenth-Century Congo*. New York: Viking Press, 2002.

Kerber, Linda. *Women of the Republic: Intellect and Ideology in Revolutionary America*. Chapel Hill: University of North Carolina Press, 1980.

Klepp, Susan E. *Revolutionary Conceptions: Women, Fertility, and Family Limitation in America, 1760–1820*. Chapel Hill: University of North Carolina Press, 2009.

Koven, Seth, and Sonya Michel, eds. *Mothers of New World: Maternalist Politics and the Origins of Welfare States*. New York: Routledge, 1993.

Ladd-Taylor, Molly. *Mother-work: Women, Child Welfare, and the State, 1890–1930*. Urbana: University of Illinois Press, 1994.

Lasch-Quinn, Elizabeth. *Black Neighbors: Race and the Limits of Reform in the American Settlement House Movement, 1890–1945*. Chapel Hill: University of North Carolina Press, 1993.

Lears, T. J. Jackson. *No Place of Grace: Antimodernism and the Transformation of American Culture, 1880–1920*. New York: Pantheon Books, 1981.

Lefever, Harry G. *Undaunted by the Fight: Spelman College and the Civil Rights Movement, 1957–1967*. Macon: Mercer University Press, 2005.

Leloudis, James. *Schooling the New South: Pedagogy, Self, and Society in North Carolina, 1880–1920*. Chapel Hill: University of North Carolina Press, 1996.

Lewis, David Levering, ed. *W.E.B. DuBois: A Reader*. New York: Henry Holt and Co., 1995.

Lewis, Earl. *In Their Own Interests: Race, Class and Power in Twentieth-Century Norfolk, Virginia*. Berkeley: University of California Press, 1991.

Lindgren, James M. *Preserving Historic New England: Preservation, Progressivism, and the Remaking of Memory*. New York: Oxford University Press, 1995.

———. *Preserving the Old Dominion: Historic Preservation and Virginia Traditionalism*. Charlottesville: University of Virginia Press, 1993.

Link, William. *Atlanta: Cradle of the New South: Race and Remembering in the Civil War's Aftermath*. Chapel Hill: University of North Carolina Press, 2013.

———. *A Hard Country and a Lonely Place: Schooling, Society, and Reform in Rural Virginia, 1870–1920*. Chapel Hill: University of North Carolina Press, 1986.

———. *The Paradox of Southern Progressivism, 1880–1930*. Chapel Hill: University of North Carolina Press, 1992.

Lowe, Margaret A. *Looking Good: College Women and Body Image, 1875–1930*. Baltimore: Johns Hopkins University Press, 2003.

Mancini, Matthew J. *One Dies, Get Another: Convict Leasing in the American South, 1866–1928*. Columbia: University of South Carolina Press, 1996.

Marshall, Susan. *Splintered Sisterhood: Gender and Class in the Campaign against Woman Suffrage*. Madison: University of Wisconsin Press, 1997.

Martin, Harold H. *Georgia: A Bicentennial History*. Nashville, Tenn.: American Association of State and Local History, 1977.

Materson, Lisa. *For the Freedom of Her Race: Black Women and Electoral Politics in Illinois, 1877–1932*. Chapel Hill: University of North Carolina Press, 2009.

May, Ann Mari, ed. *The "Woman Question" and Higher Education: Perspectives on Gender and Knowledge Production in America*. Cheltenham, UK: Edward Elgar, 2008.

McCandless, Amy. *The Past in the Present: Women's Higher Education in the Twentieth-Century South*. Tuscaloosa: University of Alabama Press, 1999.

McCurry, Stephanie. *Masters of Small Worlds: Yeoman Households, Gender Relations, and the Political Culture of the Antebellum South Carolina Low Country*. New York: Oxford University Press, 1995.

McNeil, W. K., editor. *Appalachian Images in Folk and Popular Culture*. Ann Arbor: University of Michigan Press, 1989.

McPherson, James M. *The Abolitionist Legacy, from Reconstruction to the NAACP*. Princeton: Princeton University Press, 1975.

Meier, August. *Negro Thought in America, 1880–1915: Racial Ideologies in the Age of Booker T. Washington*. Ann Arbor: University of Michigan Press, 1963.

Mink, Gwendolyn. *Wages of Motherhood: Inequality in the Welfare State, 1917–1942.* Ithaca: Cornell University Press, 1995.

Mitchell, Michele. *Righteous Propagation: African Americans and the Politics of Racial Destiny after Reconstruction.* Chapel Hill: University of North Carolina Press, 2004.

Mixon, Gregory. *The Atlanta Race Riot: Race, Class, and Violence in a New South City.* Gainesville: University Press of Florida, 2005.

Montgomery, Rebecca S. *The Politics of Education in the New South: Women and Reform in Georgia.* Baton Rouge: Louisiana State University Press, 2006.

Moore, Jacqueline M. *Booker T. Washington, W.E.B. Dubois, and the Struggle for Racial Uplift.* Wilmington, Del.: Scholarly Resources, Inc., 2003.

Morgan, Francesca. *Women and Patriotism in Jim Crow America,* Chapel Hill: University of North Carolina Press, 2005.

Muncy, Robyn. *Creating a Female Dominion in American Reform, 1890–1935.* New York: Oxford University Press, 1991.

Nash, Margaret A. *Women's Education in the United States, 1780–1840.* New York: Palgrave Macmillan, 2005.

Neff, John R. *Honoring the Confederate Dead: Commemoration and the Problem of Reconciliation.* Lawrence: University Press of Kansas, 2005.

Neverdon-Morton, Cynthia. *Afro-American Women of the South and the Advancement of the Race.* Knoxville: University of Tennessee Press, 1989.

Nevins, Allan. *Study in Power: John D. Rockfeller, Industrialist and Philanthropist.* 2 vols. New York: Charles Scribner's Sons, 1953.

Nevins, James B., ed. *Prominent Women of Georgia.* Atlanta: National Biographical Publishers, [1928?].

Norton, Mary Beth. *Liberty's Daughters: The Revolutionary Experience of American Women, 1750–1800.* Boston: Little, Brown, 1980.

O'Brien, Thomas V. *The Politics of Race and Schooling: Public Education in Georgia, 1900–1961.* New York: Lexington Books, 1999.

O'Connor, Alice. *Poverty Knowledge: Social Science, Social Policy, and the Poor in Twentieth-Century U.S. History.* Princeton: Princeton University Press, 2001.

Painter, Nell Irvin. *Southern History Across the Color Line.* Chapel Hill: University of North Carolina Press, 2002.

Pascoe, Peggy. *Relations of Rescue: The Search for Female Moral Authority in the American West, 1874–1939.* New York: Oxford University Press, 1990.

Perdue, Theda. *Race and the Atlanta Cotton States Exposition of 1895.* Athens: University of Georgia Press, 2010.

Plank, David N., and Rick Ginsberg. *Southern Cities, Southern Schools: Public Education in the Urban South.* Westport, Conn.: Greenwood Press, 1990.

Platt, Robert. *We Shall not be Moved: The Desegregation of the University of Georgia.* Athens: University of Georgia Press, 2002.

Pomeranz, Gary M. *Where Peachtree Meets Sweet Auburn: A Saga of Race and Family.* New York: Penguin Books, 1996.

Poppenheim, Mary B., et al. *The History of the United Daughters of the Confederacy* (3 vols. in 2). Raleigh, N.C.: Edwards and Broughton, Co., 1956.

Powdermaker, Hortense. *After Freedom: A Cultural Study of the Deep South*. New York: Viking Press, 1939.

Provenzo, Eugene F., Jr., ed. *Du Bois on Education*. Walnut Creek, Calif.: AltaMira Press, 2002.

Rabinowitz, Howard. *Race Relations in the Urban South, 1865–1890*. New York: Oxford University Press, 1978.

Rable, George. *Civil Wars: Women and the Crisis of Southern Nationalism*. Urbana: University of Illinois Press, 1989.

Read, Florence Matilda. *The Story of Spelman College*. Atlanta: United Negro College Fund with Princeton University Press, 1961.

Reeves-Ellington, Barbara, Kathryn Kish Sklar, and Connie A. Shemo, eds. *Competing Kingdoms: Women, Mission, Nation, and the American Protestant Empire, 1812–1960*. Durham: Duke University Press, 2010.

Riley, Denise. *"Am I That Name?" Feminism and the Category of "Women" in History*. Minneapolis: University of Minnesota Press, 1988.

Robertson, Nancy Marie. *Christian Sisterhood, Race Relations, and the YWCA, 1906–46*. Urbana: University of Illinois Press, 2007.

Roth, Darlene Rebecca. *Matronage: Patterns of Women's Organizations, Atlanta, Georgia, 1890–1940*. Brooklyn, N.Y.: Carlson Publishing, Inc., 1994.

Rouse, Jacqueline Anne. *Lugenia Burns Hope: Black Southern Reformer*. Athens: University of Georgia Press, 1989.

Rowe, H. J. ed. *History of Athens and Clarke County*. Athens: H. L. Rowe, 1923.

Rowson, Susanna. *Charlotte Temple*, ed. Cathy Davidson. New York: Oxford University Press, 1986.

Royster, Jacqueline Jones. *Traces of a Stream: Literacy and Social Change Among African American Women*. Pittsburgh: University of Pittsburgh Press, 2000.

Samway, Patrick H. *Walker Percy, A Life*. New York: Farrar, Straus and Giroux, 1997.

Sanders, Lynn Moss. *Howard W. Odum's Folklore Odyssey: Transformation to Tolerance through African American Folk Studies*. Athens: University of Georgia Press, 2003.

Schechter, Patricia. *Ida B. Wells-Barnett and American Reform, 1880–1930*. Chapel Hill: University of North Carolina Press, 2001.

Scott, Anne Firor. *The Southern Lady: From Pedestal to Politics, 1830–1930*. Chicago: University of Chicago Press, 1970.

Scott, Joan Wallach. *Gender and the Politics of History*. New York: Columbia University Press, 1988.

Shapiro, Henry. *Appalachia on Our Mind: The Southern Mountains and Mountaineers in the American Consciousness, 1870–1920*. Chapel Hill: University of North Carolina Press, 1978.

Shaw, Stephanie J. *What a Woman Ought to Be and Do: Black Professional Women Workers During the Jim Crow Era*. Chicago: University of Chicago Press, 1996.

Silber, Nina. *The Romance of Reunion: Northerners and the South, 1865–1900*. Chapel Hill: University of North Carolina Press, 1993.

Sims, Anastasia. *The Power of Femininity in the New South: Women's Organizations and Politics in North Carolina, 1880–1930.* Columbia: University of South Carolina Press, 1997.

Smith, John David. *An Old Creed for the New South: Proslavery Ideology and Historiography, 1865–1918.* Westport, Conn.: Wesleyan University Press, 1985.

Smith, Trudi. *Building Bridges to Common Ground.* Boston, Mass.: The Thurman Center, Boston University, 1985.

Solomon, Barbara Miller. *In the Company of Women: A History of Women and Higher Education in America.* New Haven: Yale University Press, 1985.

Sorley, Merrow Egerton. *Lewis of Warner Hall: The History of a Family* (Reprint, Baltimore: Geneological Publishing, 2000).

Sosna, Morton. *In Search of the Silent South: Southern Liberals and the Race Issue.* New York: Columbia University Press, 1977.

Spain, Rufus B. *At Ease in Zion: A Social History of Southern Baptists, 1865–1900.* Tuscaloosa: The University of Alabama Press, 2003.

Spalding, Phinizy, comp. and ed. *Higher Education in the South: A History of Lucy Cobb Institute, 1858–1994.* Athens: Georgia Southern Press, 1994.

Spivey, Donald. *Schooling for the New Slavery: Black Industrial Education, 1868–1915.* Westport, Conn.: Greenwood Press, 1978.

Stage, Sarah, and Virginia B. Vincenti, *Rethinking Home Economics: Women and the History of a Profession.* Ithaca and London: Cornell University Press, 1997.

Stampp, Kenneth M. *The Era of Reconstruction, 1865–1877.* New York: Knopf, 1965.

Stowell, Daniel W. *Rebuilding Zion: The Religious Reconstruction of the South, 1863–1877.* New York and Oxford: Oxford University Press, 1998.

Strahan, Charles Morton. *Clarke County, Ga. and the City of Athens.* Athens, Ga.: copyrighted by author, no publisher, 1893.

Terborg-Penn, Rosalyn. *African American Women in the Struggle for the Vote, 1850–1920.* Bloomington: Indiana University Press, 1998.

Thelen, David, ed. *Memory and American History.* Bloomington: Indiana University Press, 1990.

Thomas, Frances Taliaferro. *A Portrait of Historic Athens & Clarke County.* Athens: University of Georgia Press, 1992.

Tindall, George Brown. *The Emergence of the New South 1913–1945.* Baton Rouge: Louisiana State University Press, 1967.

Torbet, Robert G. *A History of the Baptists.* Valley Forge, Penn.: Judson Press, 1963 [1950].

Turner, Elizabeth Hayes. *Women, Culture, and Community: Religion and Reform in Galveston, 1880–1920.* New York: Oxford University Press, 1997.

Tyack, David. *The One Best System: A History of American Urban Education.* Cambridge, Mass.: Harvard University Press, 1974.

Urban, Wayne J., ed. *Essays in Twentieth-Century Southern Education: Exceptionalism and Its Limits.* New York: Garland Publishing, 1999.

Varon, Elizabeth. *"We Mean to be Counted": White Women and Politics in Antebellum Virginia*. Chapel Hill: University of North Carolina Press, 1998.

Watkins, William H. *The White Architects of Black Education: Ideology and Power in America, 1865–1954*. New York: Teachers College, Columbia University, 2001.

Watson, Yolanda L., and Sheila T. Gregory. *Daring to Educate: The Legacy of the Early Spelman College Presidents*. Sterling, Va.: Stylus Publishing, LLC, 2005.

Wheeler, Marjorie Spruill. *New Women of the New South: The Leaders of the Woman Suffrage Movement in the Southern States*. New York: Oxford University Press, 1993.

———. *One Woman, One Vote: Rediscovering the Woman Suffrage Movement*. Troutdale, Ore.: NewSage Press, 1995.

———, ed. *Votes for Women! The Woman Suffrage Movement in Tennessee, the South, and the Nation*. Knoxville: University of Tennessee Press, 1995.

Whisnant, David E. *All That Is Native and Fine: The Politics of Culture in an American Region*. Chapel Hill: University of North Carolina Press, 1983.

———. *Modernizing the Mountaineer: People, Power, and Planning in Appalachia*. Boone, N.C.: Appalachia Consortium Press, 1980.

White, Deborah Gray. *Ar'n't I a Woman? Female Slaves in the Plantation South*, rev. ed. New York: W. W. Norton, 1985.

Williams, Heather Andrea. *African American Education in Slavery and Freedom*. Chapel Hill: University of North Carolina Press, 2005.

Williamson, Joel. *A Rage for Order: Black-White Relations in the American South Since Emancipation*. New York: Oxford University Press, 1986.

Wilson, Charles. *Baptized in Blood: The Religion of the Lost Cause, 1865–1920*. Athens: University of Georgia Press, 1980.

Wolcott, Victoria W. *Remaking Respectability: African American Women in Interwar Detroit*. Chapel Hill: University of North Carolina Press, 2001.

Wolfe, Margret Ripley. *Daughters of Canaan: A Saga of Southern Women*. Lexington: The University Press of Kentucky, 1995.

Wolters, Raymond. *The New Negro on Campus: Black College Rebellions of the 1920s*. Princeton: Princeton University Press, 1975.

Women of Georgia: A Ready and Accurate Reference Book for Newspapers and Librarian[s]. Atlanta: Georgia Press Reference Association, 1927.

Woodward, C. Vann. *Origins of the New South, 1877–1913*. Baton Rouge: Louisiana State University Press, 1951.

Wright, Gavin. *Old South, New South: Revolutions in the Southern Economy Since the Civil War*. New York: Basic Books, Inc., 1986.

Wynne, Lewis Nicholas. *The Continuity of Cotton: Planter Politics in Georgia, 1865–1892*. Macon, Ga.: Mercer University Press, 1986.

ARTICLES

Alexander, Adele Logan. "Adella Hunt Logan, the Tuskegee Woman's Club, and African Americans in the Suffrage Movement." In *Votes for Women! The Woman Suffrage Movement in Tennessee, the South, and the Nation*, ed. Marjorie Spruill Wheeler, 71–104. Knoxville: University of Tennessee Press, 1995.

Bailey, Fred Arthur. "Free Speech and the Lost Cause in the Old Dominion." *Virginia Magazine of History and Biography* 103 (April 1995): 237–266.

———. "Free Speech at the University of Florida: The Enoch Marvin Banks Case." *Florida Historical Quarterly* 71 (July 1992): 1–17.

———. "Mildred Lewis Rutherford and the Patrician Cult of the Old South." *Georgia Historical Quarterly* 77 (Fall 1994): 509–35.

———. "Textbooks of the 'Lost Cause': Censorship and the Creation of Southern State Histories." *Georgia Historical Quarterly* 75 (Fall 1991): 507–33.

Berkeley, Kathleen C. "'Colored Ladies Also Contributed': Black Women's Activities from Benevolence to Social Welfare, 1866–1896." In *The Web of Southern Social Relations: Women, Family, and Education*, eds. Walter J. Fraser, Jr., R. Frank Saunders, Jr., and Jon L. Wakelyn, 181–203. Athens: University of Georgia Press, 1985.

Best, John Hardin. "Education in the Forming of the American South." In *Essays in Twentieth-Century Southern Education: Exceptionalism and Its Limits*, ed. Wayne J. Urban, 3–18. New York: Garland Publishing, 1999.

Birnbaum, Shira. "Making Southern Belles in Progressive Era Florida: Gender in the Formal and Hidden Curriculum of the Florida Female College." *Frontiers* 16, no. 2/3 (1996): 218–46.

Bloch, Ruth. "The Gendered Meaning of Virtue in Revolutionary America." *Signs* 13 (Autumn 1987): 37–58.

Brazzell, Johnetta Cross. "Bricks without Straw: Missionary-Sponsored Black Higher Education in the Post-Emancipation Era." *Journal of Higher Education* 63 (January/February 1992): 26–49.

Brown, Elsa Barkley. "Womanist Consciousness: Maggie Lena Walker and the Independent Order of Saint Luke." *Signs* 14 (Spring 1989): 610–33.

Brown, W. O. "Role of Poor Whites in Race Contacts of the South." *Social Forces* 19 no. 2 (December 1940): 258–68.

Buchanan, Linda R., and Philip A. Hutchenson. "Reconsidering the Washington-Du Bois Debate: Two Black Colleges in 1910–11." In *Essays in Twentieth-Century Southern Education: Exceptionalism and Its Limits*, ed. Wayne J. Urban, 77–99. New York: Garland Publishing, 1999.

Chirhart, Ann Short. "'Gardens of Education': Beulah Rucker and African-American Culture in the Twentieth-Century Georgia Upcountry." *Georgia Historical Quarterly* 82 no. 4 (Winter 1998): 829–47.

———. "Gender, Jim Crow, and Eugene Talmadge: The Politics of Social Policy in Georgia." In *The New Deal and Beyond: Social Welfare in the South since 1930*, ed. Elna C. Green, 71–99. Athens: University of Georgia Press, 2003.

Cobb, James C. "Beyond Planters and Industrialists: A New Perspective on the New South." *Journal of Southern History* 54 (February 1988): 45–68.

Cowan, Ruth Schwartz. "The 'Industrial Revolution' in the Home: Household Technology and Social Change in the Twentieth Century." *Technology and Culture* 17 (1976): 1–23.

Dean, Pamela. "Learning to Be New Women: Campus Culture at the North Carolina Normal and Industrial College." *The North Carolina Historical Review* 68, no. 3 (July 1991): 286–306.

Donaldson, Bobby J. "Standing on a Volcano: The Leadership of William Jefferson White." In *Paternalism in a Southern City: Race, Religion and Gender in Augusta, Georgia*, eds. Edward J. Cashin and Glenn T. Eskew, 135–176. Athens: University of Georgia Press, 2001.

Faust, Drew Gilpin. "Altars of Sacrifice: Confederate Women and the Narratives of War." *Journal of American History* 76 (March 1990), 1200–1228.

———, Thavolia Glymph, and George C. Rable. "A Woman's War: Southern Women in the Civil War." In *A Woman's War: Southern Women, Civil War, and the Confederate Legacy*, eds. Edward D. C. Campbell Jr. and Kym S. Rice, 1–27. Richmond: The Museum of the Confederacy, 1996.

Fields, Barbara. "Ideology and Race in American History." In *Region, Race, and Reconstruction: Essays in Honor of C. Vann Woodward*, eds. J. Morgan Kousser and James M. McPherson, 143–77. New York: Oxford University Press, 1982.

Finkenbine, Roy E. "'Our Little Circle': Benevolent Reformers, the Slater Fund, and the Argument for Black Industrial Education, 1882–1908." In *African-Americans and Education in the South, 1865–1900,* ed. Donald G. Nieman, 70–86. New York: Garland Publishing, Inc., 1994 (reprinted from *Hayes Historical Journal* 6 [1986], 6–22).

Friedlander, Amy. "A More Perfect Christian Womanhood: Higher Learning for a New South." In *Education and the Rise of the New South*, eds. Ronald K. Goodenow and Arthur O. White, 72–91. Boston: G. K. Hall & Co., 1981.

Gordon, Fon. "'A Generous and Exemplary Womanhood': Hattie Rutherford Watson and NYA Camp Bethune in Pine Bluff, Arkansas." In *The Southern Elite and Social Change: Essays in Honor of Willard B. Gatewood, Jr.,* eds. Randy Finley and Thomas A. DeBlack. Fayetteville: University of Arkansas Press, 2002.

Guy-Sheftall, Beverly. "Black Women in Higher Education: Spelman and Bennett Colleges Revisited." *Journal of Negro Education* 51 (Summer 1982): 279–89.

Hackney, Sheldon. "Origins of the New South in Retrospect." *Journal of Southern History* 38 (May 1972): 191–216.

Hale, Grace Elizabeth. "'Some Women Have Never Been Reconstructed': Mildred Lewis Rutherford, Lucy M. Stanton, and the Racial Politics of White Southern Womanhood, 1900–1930." In *Georgia in Black and White: Explorations in the Race Relations of a Southern State, 1865–1950*, ed. John C. Inscoe, 173–201. Athens: University of Georgia Press, 1994.

Harlan, Louis R. "Booker T. Washington and the *Voice of the Negro*, 1904–1907." *Journal of Southern History* 45 (February 1979): 45–62.

Harley, Sharon. "For the Good of Family and Race: Gender, Work, and Domestic Roles in the Black Community, 1880–1930." *Signs* 15 (Winter 1990): 336–49.

———. "Nannie Helen Burroughs: 'The Black Goddess of Liberty.'" *The Journal of Negro History* 81, no. 1–4 (Winter-Autumn 1996): 62–71.

———. "When Your Work is Not Who You Are: The Development of a Working-Class Consciousness among Afro-American Women." In *"We Specialize in the Wholly Impossible": A Reader in Black Women's History*, eds. Darlene Clark Hine, Wilma King, and Linda Reed, 25–37. Brooklyn, N.Y.: Carlson Publishing, 1995.

Harris, Carl V. "Stability and Change in Discrimination against Black Public Schools: Birmingham, Alabama, 1871–1931." *Journal of Southern History* 51 (August 1985): 375–416.

Hewitt, Nancy. "Beyond the Search for Sisterhood: American Women's History in the 1980s." *Social History* 10 (October 1985): 299–321.

———. "Compounding Differences." *Feminist Studies* 18 (Summer 1992): 313–26.

Hickey, Georgina. "Disease, Disorder, and Motherhood: Working-Class Women, Social Welfare, and the Process of Urban Development in Atlanta." In *Before the New Deal: Social Welfare in the South, 1830–1930*, ed. Elna Green, 181–207. Athens: University of Georgia Press, 1999.

Hicks, Paul DeForest. "Caroline O'Day: The Gentlewoman from New York." *New York History* (Summer 2007): 287–305.

Higginbotham, Evelyn Brooks. "African-American Women's History and the Meta-language of Race." *Signs* 17 (Winter 1992): 251–74.

———. "Beyond the Sound of Silence: Afro-American Women's History." *Gender and History* 1 (Spring 1989): 50–67.

Hine, Darlene Clark. "Rape and the Inner Lives of Black Women in the Middle West." *Signs* 14 (Summer 1989): 912–920.

———. "'They Shall Mount Up with Wings as Eagles': Historical Images of Black Nurses, 1890–1950." In *Hine Sight: Black Women and the Re-Construction of American History*, ed. Darlene Clark Hine, 163–81. Brooklyn, N.Y.: Carlson Publishing, 1994.

———. "'We Specialize in the Wholly Impossible': Philanthropic Work of Black Women." In *Hine Sight: Black Women and the Re-Construction of American History*, ed. Darlene Clark Hine, 109–128. Brooklyn, N.Y.: Carlson Publishing, 1994.

Hodes, Martha. "The Sexualization of Reconstruction Politics: White Women and Black Men in the South after the Civil War." *Journal of the History of Sexuality* 3 (January 1993): 402–417.

Holmes, Catherine L. "The Darling Offspring of her Brain: The Quilts of Harriet Powers." In *Georgia Quilts: Piecing Together a History*, ed. Anita Zaleski Weinraub. Athens: University of Georgia Press, 2006.

Horowitz, Helen Lefkowitz. "The Body in the Library." In *The "Woman Question" and Higher Education: Perspectives on Gender and Knowledge Production in America*, ed. Ann Mari May, 11–31. Cheltenham, UK: Edward Elgar, 2008.

Hunt, Patricia K. "Clothing as an Expression of History: The Dress of African-American Women in Georgia, 1880–1915." In *"We Specialize in the Wholly Impossible": A Reader in Black Women's History*, eds. Darlene Clark Hine, Wilma King, and Linda Reed, 393–404. Brooklyn, N.Y.: Carlson Publishing, 1995.

Hunter, Tera W. "Domination and Resistance: The Politics of Wage Household Labor in New South Atlanta." In *"We Specialize in the Wholly Impossible": A Reader in Black Women's History*, eds. Darlene Clark Hine, Wilma King, and Linda Reed, 343–57. Brooklyn, N.Y.: Carlson Publishing, 1995.

Jabour, Anya. "Sophonisba Preston Breckinridge: Homegrown Heroine." In *Kentucky Women: Their Lives and Times*, eds. Melissa McEuen and Thomas H. Appleton Jr., 140–67. Athens: University of Georgia Press, 2015.

Jackson, Harvey H., III, "Billups Phinizy Spalding: A Tribute." *Georgia Historical Quarterly* 78 (Fall 1994): [pages unnumbered].

Jacobs, Sylvia M. "Give a Thought to Africa: Black Women Missionaries in Southern Africa." In *"We Specialize in the Wholly Impossible": A Reader in Black Women's History*, eds. Darlene Clark Hine, Wilma King, and Linda Reed, 103–23. Brooklyn, N.Y.: Carlson Publishing, 1995.

Jennings, Thelma. "'Us Colored Women Had to Go Through a Plenty': Sexual Exploitation of African-American Slave Women." *Journal of Women's History* 1 (Winter 1990): 45–74.

Keer, Andrea Moore. "White Women's Rights, Black Men's Wrongs, Free Love, Blackmail, and the Formation of the American Woman Suffrage Association." In *One Woman, One Vote: Rediscovering the Woman Suffrage Movement*, ed. Marjorie Spruill Wheeler, 61–79. Troutdale, Ore.: NewSage Press, 1995.

Kerber, Linda. "'Why Should Girls be Learn'd and Wise?': Two Centuries of Higher Education for Women as Seen through the Unfinished Work of Alice Mary Baldwin." In *Women and Higher Education in American History*, eds. John Mack Faragher and Florence Howe, 25–26. New York: Norton, 1988.

Kett, Joseph F. "Women and the Progressive Impulse in Southern Education." In *The Web of Southern Social Relations: Women, Family, and Education*, eds. Walter J. Fraser Jr., R. Frank Saunders Jr., and Jon L. Wakelyn, 166–80. Athens: University of Georgia Press, 1985.

Kousser, J. Morgan. "Progressivism—For Middle Class Whites Only: North Carolina Education, 1880–1910." *Journal of Southern History* 46 (May 1980): 168–94.

Lebsock, Suzanne. "Woman Suffrage and White Supremacy: A Virginia Case Study." In *Visible Women: New Essays on American Activism*, eds. Nancy A. Hewitt and Suzanne Lebsock, 62–100. Urbana: University of Illinois Press, 1993.

Lewis, Jan. "The Republican Wife: Virtue and Seduction in the Early Republic." *The William and Mary Quarterly* 44 (October 1987): 689–721.

MacLean, Nancy. "The Leo Frank Case Reconsidered: Gender and Sexual Politics in the Making of Reactionary Populism." *Journal of Southern History* 78 (December 1991): 917–48.

Marshall, Susan. "In Defense of Separate Spheres: Class and Status Politics in the Anti-Suffrage Movement." *Social Forces* 65 (December 1986): 327–35.

Martin, Sandy Dwayne. "The American Baptist Home Mission Society and Black Higher Education in the South, 1865–1920." *Foundations* 24 (1981): 310–327.

Materson, Lisa G. "African American Women, Prohibition, and the 1928 Presidential Election." *Journal of Women's History* 21 (2009): 63–86.

McClusky, Audrey Thomas. "'We Specialize in the Wholly Impossible': Black Women School Founders and Their Mission." *Signs* 22 no. 2 (Winter 1997): 403–26.

McDonald. "'To Educate Neither Belles Nor Bluestockings': Women and Higher Education in the South During the Progressive Era." *Studies in Popular Culture* 20 no. 2 (October 1997): 59–70.

McRae, Elizabeth Gillespie. "Caretakers of Southern Civilization: Georgia Women and the Anti-Suffrage Campaign, 1914–1920." *Georgia Historical Quarterly* 82, no. 4 (Winter 1991): 801–28.

Meier, August, and David Lewis. "History of the Negro Upper Class in Atlanta, Georgia, 1890–1958." *Journal of Negro Education* 28 (Spring 1958): 128–39.

Miller, Mary Morris. "Madame Sophie Sosnowski." *Georgia Historical Quarterly* 38, no. 3 (September 1954): 249–52.

Moss, Margaret Anne. "Miss Mille Rutherford, Southerner." *Georgia Review* 7 (Spring 1953): 57–66.

Office of History & Preservation, U.S. House of Representatives, "Caroline Love Goodwin O'Day." In *Women in Congress, 1917–2006*, 155–59. Washington: Government Printing Office, 2006, .

Parrott, Angie. "'Love Makes Memory Eternal': The United Daughters of the Confederacy in Richmond, Virginia 1897–1920." In *The Edge of the South: Life in Nineteenth Century Virginia*, eds. Edward L. Ayers and John C. Willis, 219–238. Charlottesville: University of Virginia Press, 1991.

Patton, June O. "Moonlight and Magnolias in Southern Education: The Black Mammy Memorial Institute." *Journal of Negro History* 65, no. 2 (Spring 1980): 149–155.

Racine, Philip N. "Public Education in the New South: A School System for Atlanta, 1868–1879." In *Southern Cities, Southern Schools: Public Education in the Urban South*, eds., David N. Plank and Rick Ginsberg, 37–58. Westport, Conn.: Greenwood Press, 1990.

Renner, Karen J. "Seduction, Prostitution, and the Control of Female Desire in Popular Antebellum Fiction." *Nineteenth-Century Literature* 65 (September 2010): 166–191.

Rice, Kym S., and Edward D. C. Campbell Jr. "Voices from the Tempest: Southern Women's Wartime Experience." In *A Woman's War: Southern Women, Civil War, and the Confederate Legacy*, eds. Edward D. C. Campbell Jr., and Kym S. Rice, 73–111. Richmond: The Museum of the Confederacy, 1996.

Scott, Anne Firor. "Most Invisible of All: Black Women's Voluntary Associations." *Journal of Southern History* 56 (February 1990): 3–22.

Shaw, Stephanie. "Black Club Women and the Creation of the National Association of Colored Women." In *"We Specialize in the Wholly Impossible": A Reader in Black Women's History*, eds. Darlene Clark Hine, Wilma King, and Linda Reed, 433–47. Brooklyn, N.Y.: Carlson Publishing, 1995.

Sklar, Kathryn Kish. "The Historical Foundations of a Women's Power in the Creation of the American Welfare State, 1830–1930." In *Mothers of a New World: Maternalist Politics and the Origins of Welfare States*, eds. Seth Koven and Sonya Michel, 43–93. New York: Routledge, 1993.

Smith, Jennifer Lund. "Ties that Bind: Educated African-American Women in Post-Emancipation Atlanta." In *Georgia in Black and White: Explorations in the Race Relations of a Southern State, 1865–1950*, ed. John C. Inscoe, 91–105. Athens: University of Georgia Press, 1994.

Smith, Katharine Capshaw. "Childhood, the Body, and Race Performance: Early Twentieth-Century Etiquette Books for Black Children." *African-American Review* 40 (Winter 2006): 795–811.

Smith, Patricia E. "Rhoda Kaufman: A Southern Progressive's Career, 1913–1956." *Atlanta Historical Bulletin* 8 (Spring/Summer 1973): 43–50.

Stowe, Steven M. "The Not-So-Cloistered Academy: Elite Women's Education and Family Feeling in the Old South." In *The Web of Southern Social Relations: Women, Family, and Education*, eds. Walter J. Fraser Jr., R. Frank Saunders Jr., and Jon L. Wakelyn, 90–106. Athens: University of Georgia Press, 1985.

Tindall, George. "The Significance of Howard Odum to Southern History: A Preliminary Estimate." *Journal of Southern History* 24 (August 1958): 303–304.

Townsend, Sara Bertha. "The Admission of Women to the University of Georgia." *Georgia Historical Quarterly* 43, no. 2 (June 1959): 156–169.

Ulrich, Laurel Thatcher. "'A Quilt Unlike Any Other': Rediscovering the Work of Harriet Powers." In *Writing Women's History: A Tribute to Anne Firor Scott*, ed. Elizabeth Anne Payne. Jackson: University Press of Mississippi, 2011.

Urban, Wayne J. "Educational Reform in a New South City: Atlanta, 1890–1925." In *Education and the Rise of the New South*, eds. Ronald K. Goodenow and Arthur O. White, 114–30. Boston: G.K. Hall & Co., 1981.

Wagoner, Jennings L., Jr. "The American Compromise: Charles W. Eliot, Black Education, and the New South." In *Education and the Rise of the New South*, eds. Ronald K. Goodenow and Arthur O. White. Boston: G.K. Hall & Co., 1981.

Whitby, Gary L., and Lynn K. Whitby, "John Drewry and Social Progress." In *Makers of the Media Mind: Journalism Educators and Their Ideas*, ed. Wm. David Sloan, 142–48. New York: Routledge, 1990.

White, Mary Harriet. "Madame Sophie Sosnowski, Educator of Young Ladies." *Georgia Historical Quarterly* 50, no. 3 (September 1966): 283–87.

Whites, LeeAnn. "'Stand by Your Man': The Ladies Memorial Association and the Reconstruction of Southern White Manhood." In *Women of the American South: A Multicultural Reader*, ed. Christie Anne Farnham, 133–149. New York: New York University Press, 1997.

Wilkerson-Freeman, Sarah. "The Creation of a Subversive Feminist Dominion: Interracialist Social Workers and the Georgia New Deal." *Journal of Women's History* 13 (Winter 2002): 132–154.

———. "The Second Battle for Woman Suffrage: Alabama White Women, the Poll Tax, and V. O. Key's Master Narrative of Southern Politics." *Journal of Southern History* 68 (May 2002): 333–74.

Zagarri, Rosemarie. "Morals, Manners, and the Republican Mother." *American Quarterly* 44 no. 2 (June 1992): 192–215.

DISSERTATIONS AND THESES

Barrow, Phyllis Jenkins. "History of Lucy Cobb Institute, 1858–1950." MA thesis, University of Georgia, 1951; reprinted in Phinizy Spalding, comp. and ed., *Higher*

Education in the South: A History of Lucy Cobb Institute, 1858–1994. Athens, Ga.: Georgia Southern Press, 1994.

Blackwell, Deborah L. "The Ability to "Do Much Larger Work': Gender and Reform in Appalachia." PhD dissertation, University of Kentucky, 1998.

Brazzell, Johnetta. "Education as a Tool of Socialization: Agnes Scott Institute and Spelman Seminary, 1881–1910." PhD dissertation, University of Michigan, 1991.

Brumby, Anne Wallis. "Education of Women in the United States." MA thesis, University of Georgia, 1925.

Corley, Florence Fleming. "Higher Education For Southern Women: Four Church-Related Women's Colleges in Georgia, Agnes Scott, Shorter, Spelman, and Wesleyan, 1900–1920." PhD dissertation, Georgia State University, 1985.

Knight, Monica Dellengerber. "Seeking Education for Liberation: The Development of Black Schools in Athens, Georgia, from Emancipation Through Desegregation." PhD dissertation, University of Georgia, 2007.

McPherson, Mary E. "Organizing Women: Women's Clubs and Education in Georgia, 1890–1920." PhD dissertation, Georgia State University, 2009.

Mell, Mildred. "A Definitive Study of Poor Whites in the South." PhD dissertation, University of North Carolina, 1938.

Moore, Maude. "History of the College for Women, Columbia, SC." MA thesis, University of South Carolina, 1932.

Shivery, Louise Delphia Davis. "The History of Organized Social Work Among Atlanta Negroes, 1890–1935." MA thesis, Atlanta University, 1936.

Tuthill, Hazelle Beard. "Mildred Lewis Rutherford." MA thesis, University of South Carolina, 1929.

Wilkerson-Freeman, Sarah. "The Feminization of the American State: The Odyssey of a Southern Vanguard, 1898–1940." PhD dissertation, University of North Carolina, 1995.

Womack, Margaret Anne. "Mildred Lewis Rutherford, Exponent of Southern Culture." MA thesis, University of Georgia, 1946.

Index

SARAH H. CASE is a lecturer in the department of history at University of California, Santa Barbara and is managing editor of *The Public Historian.*

Women, Gender, and Sexuality in American History

Women Doctors in Gilded-Age Washington: Race, Gender, and
Professionalization   *Gloria Moldow*

Friends and Sisters: Letters between Lucy Stone and Antoinette Brown Blackwell,
1846–93   *Edited by Carol Lasser and Marlene Deahl Merrill*

Reform, Labor, and Feminism: Margaret Dreier Robins and the Women's Trade
Union League   *Elizabeth Anne Payne*

Private Matters: American Attitudes toward Childbearing and Infant Nurture in
the Urban North, 1800–1860   *Sylvia D. Hoffert*

Civil Wars: Women and the Crisis of Southern Nationalism   *George C. Rable*

I Came a Stranger: The Story of a Hull-House Girl   *Hilda Satt Polacheck;
edited by Dena J. Polacheck Epstein*

Labor's Flaming Youth: Telephone Operators and Worker Militancy,
1878–1923   *Stephen H. Norwood*

Winter Friends: Women Growing Old in the New Republic, 1785–1835
Terri L. Premo

Better Than Second Best: Love and Work in the Life of Helen Magill
Glenn C. Altschuler

Dishing It Out: Waitresses and Their Unions in the Twentieth Century
Dorothy Sue Cobble

Natural Allies: Women's Associations in American History   *Anne Firor Scott*

Beyond the Typewriter: Gender, Class, and the Origins of Modern American
Office Work, 1900–1930   *Sharon Hartman Strom*

The Challenge of Feminist Biography: Writing the Lives of Modern American
Women   *Edited by Sara Alpern, Joyce Antler, Elisabeth Israels Perry,
and Ingrid Winther Scobie*

Working Women of Collar City: Gender, Class, and Community in Troy,
New York, 1864–86   *Carole Turbin*

Radicals of the Worst Sort: Laboring Women in Lawrence, Massachusetts,
1860–1912   *Ardis Cameron*

Visible Women: New Essays on American Activism   *Edited by Nancy A. Hewitt
and Suzanne Lebsock*

Mother-Work: Women, Child Welfare, and the State, 1890–1930
Molly Ladd-Taylor

Babe: The Life and Legend of Babe Didrikson Zaharias   *Susan E. Cayleff*

Writing Out My Heart: Selections from the Journal of Frances E. Willard,
1855–96   *Edited by Carolyn De Swarte Gifford*

U.S. Women in Struggle: A *Feminist Studies* Anthology   *Edited by Claire Goldberg
Moses and Heidi Hartmann*

In a Generous Spirit: A First-Person Biography of Myra Page
Christina Looper Baker

Mining Cultures: Men, Women, and Leisure in Butte, 1914–41   *Mary Murphy*

Gendered Strife and Confusion: The Political Culture of Reconstruction
  Laura F. Edwards
The Female Economy: The Millinery and Dressmaking Trades,
  1860–1930   *Wendy Gamber*
Mistresses and Slaves: Plantation Women in South Carolina, 1830–80
  Marli F. Weiner
A Hard Fight for We: Women's Transition from Slavery to Freedom in South
  Carolina   *Leslie A. Schwalm*
The Common Ground of Womanhood: Class, Gender, and Working Girls' Clubs,
  1884–1928   *Priscilla Murolo*
Purifying America: Women, Cultural Reform, and Pro-Censorship Activism,
  1873–1933   *Alison M. Parker*
Marching Together: Women of the Brotherhood of Sleeping Car Porters
  Melinda Chateauvert
Creating the New Woman: The Rise of Southern Women's Progressive Culture
  in Texas, 1893–1918   *Judith N. McArthur*
The Business of Charity: The Woman's Exchange Movement, 1832–1900
  Kathleen Waters Sander
The Power and Passion of M. Carey Thomas   *Helen Lefkowitz Horowitz*
For Freedom's Sake: The Life of Fannie Lou Hamer   *Chana Kai Lee*
Becoming Citizens: The Emergence and Development of the California Women's
  Movement, 1880–1911   *Gayle Gullett*
Selected Letters of Lucretia Coffin Mott   *Edited by Beverly Wilson Palmer
  with the assistance of Holly Byers Ochoa and Carol Faulkner*
Women and the Republican Party, 1854–1924   *Melanie Susan Gustafson*
Southern Discomfort: Women's Activism in Tampa, Florida, 1880s–1920s
  Nancy A. Hewitt
The Making of "Mammy Pleasant": A Black Entrepreneur in Nineteenth-Century
  San Francisco   *Lynn M. Hudson*
Sex Radicals and the Quest for Women's Equality   *Joanne E. Passet*
"We, Too, Are Americans": African American Women in Detroit and Richmond,
  1940–54   *Megan Taylor Shockley*
The Road to Seneca Falls: Elizabeth Cady Stanton and the First Woman's Rights
  Convention   *Judith Wellman*
Reinventing Marriage: The Love and Work of Alice Freeman Palmer and
  George Herbert Palmer   *Lori Kenschaft*
Southern Single Blessedness: Unmarried Women in the Urban South,
  1800–1865   *Christine Jacobson Carter*
Widows and Orphans First: The Family Economy and Social Welfare Policy,
  1865–1939   *S. J. Kleinberg*
Habits of Compassion: Irish Catholic Nuns and the Origins of the Welfare System,
  1830–1920   *Maureen Fitzgerald*

The University of Illinois Press
is a founding member of the
Association of American University Presses.

Cover illustration: (*Left photo*): Lucy Cobb Institute Collection,
Hargrett Library, University of Georgia. (*Right photo*): Teacher
Professional Training Course participants, Spelman Seminary,
1920. Courtesy of the Spelman College Archives.

University of Illinois Press
1325 South Oak Street
Champaign, IL 61820-6903
www.press.uillinois.edu